Lecture Notes in Artificial Intelligence   1195

Subseries of Lecture Notes in Computer Science
Edited by J. G. Carbonell and J. Siekmann

Lecture Notes in Computer Science

Edited by G. Goos, J. Hartmanis and J. van Leeuwen

Springer
Berlin
Heidelberg
New York
Barcelona
Budapest
Hong Kong
London
Milan
Paris
Santa Clara
Singapore
Tokyo

Robert Trappl   Paolo Petta (Eds.)

Creating Personalities for Synthetic Actors

Towards Autonomous
Personality Agents

Springer

Series Editors
Jaime G. Carbonell, Carnegie Mellon University, Pittsburgh, PA, USA
Jörg Siekmann, University of Saarland, Saarbrücken, Germany

Volume Editors

Robert Trappl
Paolo Petta
Austrian Research Institute for Artificial Intelligence
Schottengasse 3, A-1010 Vienna, Austria
E-mail: robert@ai.univie.ac.at
        paolo@ai.univie.ac.at

Cataloging-in-Publication Data applied for

Die Deutsche Bibliothek - CIP-Einheitsaufnahme

Creating personalities for synthetic actors : towards
autonomous personality agents / Robert Trappl ; Paolo Petta
(ed.). - Berlin ; Heidelberg ; New York ; Barcelona ; Budapest ;
Hong Kong ; London ; Milan ; Paris ; Santa Clara ; Singapore ;
Tokyo : Springer, 1997
  (Lecture notes in computer science ; 1195 : Lecture notes in artificial
  intelligence)
  ISBN 3-540-62735-9
NE: Trappl, Robert [Hrsg.]; GT

The cover illustration is based on Figure 7, page 109
(contribution by Barbara Hayes-Roth, Robert von Gent, and Daniel Huber)

CR Subject Classification (1991): I.2, I.3, J.5, H.5.1

ISBN 3-540-62735-9 Springer-Verlag Berlin Heidelberg New York

© Springer-Verlag Berlin Heidelberg 1997
Printed in Germany

Typesetting: Camera ready by author
SPIN 10548995   06/3142 – 5 4 3 2 1 0   Printed on acid-free paper

Preface

Progress in computer animation has attained such a speed that computer-generated human faces and figures on ubiquitous screens will soon be indistinguishable from those of real humans. The potential both for scripted films and real-time interaction with users is enormous. However, in order to cope with this potential, these faces and figures must be guided by autonomous "personality agents". But what is the current state of the art in this far less visible domain of research?

To answer this question, we decided to organise a two-day workshop which took place at the premises of the Austrian Research Institute for Artificial Intelligence in Vienna. To this workshop we invited scientists known for their work in this area, ranging from computer animation specialists, computer scientists, and specialists in AI, to psychologists and philosophers.

This book is the collection of the papers which were presented as first drafts at that occasion. The lively discussion was taped, transcribed, and sent to the participants. We are extremely grateful to them for the pains they took to consider the comments, to enhance their papers with new material, and to submit them on time. At least one author of each of the papers presented in this book was present at our workshop, with the sole exception of Barbara Hayes-Roth, who regrettably had already accepted other duties when the date of the event was set.

We want to thank all our colleagues at the Austrian Research Institute for Artificial Intelligence, especially Dr. Bernhard Pfahringer, who was not only very instrumental in the scientific preparation and organization of the workshop but also proposed its name, and thus the title of this book, and to Gerda Helscher, MA, for preparing the transcripts of the tape recordings and for her help in the finalization of this volume. Both Prof. Jörg Siekmann, one of the LNAI series editors, and Mr. Alfred Hofmann of Springer-Verlag were ideal partners in our endeavor.

We are grateful to Dr. Erhard Busek, then Federal Minister for Science and Research, for his support of an agent project of which the workshop was an integral part, and to Dr. René Fries from the same Ministry, who took great care to keep the project going. We hope we will get to be as grateful to Dr. Caspar Einem, now Federal Minister for Science and Transport, since we have applied to his Ministry for its financial support of a research project on the development of personality agents.

It is our hope that this book will serve as a useful guide to the different approaches to create personalities for synthetic actors and to stimulate future research in this promising field.

Vienna, Austria, January 1997   Robert Trappl and Paolo Petta

Contents

Why to Create Personalities
for Synthetic Actors

Paolo Petta, Robert Trappl

Austrian Research Institute for Artificial Intelligence*, Vienna, and
Department of Medical Cybernetics and Artificial Intelligence, University of Vienna
{paolo, robert}@ai.univie.ac.at

1 Introduction

The last decade has seen not only the impressive developments from the first brief appearance of a computer-generated character in a feature film[2], over the first digital performer in a movie[3], all the way to the first fully computer-generated theatrical motion picture[4]; synthetic actors have also conquered demanding real-time domains from the (co-)moderation of live television shows to the evaluation of complex real-world scenarios modeled in detail in advanced simulators.

Over this timespan the rendering of the external appearance has progressed from the basic geometrical and physical modeling and animation over the inclusion of dependencies on the simulated environment to event- and object-based behaviours. As synthetic actors were placed in simulated worlds of growing complexity, an obvious requirement that came about was to make them perform *in* these worlds: for convincing realistic behaviour they ought to perform as if they were gathering information as it became available to them and they should interact with objects -- e.g., tracking, avoiding, manipulating,...them -- in plausible ways. It soon became evident that the first approach of setting out from an omniscient position where all the data of the simulated world was made available to programs driving the actors was very inefficient in a number of respects. For instance, those pieces of information that could actually be accessed given the actor's current state in the world had to be laboriously identified and progressively singled out. Similarly, all sequences of actions making up basic behaviours of an agent had to be explicitly prescribed: take as an example an object "catching the eye" of the actor which would then turn around to inspect it more closely. Instead, taking the step forward and equipping actors with virtual sensors, turning their bodies into virtual effectors, and using these devices to guide the execution of behaviours proved to be a superior alternative, with

* The Austrian Research Institute for Artificial Intelligence is supported by the Austrian Federal Ministry of Science, Transport, and the Arts.

2 Young Sherlock Holmes, directed by Barry Levinson, visual effects by Industrial Light & Magic.

3 Casper, directed by Brad Silberling, visual effects by Industrial Light & Magic.

4 Toy Story, directed by John Lasseter, visual effects by Pixar.

the additional benefit of introducing a well defined interface between the actor and its environment, allowing to deploy actors in different worlds[5].

However, all of these external aspects still cover only part of what makes up an actor: as entities that "act a part or take part in an affair", synthetic actors also have to be endowed with internal capabilities, both affective and cognitive—i.e., in concordance with the following definition by Osherson[10]

> Cognitive Science is the study of human intelligence in all of its forms, from perception and action to language and reasoning. The exercise of intelligence is called cognition. Under the rubric of cognition fall such diverse human activities as recognizing a friend's voice over the telephone, reading a novel, jumping from stone to stone in a creek, explaining an idea to classmates, remembering the way home from work, and choosing a profession. Cognitive processes are essential to each of these activities; indeed, they are essential to everything we do. [p.ix]

From the point of view of the different applications, the actual requirements calling for these internal faculties can vary widely: feature film animators might just want to be able to instruct their puppets using high level commands (e.g., *"walk leisurely across the room"*) or be assisted in the more delicate and ephemeral task of ensuring consistent patterns of behaviour of a virtual actor over a longer time span; in other settings, achieving e.g. various degrees of agent autonomy can play an essential role in providing effective assistance to users or in achieving credible and interesting performance in virtual environments. Especially in this latter context, the inevitable limitations in terms of incompleteness of information about the world that can be perceived by the actor via its virtual sensors as well as restrictions in terms of available resources[6] become of particular relevance. Different approaches have been taken to tackle this problem. Some favour runtime performance and acceptance by a broad public even though adhering to scientifically disproved preconceptions of folk psychology — as in the Oz project directed by Joseph Bates at Carnegie Mellon University. Others place the emphasis on the soundness of the implementation of a cognitive theory resting on plausible first principles, as illustrated in the chapters by Dave Moffat and Aaron Sloman in this volume. Also, it must not be overlooked that as the exterior architecture of agents and their environments become more complex and structured, control of these worlds necessarily also becomes of a more indirect, higher-level nature, and consequently has to rely on the availability of interior mechanisms of corresponding functionality.

All of these circumstances thus give rise to concerns regarding the characteristics of the high-level behaviour of the synthetic actors, both in terms of reliability

---

[5] A related effort which gained a certain publicity was the work carried out by an undergraduate student at the MIT Media Lab who interfaced their ALIVE system to the game world of DOOM. See [12, 3] for a more detailed discussion of these topics.

[6] Computational resources and timing constraints, especially for characters "thrown" into worlds where they have to act in real time.

and predictability—ensuring that the performance remains within anticipated or prescribable limits—and interestingness—the manifestation of individual distinguishing marks due to which the actors become recognizable individuals: in other words, the design of tailored personalities. The papers included in the present collection span the range from theoretical to applied and application-specific aspects, laying a foundation for the creation of multifarious and more believable synthetic actors. From its very beginning the event at which these works were presented was characterized by an informal atmosphere which engendered animated exchanges of opinions. The results of these discussions are reflected in the contents of the revised versions of the workshop papers. In the following we will briefly summarize some key points presented in the single contributions, deferring a principled discussion of the subject domain to the final chapter of this volume.

2 Contents

2.1 Virtual Humans

An essential point of emphasis of the research supervised by Nadia Magnenat-Thalmann and Daniel Thalmann at the MIRALab in Geneva and the EPFL in Lausanne is the pursuit of the highest qualitative standards (i.e., photorealism) of the appearance of their creations: achievement of flexible real-time behaviour is subordinated to this primary goal. Consequently, special consideration is given e.g. to the simulation of different surfaces, such as clothes made of different fabrics and materials, or human hair and skin [7]. Similarly, single courses of actions—such as the grasping of objects or the facial expressions—are modeled in accurate detail [12]. These latter procedures also rely on the last focus of research to be mentioned here, namely the synthetic sensing of the environment. In particular this includes the virtual vision, tactile, and audition, which contribute decisively to a "natural" behaviour of the virtual actors. Most of this research is strongly application-oriented, with telecooperation—following the maxim that the realistic representation of Avatars[7] has a crucial impact of the acceptance of the system—and the entertainment industries (e.g., the co-moderation of prime time shows) as important application areas.

The research efforts presented by Bonnie Webber and Norman Badler [1] also direct their attention on realism: the work centered on Jack® focuses on ergonomic (e.g., of complex controls systems such as a helicopter cockpit) and logistic (e.g., in military domains) evaluations of scenarios. Jack comprises a whole family of variations on a basic theme, the biomechanical simulation of a human body in real time. The overall design of Jack follows the three-level-architecture which was popularized in robotic research: on the lowest level a *sense-control-act* loop provides the interface to the environment and ensures robust "reactive"

---

[7] This commonly adopted designation for figures representing human users in cyberspace was first introduced in the Habitat System [9].

behaviour, making Jack capable of e.g., "stumbling" over obstacles[8]. At the highest level, the behaviour of all instances of Jack in one running simulation are controlled by *parallel transition networks*, in which all possible courses of action for a given scene are defined in an abstract manner (roughly comparable to Roger Schank's *scripts*): to solve occurring partial problems, specialized problem solving methods can be activated as required (e.g., heuristics and planning procedures to chose a hiding place in the context of a game of hide-and-seek).

At New York University's Media Research Lab (NYU MRL) an alternative approach is taken for a similar subject [4]. In the framework of a procedural animation technique, single movements of human figures are defined along with parameter settings for all possible transitions between these actions. As evaluation criterion for this latter step the assessment of the "naturalness" of the resulting impression as given by human experts was drawn up. This exact modeling is subsequently softened by the superposition of stochastic noise functions, so that each repetition of a single movement is performed with slight variations; but also when at a standstill, the joints of the figures thereby feature a slight "unrest", which contributes to the realistic appearance.

Given that in this way the single movements can be recalled in an efficient manner, it is possible to control the whole animation at a higher level in real time. This functionality is provided by behavioural scripts, which define the "vocabulary" of each object (actors as well as any other entities comprised in the scene). Instead of equipping each actor e.g. with comprehensive knowledge about all possible actions, the respective relevant information is thereby stored in a distributed fashion (a tea cup "knows", that it can be sipped from, a vehicle knows that it can be mounted and driven, etc.). Among the opportunities arising from this approach, it is also easily possible to achieve the effect of a stepwise acquisition of skills in mastering recurrent tasks by instantiating and updating variables stored with the given actor. The considered application scenarios for this technology include the interactive design of virtual choreographies and virtual social environments akin to graphical Internet MUD (Multi-User Dimensions) and their more recent commercial variants.

2.2 Virtual Ethology

Bruce Blumberg and Tinsley Galyean [3] present further developments of the Hamsterdam architecture which is being applied in the context of the ALIVE (Artificial Life Interactive Video Environment) project at the MIT Media Lab. ALIVE implements the metaphor of a "magic mirror" which allows users to immerse in a virtual environment without requiring them to wear any special equipment: this mirror is realized as a wide-area screen on which the image of the user as acquired by video cameras is displayed after being composited with

---

[8] As an interesting side note, the use of reinforcement learning algorithms was found to be of indispensable help in the adjustment of the numerous parameters of this complex numerical system.

a computer generated environment. User can manipulate object of the artificial world by means of gestures and similarly interact with its synthetic actors, virtual animals. The Hamsterdam architecture underlying these creatures builds upon Pattie Maes' "action selection" algorithm and particularly also takes into account findings from ethology, thereby achieving interesting, believable, and timely behaviour. Hamsterdam obeys a strict separation of drawn appearance (*geometry layer*), the repertoire of possible movements *motor skills*), and a *behaviour system* which is responsible for the possible behaviours. The behaviour system consists of a loose hierarchy of single behaviours, which are each responsible for the pursuit of a specific goal. Within groups of mutually inhibiting behaviours the *avalanche effect* describe by Marvin Minsky in Mentopolis is used to select a particular member and to achieve an adequate degree of persistence at the same time. The strength of the inhibitory signals is influenced by local variables particular to the single behaviours ("goals and motivations") as well as by input provided by a releasing mechanism. This releasing mechanism acts as a filter that identifies relevant objects and events out of the stream of data supplied by the system of virtual sensors. Actors implemented using the Hamsterdam architecture can be influenced at different levels of control, ranging from vague motivations (by setting single state variables of behaviours) to explicit instructions (imparted to the motor skill layer). More complex directions can be imparted via a combined activation of behaviour groups and the manipulation of the releasing mechanism and virtual sensors.

2.3 Virtual Drama

David Blair and Tom Meyer [2] take on the the topic under investigation from the perspective of a "guided experiencing" of a narrative. The developments which set out from David Blair's feature film "Wax or the discovery of television among the bees" first led to the working up of the material as a hypermedia system containing a number of automated narrating systems. This system was eventually published on the World-Wide Web as "WAXweb" which was also one of the first applications drawing extensively on the capabilities offered by the first release of VRML (Virtual Reality Markup Language). WAXweb was successively integrated with a interactive environment, the HyperHotel text-based virtual environment based on the MOO technology developed at Xerox PARC. In the subsequent projects, "Jews in Space" and "Grammatron" additional steps are being taken —among other by means of the inclusion of active VRML elements— towards the realization of an implicit way of narrating that can be experienced individually: on the occasion the development of semi-intelligent tools for the design and rearrangement of the deconstructed narrative space forms an important part of the projects as well as the realization of implemented operationalisations of existing theories of drama.

The Virtual Theater project at the Knowledge Systems Lab of Stanford University aims at providing a multimedia environment in which users can interact with intelligent agents that function as synthetic actors. By virtue of this additional level of indirection, the agents are not required to *have* specific personality, they only have to be "in character", i.e., display behaviours that stand in agreement with the personalities they are expected to take on in given contexts [5]. Consequently, their work is much more strongly influenced by drama theory, and more precisely by theories of improvisation than by psychological theories. Personalities are modeled only superficially using a small of set of traits that is much more restricted than the one used in the work presented by Brian Loyall, described below. The focus on artistic models of character is reflected in the importance of an effective visualization—both CMU's Edge of Intention and the procedural animation techniques developed at NYU's MRL have been used—and the reliance on a corpus of performing heuristic rules (e.g., how to effectively convey status transactions that are assumed to govern human relationships). This contribution thereby highlights the fact that at least in this particular setting the goal of achieving the impression of a believable performance delivered by synthetic actors embodying distinct personalities can be met with the inclusion of a minimum of "cognitive machinery".

Brian Loyall [6] reports on recent extensions of the well-known "Edge of Intention" scenario developed under the supervision of Joseph Bates at CMU. The possibilities to interact with the Woggles populating this virtual world had long been limited to "body language", i.e. movement and changing of size of the user's Woggle-avatar, which were then interpreted by the other Woggles as friendly or threatening gesture, invitation or readiness to participate in play, etc. Now this repertoire is complemented with the possibility of entering texts or fragments of speech. Woggles in the vicinity of the avatar may react immediately, without necessarily waiting for the completion of the typed input. This engenders the possibility of misinterpretation of the partial information, leading to reactions which have to be corrected later on. For example, an "irritated" Woggle being addressed may take this action to be a hostile act; an interpretation which may be revised when the content of the message is seen to be a friendly one. In this way, this new means of interacting offers the opportunity to make the emotive inner life of the Woggles—a slightly extended version of the personality theory by Ortony, Clore, and Collins—even better visible to the human user of the system.

2.4 Virtual Cognition

Finally, the contributions by Dave Moffat [8] and Aaron Sloman [11] round off the broad investigation of the topic by providing a psychological-cognitive perspective. Both authors share the view that the traditional methods of psychology fail to provide an adequate framework supporting actual implementations of working "deep" cognitive models.

After reviewing a some of the more important lines of research in the area of personality, Moffat takes the important step of explicitly detaching the concept of personality from the anthropomorphic context assumed in traditional personality theories. He then illustrates how his model roots in Nico Frijda's theory of emotion: this particular theory was chosen as it was seen to be nearer to implementability than most other theories in the field, and furthermore to provide the most comprehensive coverage of the problem domain. Moffat's model, *Will*, is already a successor to a first partial implementation of Frijda's theory of emotion. A prominent design goal was to keep the model as simple as possible, using off-the-shelf AI technology: "Rather than make a big, sophisticated architecture that models everything, the idea is to include as *few* design features as possible because they correspond to theoretical assumptions, and like many others, I prefer theories ... to be simple, economical, and parsimonious".

Aaron Sloman, on the other hand, takes on a much more radical stance, virtually dismissing all of the hitherto conducted psychological research which, among other things, he accuses to be sorely lacking of such basic essentials as a well-defined terminology. In stark contrast to Moffat's attitude cited above, the complex holistic architecture designed by Aaron Sloman ("Personality belongs to a whole agent") lays claim to be a comprehensive model of cognition, at which the realization of exemplary instances proves to be rather difficult because of the assumed very flexible components (e.g. the open set of representation formalisms and associated virtual machines operating on them, or the complex mechanisms of meta-control) and the *necessarily* rich content that has to be covered. The interpretation of emotion as an emergent phenomenon of *breakdown* following from the limitation of the available resources is just another proposition that will doubtlessly spark many further discussions, such as the ones that took place during the workshop and which are partly reproduced in this volume as appendix to Aaron Sloman's contribution.

3 Concluding Remarks

This brief overview of the topics covered in the contributions comprised in this collection cannot be expected but to convey a first impression of the plethora of facets under which the topic of creating personalities for synthetic actors is being researched. At the same time, within this wide range of diverse approaches pursued to tackle the posed challenges there are evident strong interrelations of which we have tried to point out just a few. This circumstance corroborates the importance of furthering the exchange of ideas between researchers from different backgrounds in this rapidly growing area.

References

1. Badler N., Reich B.D., Webber B.L. (1997) Towards Personalities for Animated Agents with Reactive and Planning Behaviors. In: Trappl R., Petta P. (eds.) *Creating Personalities for Synthetic Actors* (In this volume)

2. Blair D., Meyer T. (1997) Tools for an Interactive Virtual Cinema. In: Trappl R., Petta P. (eds.) *Creating Personalities for Synthetic Actors* (In this volume)

3. Blumberg B. (1997) Multi-level Control for Animated Autonomous Agents: Do the Right Thing... Oh, Not That... In: Trappl R., Petta P. (eds.) *Creating Personalities for Synthetic Actors* (In this volume)

4. Goldberg A. (1997) IMPROV: A System for Real-Time Animation of Behavior-based Interactive Synthetic Actors. In: Trappl R., Petta P. (eds.) *Creating Personalities for Synthetic Actors* (In this volume)

5. Hayes-Roth B., Gent R.van, Huber D. (1997) Acting in Character. In: Trappl R., Petta P. (eds.) *Creating Personalities for Synthetic Actors* (In this volume)

6. Loyall B. (1997) Some Requirements and Approaches for Natural Language in a Believable Agent. In: Trappl R., Petta P. (eds.) *Creating Personalities for Synthetic Actors* (In this volume)

7. Magnenat-Thalmann N., Volino P. (1997) Dressing Virtual Humans. In: Trappl R., Petta P. (eds.) *Creating Personalities for Synthetic Actors* (In this volume)

8. Moffat D. (1997) Personality Parameters and Programs. In: Trappl R., Petta P. (eds.) *Creating Personalities for Synthetic Actors* (In this volume)

9. Morningstar C., Farmer F.R. (1990) The Lessons of Lucasfilm's Habitat. In: Benedikt M. (ed.) *Cyberspace: First Steps*, MIT Press, Cambridge, MA

10. Osherson D.N., Lasnik H. (eds.) (1990) *An Invitation to Cognitive Science*, MIT Press, Cambridge, MA

11. Sloman A. (1997) What Sort of Control System is Able to Have a Personality? In: Trappl R., Petta P. (eds.) *Creating Personalities for Synthetic Actors* (In this volume)

12. Thalmann D., Noser H., Huang Z. (1997) Autonomous Virtual Actors based on Virtual Sensors. In: Trappl R., Petta P. (eds.) *Creating Personalities for Synthetic Actors* (In this volume)

Dressing Virtual Humans

Nadia Magnenat Thalmann, Pascal Volino

MIRALab, University of Geneva, Switzerland
thalmann@cui.unige.ch

Abstract. Scenes involving virtual humans imply many complex problems to manage. We slowly come to the point of simulating real-looking virtual humans. In a short future, we will not be able to see any difference between a real person and a virtual one. However, the synthesis of realistic virtual humans leads to obtain and include the specific features of the character of interest. For well-known personalities such as Marilyn, Humphrey, or Elvis, there is less scope for mistakes as the deviations will be very easily detected by the spectator. In this paper, we emphasize an important issue in the creation of realistic virtual actors: the creation and animation of their clothes.

1 State-of-the-Art in Cloth Modeling and Animation

In most computer-generated films involving virtual humans, clothes are simulated as a part of the body with no autonomous motion. However, in recent years, software has been developed and applied to the interactive design of 2D garment panels and to optimizing the layout of garment panels on the fabric. In Hinds and McCartney's work [9], a static trunk of a mannequin's body is represented by bicubic B-spline surfaces. Garment panels are considered to be surfaces of complex shapes in 3D. The garment panels are designed around the static mannequin body, and then are reduced to 2D cutting patterns. This approach is contrary to the traditional approach to garment design. The garment is modeled by geometric methods. To visualize the folds and drapes, harmonic functions and sinusoidal functions are superimposed on the garment panels. Mangen and Lasudry [16] proposed an algorithm for finding the intersection polygon of any two polygons. This is applied to the automatic optimization of the layout of polygonal garment panels in 2D rectangular fabrics. Both of these projects concern stages of garment design and manufacturing in real industrial contexts.

Previous works on deformable object animation using physically based models have permitted animation of cloth-like objects in many kinds of situations. Weil [24] pioneered cloth animation using an approximated model based on relaxation of the surface. Haumann and Parent [8] produced animations with flags or leaves moving in the wind, or curtains blowing in a breeze. Kunii and Godota [10] used a hybrid model incorporating physical and geometrical techniques to model garment wrinkles. Aono [1] simulated wrinkle propagation on a handkerchief using an elastic model. Terzopoulos et al. [21] developed a general elastic model and applied it to a wide range of objects including cloth. Interaction of clothes with synthetic actors in motion [11, 5, 27] marked the beginning of a new era in cloth animation in more complex situations. However, there were still a number of restrictions on the simulation conditions on the geometrical structure and the mechanical situations, imposed by the simulation model or the collision detection.

Deformable objects may be represented by different geometrical models, Triangular grids are most common, but polynomial surfaces [26, 3] and particle systems [4] are also used for solutions to specific mechanical simulations. Yielding nice and accurate deformations, they constrain both the initial shape and the allowed deformations. Each model requires different techniques for modeling complex objects such as panels-and-seaming for cloth objects [27]. Furthermore, global mechanical models such as finite elements and finite difference are not suitable for situations involving constraints and nonlinearities as non-marginal situations all over the surfaces. These situations happen when modeling the highly nonlinear deformations required for wrinkles and crumples [6], and when there are numerous collisions and much friction.

Collision detection and response has been used mainly for stopping cloth from penetrating the body and, more marginally, for preventing self-collisions between different parts of the cloth. The first time-consuming problem was to extract the possible colliding elements from the whole set of elements composing the cloth and the body surfaces. Many techniques have been developed, based on different ideas and adapted for various surface representations. For example, mathematical algorithms have been developed for situations where the surfaces are represented by curved patches or parametric surfaces, as described in [2, 3, 23, 7, 20]. In the case of representing surfaces by a huge set of flat polygons, techniques based on rasterisation [19] or the tracking of the closest distance on the convex hull [17, 12] have been developed. Unfortunately, these techniques are not well suited for efficient detection on deformable surface animations, as they require either expensive z-buffer rendering or constructing the convex hull of the objects at each frame. We have also described a method of collision avoidance [11] that creates a very thin force field around the surface of the obstacle to be avoided. This force field acts like a shield rejecting the points. Although the method works for a simple case of a skirt, use of this type of force is somewhat artificial and cannot provide realistic simulation with complex clothes. In fact, the effect degrades when the force becomes very strong, looking like a "kick" given to the cloth. Figure 1 shows an example from the film Flashback [13]. To improve realism, we have proposed [5] to use the law of conservation of momentum for perfectly inelastic bodies. This means we consider all energy to be lost within a collision.

After some comparisons [15], Terzopoulos' elastic surface model [21] was chosen for our first system with the damping term replaced by a more accurate [5]. The fundamental equation of motion corresponds to an equilibrium between internal forces (Newton term, resistance to stretching, dissipative force, resistance to bending) and external forces (collision forces, gravity, seaming and attaching forces, wind force). In the animation of deformable objects consisting of many surface panels, the constraints that join different panels together and attach them to other objects are very important. In our case, two kinds of dynamic constraints are used in two different stages. When deformable panels are separated, forces are applied to the elements in the panels to join them according to the seaming information. The same method is used to attach the elements of deformable objects to other rigid objects. After the creation of deformable objects, another kind of dynamic constraint is used to guarantee seaming and attaching. For the attaching, the elements of the deformable objects are always kept on the rigid object, so they have the same position and velocity as the elements of the rigid object to which they are attached. For the seaming and joining of the panels themselves, two seamed elements move with the same velocity and position, but the velocity and position depend on those of the individual elements. According to the law of momentum conservation, total momentum of the elements before and after seaming should remain the same. Figure 2 shows an example of dressed actress.

Fig. 1. Collision detection in the film Flashback

2 Simulating Autonomous Clothes Using Physics-Based Models

2.1 History and Evolution

Until now, cloth simulation programs have tried to get realistic results for garments worn by an animated body. The garments were considered as a set of flat polygons made of a regular triangle mesh, that were held together by seaming forces. For calculation speed, geometrical assumptions were made to reduce collision detection time according to the specific situation where an actor wears a garment. That situation is in fact a rather "simple" mechanical context with well-defined collision situations, and quite smooth deformation.

Now, animation goals have evolved. Before, focus was put on realistic cloth deformation and appearance on the animated actor. Now, focus is more oriented toward extending the simulation possibilities and animating cloth in very diversified situations, such as clothes worn on several layers, clothes being put on and taken off by an actor, and folded, piled, or crumpled clothes.

Fig. 2. A synthetic actress with clothes

The new situations required for such simulations are quite different from those required when an actor simply wears clothes. The model should now be able to handle clothes more like an independent object, rather than a set of panels dependent on the actor's body. Furthermore, several new mechanical situations should be considered, such as high deformation and bending. Collision and self-collision detection should also be very efficient for detecting collisions on the multilayers of crumpled situations.

Generalizing the application range of the software, the simulation engine could be extended for animating a very wide range of deformable objects simply by importing triangular meshes and giving them mechanical properties. Rigid object simulation could also be included (as a new class of animated objects) in the system.

2.2 Improvements of the New Software

In order to cope with these new possibilities, the simulation engine, the collision detection procedures, and the modeling of the human bodies have been completely rewritten [22].

The main concern is to be able to handle clothes as independent objects that do not rely on the underlying body. Thus, the data structure has been completely changed, and any triangular mesh surface, whether regular or not, can be handled by the simulation engine. A garment may still be generated by an assembly of panels, but when the panels are seamed together, it becomes a single and independent object.

Such a clothes model may interact with the body or other clothes using collision response and attach points, but the body may also be removed and the cloth simulated on its own as, for example, when cloth falls down and gets crumpled on the ground.

Generally, crumpling, high deformation and important collision interaction are the primary difficulties encountered in cloth simulation. These problems are dealt with as follows:

- A new collision detection algorithm was used for high efficiency in detecting collisions, particularly self-collisions. This algorithm uses hierarchisation of the surface mesh and takes advantage of curvature regularity within surface regions for determining the possibility of self-collision within these regions. Using such an algorithm, self-collision detection is no longer a time critical process, and can be fully performed for accurate handling of cases including numerous self-collisions, such as crumpling.
- The mechanical model has been modified for robust handling of cases implying high nonlinear deformations resulting from severe elongation and bending, despite a discretisation that may be irregular and rough. Rather than using global integration methods such as finite elements in which nonlinearities and discontinuous behaviors can not easily be integrated, direct integration of Newton's second law was implemented. Several possibilities result from such an approach, including acting directly on position and speed (for

direct and interactive manipulation), and integrating highly non linear and time-varying behaviors (high deformations, collision response, stability control).

– Particular attention has been given to the efficiency of collision response. In order to handle in an accurate and stable way complex situations with numerous interacting collisions such as crumpling and multilayer surfaces, response is not computed using force feedback. Instead response is directly performed using position and velocity correction according to the mechanical conservation laws. Thus, we avoid the use of strong discontinuous fields requiring very small time steps for accurate handling, and all collisions can be handled independently of other mechanical computation within the same unaltered time step. An iterative process is then used locally on elements involved in several collisions. With such a technique, we obtain good stability even in complex situations and the global computation time is not severely affected by extra forces and the reduced time step otherwise created by collisions.

– The data structure has been unified between all the different kinds of objects, providing increased simulation versatility. Any object of the scene can be animated as a deformable surface, as a rigid body, as a pre computed animation or as an immobile scene object. All these different objects share the same file format.

– The interface has been completely rebuilt in order to take advantage of all the possibilities brought by the new simulation engine.

Thus, the improvements mainly address versatility and provide the tools for simulating clothes and other deformable objects in many different conditions.

Our model can be easily integrated into existing environments, producing a body mesh with fixed topology. Since files for implicit models are typically at least two to three orders of magnitude smaller than those modeled with polygon or parametric patches, a compact, parameterized body model, suitable for communication, can be obtained.

3   General Description of the Simulation Software

3.1   The Software Architecture

The whole software is divided into several parts (see Fig.3):

– The data structure, storing all object information.
– The collision detection engine, which computes the collisions between all the objects in the structure.
– The mechanical simulation engine, which animates objects according to different mechanical models for rigid or deformable objects.
– The software for human body modeling and deformation.
– Display modules, handling either window management or object display, which also provide feedback on user graphical interaction (selection, displacements).

-- A set of object and event managers, handling all the object attributes and visualization parameters, which processes the interface events and the scripting.

-- A Motif-based interface, providing the high-level interactive control to the user.

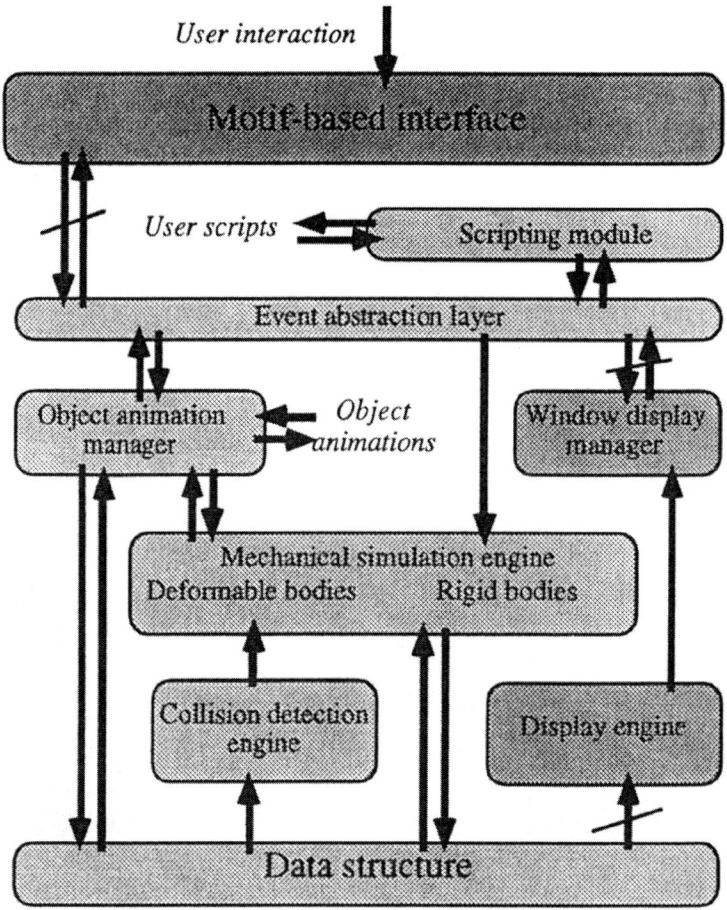

Fig. 3. The software modules

The scripting system allows the program to run without any user interaction. The interface component, at well as the display components, may be suppressed, and the resulting program will run in a complete non-graphical context, allowing, for example, batch-processing on remote sites.

For the whole software, modularity and abstraction has been an important development idea. For example, using event abstraction, an interface system substitution would only require modifying a small number of high-level modules.

The data flow (Fig.4) is basically a computation loop where several animation engines animate their respective types of objects, which are deformable surfaces, rigid objects, animated sequences, transformation-based animations and immobile scene objects. Collision detection is performed for all the objects, and provides collision response for the mechanical simulation engines. The objects are imported from several sources, including animations, static objects in various formats, and cloth panel descriptions. The output is a collection of frames of the computed animation.

3.2   The Mechanical Simulation Engine

The mechanical engine is specially designed for handling deformable surfaces in very severe mechanical situations, such as those encountered in crumpling surfaces. It has to deal with high deformations and nonlinear mechanical behaviors. Despite severe bending and wrinkling, the discretisation has to remain coarse enough to be able to simulate several garments concurrently with reasonable computation time. Furthermore, numerous and interacting collisions resulting from crumpling or multilayer cloth have to be handled efficiently and in robustly.

To comply with all these constraints, the model is based on the direct integration of Newton's second law applied to a particle system model [29]. Such a model allows us to handle each surface element independently, including independent manipulation for simulating position and speed constraints, and linearities such as collision response. Furthermore, such a model allows explicit and simple formulation of any kind of complex and non linear behavior, allowing precise modelling for big deformations.

Such a model provides particularly efficient collision response processing. After performing deformation calculations without taking into account constraints, a second step performs direct position and speed correction on the colliding elements according to mechanical conservation laws. All the collisions are thus processed independently from the deformation computation, leaving the time step unaltered. By using such a technique, we also avoid the use of strong and discontinuous force fields that alter the simulation efficiency.

Several other facilities have been implemented taking advantage of the model's flexibility. For instance, direct and interactive manipulation is possible as the computation is running. "Elastics" that bring together couples of vertices can be added interactively, providing an efficient technique for adding attachments and seaming lines.

3.3   Collision Detection

Collision detection is often the bottleneck of deformable surface simulation programs that handle highly discretized objects, particularly when complete self-collision detection is required, as in wrinkle and crumple situations.

The program takes advantage of an efficient collision detection algorithm, which is based on hierarchisation and takes advantage of surface curvature within and between adjacent surface regions for optimizing self-collision detection. The

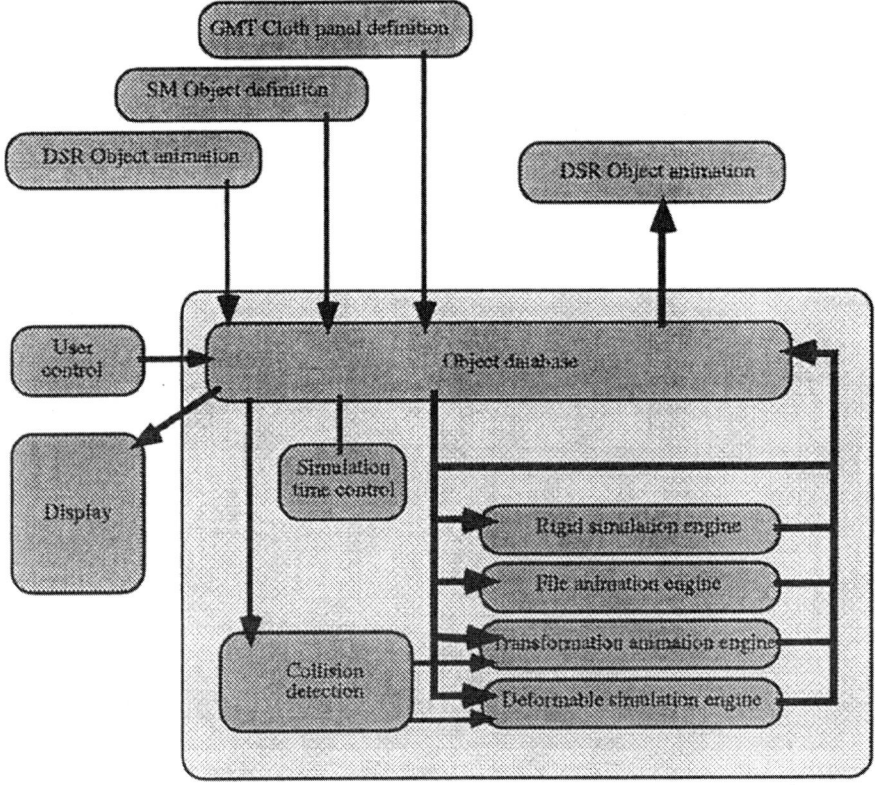

Fig. 4. The simulation data flow

hierarchisation is performed once at the beginning of the simulation. After this, only bounding boxes and normals are recomputed for all the hierarchy elements and the detection is performed within an element or between two adjacent elements only if their curvature is compatible with the existence of collisions.

Such an algorithm is particularly efficient for huge and regular surfaces, independent of the refinement of the discretisation. In normal cloth simulations, full self-collision detection shows up to be less than 10% of the total collision detection time. This algorithm allows the program to make extensive use of self-collision detection without making any hypothesis about which surface parts may collide, providing a great flexibility on the difficult situations involving complex wrinkling and crumpling.

Because we deal with both dressed bodies and wrinkling, there is no way to define an "inside-outside orientation" for all the simulated surfaces. Thus, it is not possible to say what side should be repelled from the surface in the case of collision. Additionally, some situations may occur where interacting collisions and high deformation cause the collision response to temporarily fail from preventing surface crossover. However, in such case, the system should be robust enough to correct the situation during the next simulation steps. To do this, extra algorithms have been implemented for correcting collision orientations in case of crossover by statistically analyzing the orientations of the neighboring collisions. Such a system allows the simulation to recover from crossover situations, despite the lack of preset orientation information.

Associated with the previously described mechanical simulation engine, this collision detection algorithm preserves its efficiency and robustness in most kinds of situations encountered in cloth simulation.

3.4 The Mechanical Model

Models based on global minimization or Lagrangian dynamics formulations are not suited for highly nonlinear situations where discontinuities generated by collisions are numerous. The main idea of our model is to integrate Newton's motion equation $F = ma$ in a direct way to keep quickly evaluated time steps small. Thus, nonlinear behaviors and discontinuous responses such as collisions will be handled in an accurate way. Furthermore, this direct formulation allows us easy and precise inclusion of any nonlinear mechanical behavior. With such a model, we can also act directly on the position and speed of the elements, and thus avoid handling collisions through strong repulsion forces that perturbate the simulation.

The animated deformable object is represented as a particle system by sets of vertices forming heterogeneous triangles, thus allowing surfaces of any shape to be easily modeled and simulated.

The object is considered to be isotropic and of constant thickness. Elastic properties of the object are partially described by the standard parameters [18] that are:

- E_0 the Young modulus
- ν the Poisson coefficient
- ρ the density
- T the thickness

To avoid textile to behave like a rubber sheet, non linearity is added to textile's response through Young Modulus which will be represented locally as a function of the unit elongation (ε):

$$E_{(\varepsilon)} = \begin{array}{ll} E_0(1 + A_\varepsilon) & 0 < \varepsilon < \varepsilon_{\max} \\ E_0(1 + B_\varepsilon) & \varepsilon_{\min} < \varepsilon < 0 \\ E_{\max} & \varepsilon < \varepsilon_{\min}, \varepsilon > \varepsilon_{\max} \end{array}$$

A, B, E_{max} and E_0 are defined from discretisation size and real textile rigidity. Since buckle formation requires a change of area that increases with the size of the discretized elements, the discretisation size alters the textile's easiness to buckle into double curvature. E_0 is then settled slightly below the real textile's rigidity. Choosing A>B will help compression during double curvature manifestation without losing too much textile stretching stiffness. E_{max} is used only to limit internal force since the textile would have to break before reaching such a value. It is difficult to find a function that rules those parameters and this have not been done yet, we only adjust the parameters to get visual realism. Further work would allow a more precise adjustment of these parameters to represent more accurately specific types of textile.

Using Newton's second law F=ma, the motion equation consists of a pair of coupled first-order differential equations, for position and velocity. The system of equations is resolved using second order (midpoint method) of the Euler-Cromer method.

4 The Interface

The new clothing software is more than just a cloth program designed for dressing an actor. It is indeed a complete and very general tool for performing rigid or deformable mechanical simulation on any kind of object, whether cloth or not.

4.1 Interface Principle

The software is basically an object animator that simultaneously moves and deforms several objects concurrently with interactions such as collisions and attachments.

The software handles four types of objects:

- Static objects.
- Animated objects, moved either by an animation sequence or a geometrical transformation.
- Rigid mechanical objects animated by mechanical computation.
- Deformable mechanical objects animated and deformed by mechanical computation.

Each object may be loaded from different sources (various file formats). They are all concurrently animated and collision detection is performed accordingly.

Animation is then run and mechanical computation is performed for the rigid and deformable objects. At each frame instance, the animated objects are saved with their respective frame numbers. User interaction such as modifying parameters or manipulating objects, is possible at any time.

4.2 The Cloth Design and Simulation Process

Cloth are animated as any kind of deformable objects. They differ only by how they are constructed, that is by assembling 2D panels. The clothing design and simulation process is divided into two parts:

- The 2D panel design process [25], consisting of designing garment models as flat fabric panels, using a 2D drawing software. Seams are defined around the borders of the panels. Figure 5 shows an example of a panel.
- The 3D simulation process, that basically consists of assembling the garment panels in the context where the animation will take place using mechanical simulation, and then continuing the simulation on the animated scene and characters.

The scene may contain several objects, static or animated, that will interact with the garments through collision. In particular, the actor to be dressed is an animated object.

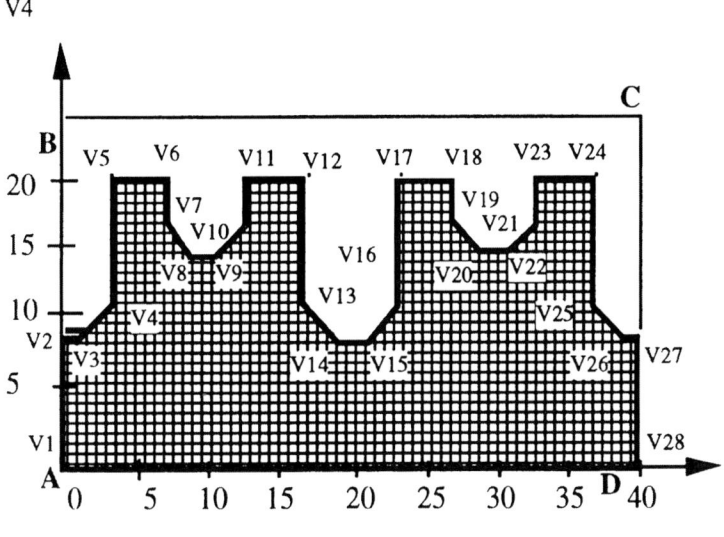

Fig. 5. Panel

Garments are then loaded from a file containing the description of the 2D panels. The panels are discretized into triangle meshes and then interactively placed in an initial position that is suitable for seaming. When dressing an actor, the initial position is around the actor body. Then, using mechanical simulation, the panels are pulled together along the seaming lines using "elastics". Once the seaming lines are close enough, they are topologically merged, and the set of panels becomes one unique object. Such an object can then be handled independently and relies neither on the former panel definition, nor on the body that supported it when it was built. Figure 6 shows the seaming process.

Once garment is defined in this way, the mechanical computation may proceed with the animated scene for computing the final animation. At any time, extra elastics may be added as attach points within the cloth or between the cloth and other objects, adding new design possibilities.

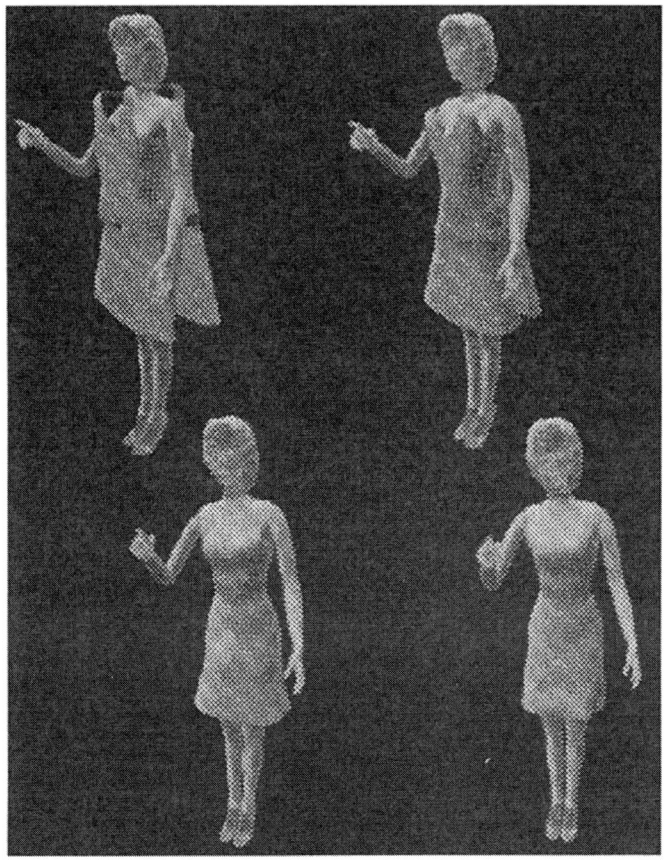

Fig. 6. Seaming garment panels around the body

Complex dressings containing several garments are animated concurrently by the program. Full interaction is provided by collision detection, and optimization for multilayer animated objects provides stability of the overall system. Incremental collision detection is also used when relative movements are slow enough.

All the operations performed during simulation can be recorded in scripts, that are executed for setting up subsequent automatical simulations. Scripts can also be organized into specialized libraries, providing tools for setting up materials, fabric types, simulation conditions,etc.

The animated garments are finally recorded frame by frame as animations, which can be re-used as input data for subsequent computations. This allows incremental garment design for complex cloth. Figure 7 shows an example.

The interface was designed for providing maximal interaction for controlling the simulation. The user can, at any time, block some points of the animated

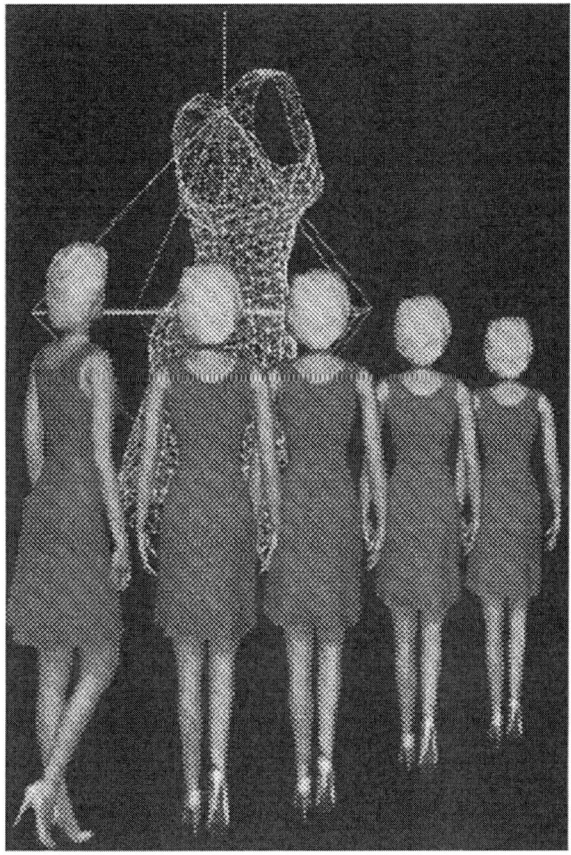

Fig. 7. Animation sequence

objects, add or remove elastics, move interactively vertices of the deformable objects interactively, and move whole objects.

5 Acknowledgements

The research was sponsored by the "Fonds National pour la Recherche Scientifique."

References

1. Aono M. (1990) "A Wrinkle Propagation Model for Cloth". In: *Proc. Computer Graphics International*, Springer-Verlag, pp.96–115
2. Baraff D. (1990) "Curved Surfaces and Coherence for Non-Penetrating Rigid Body Simulation". *Proc. SIGGRAPH'90, Computer Graphics* **24(4)**, pp.19–28

3. Baraff D., Witkin A. (1992) "Dynamic Simulation of Non-Penetrating Flexible Bodies", In: *Proc. SIGGRAPH '92, Computer Graphics* **26(2)**, pp.303–308

4. Breen D.E., House D.H., Wozny M.J. (1994) "Predicting the Drape of Woven Cloth using Interacting Particles. In: *Proc. SIGGRAPH'94, Computer Graphics* **28(4)**, pp.365–372

5. Carignan M., Yang Y., Magnenat Thalmann N., Thalmann D. (1992) "Dressing Animated Synthetic Actors with Complex Deformable Clothes". In: *Proc. SIGGRAPH'92, Computer Graphics* **26(2)**, pp.99–104

6. Denby E.F. (1976) "The Deformation of Fabrics during Wrinkling - A Theoretical Approach", *Textile Research Journal*, Lancaster PA., 46, pp.667–670

7. Duff T. (1992) "Interval Arithmetic and Recursive Subdivision for Implicit Functions and Constructive Solid Geometry". In: *Proc. SIGGRAPH'92, Computer Graphics*, **26(2)**, pp.131–138

8. Haumann D.R., Parent R.E. (1988) "The Behavioral Test-Bed: Obtaining Complex Behavior With Simple Rules". *The Visual Computer*, Springer-Verlag, 4, pp.332–347

9. Hinds B.K., McCartney J. (1990) "Interactive garment design", *The Visual Computer*, Springer-Verlag, 6, pp.53–61

10. Kunii T.L., Gotoda H. (1990) "Modeling and Animation of Garment Wrinkle Formation processes". In: *Proc. Computer Animation '90*, Springer-Verlag, pp.131–146

11. Lafleur B., Magnenat Thalmann N., Thalmann D. (1991) "Cloth Animation with Self-Collision Detection". In: *Proc. IFIP Conference on Modeling in Computer Graphics*, Springer, pp.179–187

12. Lin M.C., Manocha D. (1993) "Interference Detection between Curved Objects for Computer Animation". In: *Proc. Computer Animation '93*, Springer-Verlag, pp.43–55

13. Magnenat-Thalmann N., Thalmann D. (1991) "Flashback", video, 1 min., SIGGRAPH Video Review

14. Magnenat-Thalmann N., Thalmann D. (1992) "Fashion Show", video, 1 min

15. Magnenat-Thalmann N., Yang Y. (1991) "Techniques for Cloth Animation". In: Magnenat-Thalmann N., Thalmann D. (eds.) *New Trends in Animation and Visualization*. John Wiley & Sons Ltd., pp.243–256

16. Mangen A., Lasudry N. (1991) Search for the Intersection Polygon of any Two Polygons: Application to the Garment Industry. *Computer Graphics Forum* **10**, pp.19–208

17. Moore M., Wilhelms J. (1988) "Collision Detection and Response for Computer Animation". In: *Proc. SIGGRAPH'88 Computer Graphics* **22(4)**, pp.289–298

18. Morton W.E., Hearle J.W.S. (1962) "Physical properties of textile fibers", Manchester and London, The Textile Institute, Butterworths

19. Shinya M., Forgue M.C. (1991) "Interference Detection through Rasterisation". *Journal of Visualisation and Computer Animation*, J. Wiley & Sons, **4(2)**, pp.132–134

20. Snyder J.M., Woodbury A.R., Fleisher K., Currin B., Barr A.H. (1993) "Interval Methods for Multi-Point Collisions between Time-Dependant Curved Surfaces". *Computer Graphics annual series*, pp.321–334

21. Terzopoulos D., Platt J.C., Barr A.H. (1987) "Elastically Deformable Models". In: *Proc. SIGGRAPH'87, Computer Graphics* **21**, pp.205–214

22. Volino P., Courchesne M., Magnenat Thalmann N. (1995) "Versatile and Efficient Techniques for Simulating Cloth and Other Deformable Objects". *Computer Graphics* **29**, pp.137–144

23. Von Herzen B., Barr A.H., Zatz H.R. (1990) "Geometric Collisions for Time-Dependant Parametric Surfaces". In: *Proc. SIGGRAPH'90, Computer Graphics* **24(4)**, pp.39–48

24. Weil J. (1986) "The synthesis of Cloth Objects", *Proc. SIGGRAPH'86, Computer Graphics* **4**, pp.49–54

25. Werner H.M., Magnenat Thalmann N., Thalmann D. (1993) "User Interface for Fashion Design", *Graphics Design and Visualisation*, IFIP Trans. North Holland, pp.197–204

26. Witkin A., Welch W. (1990) "Fast Animation and Control of Non-Rigid Structures". In: *Proc. SIGGRAPH'90, Computer Graphics* **24**, pp.243–252

27. Yang Y., Magnenat Thalmann N. (1993) "An Improved Algorithm for Collision Detection in Cloth Animation with Human Body". In: *Proc. Pacific Graphics '93, Computer Graphics and Applications*, World Scientific Publishing, **1**, pp.237–251

Autonomous Virtual Actors Based on Virtual Sensors

Daniel Thalmann, Hansrudi Noser, Zhiyong Huang

Computer Graphics Lab, Swiss Federal Institute of Technology
Lausanne, Switzerland
{thalmann, noser, huang}@lig.di.epfl.ch

Abstract. In this paper, we present current research developments in the Virtual Life of autonomous synthetic actors. After a brief description of the perception action principles with a few simple examples, we emphasize the concept of virtual sensors for virtual humans. In particular, we describe in detail our experiences in implementing virtual vision, tactile, and audition. We then describe perception-based locomotion, a multisensor based method of automatic grasping, and vision-based ball games.

1 Introduction

As a virtual world is completely generated by computer, it expresses itself visually, with sounds and feelings. Virtual worlds deal with all the models describing physical laws of the real world as well as the physical, biological, and psychological laws of life. Virtual Life is linked to problems in artificial life but differs in the sense that these problems are specific to virtual worlds. It does not deal with physical or biological objects in real life but only with the simulation of biological virtual creatures. Virtual Life is at the intersection of Virtual Reality and Artificial Life [22], it is an interdisciplinary area strongly based on concepts of real-time computer animation, autonomous agents, and mobile robotics. Virtual Life cannot exist without the growing development of Computer Animation techniques and corresponds to the most advanced concepts and techniques of it.

In this paper, we first review the state-of-the-art in this emerging field of Virtual Life, then we emphasize the aspect of Virtual Life of Synthetic Actors, relating the topics to the previous chapters. The objective is to provide autonomous virtual humans with the skills necessary to perform stand-alone role in films, games [2] and interactive television ([23]). By autonomous we mean that the actor does not require the continual intervention of a user. Our autonomous actors should react to their environment and make decisions based on perception, memory and reasoning. With such an approach, we should be able to create simulations of situations such as virtual humans moving in a complex environment they may know and recognize, or playing ball games based on their visual and tactile perception.

1.1 State-of-the-Art in Virtual Life

This kind of research is strongly related to the research efforts in behavioral animation as introduced by Reynolds [30] to study the problem of group trajectories: flocks of birds, herds of land animals and fish schools. This kind of animation using a traditional approach (keyframe or procedural laws) is almost impossible. In the Reynolds approach, each bird of the flock decides its own trajectory without animator intervention. Reynolds introduces a distributed behavioral model to simulate flocks. The simulated flock is an elaboration of a particle system with the simulated birds being the particles. A flock is assumed to be the result of the interaction between the behaviors of individual birds. Working independently, the birds try both to stick together and avoid collisions with one another and with other objects in their environment. In a module of behavioral animation, positions, velocities and orientations of the actors are known from the system at any time. The animator may control several global parameters: e.g. weight of the obstacle avoidance component, weight of the convergence to the goal, weight of the centering of the group, maximum velocity, maximum acceleration, minimum distance between actors. The animator provides data about the leader trajectory and the behavior of other birds relatively to the leader. A computer-generated film has been produced using this distributed behavioral model: *Stanley and Stella*.

Haumann and Parent [13] describe behavioral simulation as a means to obtain global motion by simulating simple rules of behavior between locally related actors. Lethebridge and Ware [18] propose a simple heuristically-based method for expressive stimulus-response animation. Wilhelms [41] proposes a system based on a network of sensors and effectors. Ridsdale [33] proposes a method that guides lower-level motor skills from a connectionist model of skill memory, implemented as collections of trained neural networks.

We should also mention the huge literature about autonomous agents [19] which represents a background theory for behavioral animation. More recently, genetic algorithms were also proposed by Sims [36] to automatically generate morphologies for artificial creatures and the neural systems for controlling their muscle forces. Tu and Terzopoulos [39] described a world inhabited by artificial fishes

2 Virtual Sensors

2.1 Perception through Virtual Sensors

The problem of simulating the behavior of a synthetic actor in an environment may be divided into two parts: 1) provide to the actor a knowledge of his environment, and 2) to make him react to this environment.

The first problem consists of creating an information flow from the environment to the actor. This synthetic environment is made of 3D geometric shapes.

One solution is to give the actor access to the exact position of each object in the complete environment database corresponding to the synthetic world. This solution could work for a very "small world", but it becomes impracticable when the number of objects increases. Moreover, this approach does not correspond to reality where people do not have knowledge about the complete environment.

Another approach has been proposed by Reynolds [30]: the synthetic actor has knowledge about the environment located in a sphere centered on him. Moreover, the accuracy of the knowledge about the objects of the environment decreases with the distance. This is of course a more realistic approach, but as mentioned by Reynolds, an animal or a human being has always around him areas where his sensitivity is more important. Consider, for example, the vision of birds (birds have been simulated by Reynolds), they have a view angle of 300° and a stereoscopic view of only 15°. The sphere model does not correspond to the sensitivity area of the vision. Reynolds goes one step further and states that if actors can see their environment, they will improve their trajectory planning.

This means that the vision is a realistic information flow. Unfortunately, what is realistic to do for a human being walking in a corridor seems unrealistic to do for a computer. However, using hardware developments like the *graphic engine* [8], it is possible to give a geometric description of 3D objects together with the viewpoint and the interest point of a synthetic actor in order to get the vision on the screen. This vision may then be interpreted like the synthetic actor vision. This is our approach as described in this paper. More generally, in order to implement perception, virtual humans should be equipped with visual, tactile and auditory sensors. These sensors should be used as a basis for implementing everyday human behaviour such as visually directed locomotion, handling objects, and responding to sounds and utterances. For synthetic audition, in a first step, we model a sound environment where the synthetic actor can directly access to positional and semantic sound source information of an audible sound event. Simulating the haptic system corresponds roughly to a collision detection process. But, the most important perceptual subsystem is the vision system. A vision based approach for virtual humans is a very important perceptual subsystem and is for example essential for navigation in virtual worlds. It is an ideal approach for modeling a behavioral animation and offers a universal approach to pass the necessary information from the environment to the virtual human in the problems of path searching, obstacle avoidance, and internal knowledge representation with learning and forgetting. In the next sections, we describe our approach for the three types of virtual sensors: vision, audition and haptic.

2.2 Virtual Vision

Although the use of vision to give behavior to synthetic actors seems similar to the use of vision for intelligent mobile robots [14, 38], it is quite different. This is because the vision of the synthetic actor is itself a synthetic vision. Using a synthetic vision allow us to skip all the problems of pattern recognition and distance detection, problems which still are the most difficult parts in robotics vision. However some interesting work has been done in the topic of intelligent mobile robots, especially for action-perception coordination problems. For example, Crowley [9] working with surveillance robots states that "most low level perception and navigation tasks are algorithmic in nature; at the highest levels, decisions regarding which actions to perform are based on knowledge relevant to each situation". This remark gives us the hypothesis on which our vision-based model of behavioral animation is built.

We first introduced [29] the concept of synthetic vision as a main information channel between the environment and the virtual actor. Reynolds [31, 32] more recently described an evolved, vision-based behavioral model of coordinated group motion, he also showed how obstacle avoidance behavior can emerge from evolution under selection pressure from an appropriate measure using a simple computational model of visual perception and locomotion. The Genetic Programming is used to model evolution. Tu and Terzopoulos [39, 40] also use a kind of synthetic vision for their artificial fishes.

In [29], each pixel of the vision input has the semantic information giving the object projected on this pixel, and numerical information giving the distance to this object. So, it is easy to know, for example, that there is a table just in front at 3 meters. With this information, we can directly deal with the problematic question: "what do I do with such information in a navigation system?" The synthetic actor perceives his environment from a small window of typically 30x30 pixels in which the environment is rendered from his point of view. As he can access z buffer values of the pixels, the color of the pixels and his own position he can locate visible objects in his 3D environment. This information is sufficient for some local navigation.

We can model a certain type of virtual world representation where the actor maintains a low level fast synthetic vision system but where he can access some important information directly from the environment without having to extract it from the vision image. In vision based grasping for example, an actor can recognize in the image the object to grasp. From the environment he can get the exact position, type and size of the object which allows him to walk to the correct position where he can start the grasping procedure of the object based on geometrical data of the object representation in the world. This mix of vision based recognition and world representation access will make him fast enough to react in real time. The role of synthetic vision can even be reduced to a visibility test and the semantic information recognition in the image can be done by simple color coding and non shading rendering techniques. Thus, position and semantic information of an object can be obtained directly form the environment world after being filtered.

2.3 Virtual Audition

In real life, the behavior of persons or animals is very often influenced by sounds. For this reason, we developed a framework for modeling a 3D acoustic environment with sound sources and microphones. Now, our virtual actors are able to hear [28]. Any sound source (synthetic or real) should be converted to the AIFF format and processed by the sound renderer. The sound renderer takes into account the real time constraints. So it is capable to render each time increment for each microphone in "real time" by taking into account the final propagation speed of sound and the moving sound sources and microphones. So, the Doppler effect, for example, is audible.

In sound event generation, we integrated in our L-system-based software ([26, 25]) a peak detector of a force field which allows to detect collision between physical objects. These collisions can be coupled to sound emission events. For example, tennis playing with sound effects (ball-floor and ball-racket collision) has been realized.

The acoustic environment is composed of sound sources and a propagation medium. The sound sources can produce sound events composed of a position in the world, a type of sound, and a start and an end time of the sound. The propagation medium corresponds to the sound event handler which controls the sound events and transmits the sounds to the ears of the actors and/or to a user and/or a soundtrack file. We suppose an infinite sound propagation speed of the sound without weakening of the signal. The sound sources are all omnidirectional, and the environment is non reverberant.

2.4 Virtual Tactile

One of our aims is to build a behavioral model based on tactile sensory input received at the level of skin from the environment. This sensory information can be used in tasks as touching objects, pressing buttons or kicking objects For example at basic level, human should sense physical objects if any part of the body touches them and gather sensory information. This sensory information is made use of in such tasks as reaching out for an object, navigation etc. For example if a human is standing, the feet are in constant contact with the supporting floor. But during walking motion each foot alternately experiences the loss of this contact. Traditionally these motions are simulated using dynamic and kinematic constraints on human joints. But there are cases where information from external environment is needed. For example when a human descends a stair case, the motion should change from walk to descent based on achieving contact with the steps of the stairway. Thus the environment imposes constraints on the human locomotion. We propose to encapsulate these constraints using tactile sensors to guide the human figure in various complex situations other than the normal walking.

As already mentioned, simulating the haptic system corresponds roughly to a collision detection process. In order to simulate sensorial tactile events, a module has been designed to define a set solid objects and a set of sensor points attached to an actor. The sensor points can move around in space and collide with the above mentioned solid objects. Collisions with other objects out of this set are not detected. The only objective of collision detection is to inform the actor that there is a contact detected with an object and which object it is. Standard collision detection tests rely on bounding boxes or bounding spheres for efficient simulation of object interactions. But when highly irregular objects are present, such tests are bound to be ineffective. We need much 'tighter' bounding space than a box or a sphere could provide. We make use [1] of a variant of a digital line drawing technique called DDA [12] to digitize the surface of such objects to get very tight fitting bounds that can be used in preliminary collision detection.

3 Perception-based Actions

3.1 Action Level

Synthetic vision, audition and tactile allow the actor to perceive the environment. Based on this information, his behavioral mechanism will determine the actions he will perform. Actions may be at several degrees of complexity. An actor may simply evolve in his environment or he may interact with this environment or even communicate with other actors. We will emphasize three types of actions: navigation and locomotion, grasping and ball games.

Actions are performed using the common architecture for motion control developed in the European projects HUMANOID [3] and HUMANOID-2. HU-MANOID has led to the development of a complete system for animating virtual actors for film production. HUMANOID-2 currently extends the project for real-time applications and behavioral aspects as described in this paper. The heart of the HUMANOID software is the motion control part which includes 5 generators: keyframing, inverse kinematics, dynamics (see Fig.1), walking and grasping and high-level tools to combine and blend them. An interactive application TRACK [4] has been also developed to create films and sequences to be played in realtime playback for multimedia applications.

3.2 Perception-based Navigation and Locomotion

When the actor evolves in his environment, a simple walking model is not sufficient, the actor has to adapt his trajectory based on the variations of terrain by bypassing, jumping or climbing the obstacles he meets. The bypassing of obstacles consists in changing the direction and velocity of the walking of the actor. Jumping and climbing correspond to more complex motion. These actions should generate parameterized motion depending on the height and the length of the obstacle for a jump and the height and location of the feet for climbing the obstacle. These characteristics are determined by the actor from his perception.

The actor can be directed by giving his linear speed and his angular speed or by giving a position to reach. In the first case, the actor makes no perception (virtual vision). He just walks at the given linear speed and turns at the given angular speed. In the second case, the actor makes use of virtual vision enabling him to avoid obstacles. The vision based navigation can be local or global. With a local navigation, the agent goes straight on to his goal and it is possible that he cannot reach it. With a global navigation, the actor first tries to find a path to his goal and if the path exists, the actor follows it until he reaches the goal position or until he detects a collision by his vision. During global navigation the actor memorizes his perceived environment by voxelizing it, based on his synthetic vision. In the next section we will give more details on local and global navigation.

Fig. 1. Dynamics-based motion

We developed a special automaton for walking in complex environments with local vision based path optimization. So an actor continues walking even if he detects a future collision in front of him. By dynamically figuring out a new path during walking he can avoid the collision without halting. We also proposed a system for the automatic derivation of a human curved walking trajectory [6] from the analysis provided by its synthetic vision module. A general methodology associates the two low-level modules of vision and walking with a planning module which establishes the middle term path from the knowledge of the visualized environment. The planning is made under the constraint of minimizing the distance, the speed variation and the curvature cost. Moreover, the planning may trigger the alternate walking motion whenever the decreasing in curvature cost is higher than the associated increasing in speed variation cost due to the corresponding halt and restart. The analysis of walking trajectories on a discrete environment with sparse foothold locations has been also completed [5] regarding the vision-based recognition of footholds, the local path planning, the next step selection and the curved body trajectory. The walking model used is based on biomechanical studies of specific motion pattern [7]. Figure 2 shows an example of walking from the film *Still Walking* [21].

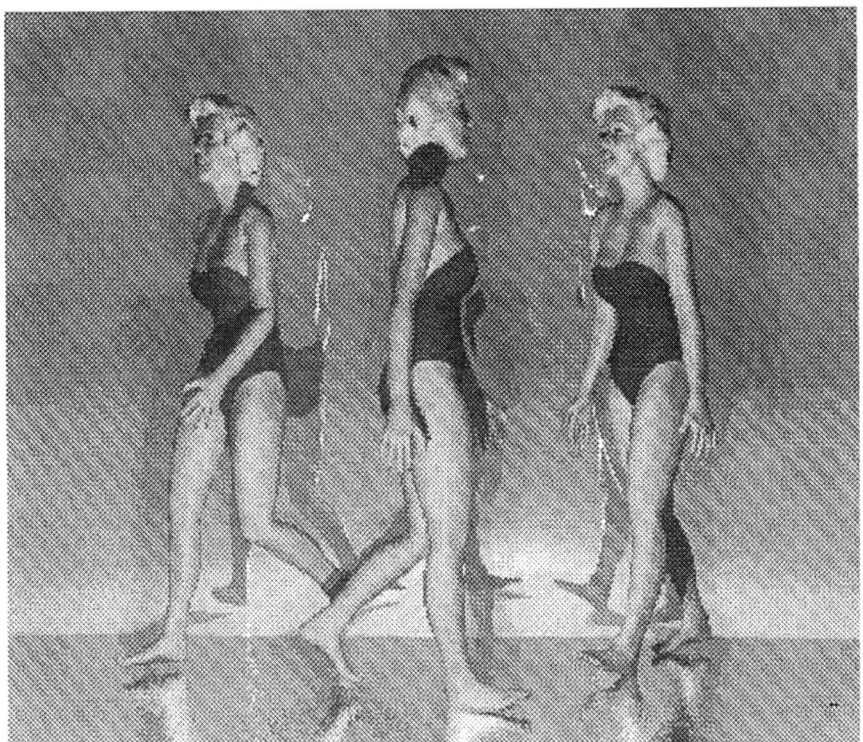

Fig. 2. Biomechanical model for walking from the film *Still Walking*

3.3 Global and Local Navigation

The task of a navigation system is to plan a path to a specified goal and to execute this plan, modifying it as necessary to avoid unexpected obstacles [9]. This task can be decomposed into global navigation and local navigation. The global navigation uses a prelearned model of the domain which may be a somewhat simplified description of the synthetic world and might not reflect recent changes in the environment. This prelearned model, or map, is used to perform a path planning algorithm.

The local navigation algorithm uses the direct input information from the environment to reach goals and sub-goals given by the global navigation and to avoid unexpected obstacles. The local navigation algorithm has no model of the environment, and doesn't know the position of the actor in the world. To make a comparison with a human being, close your eyes, try to see the corridor near your room, and how to follow it. No problem, you were using your "visual memory," which corresponds to the global navigation in our system. Now stand up and go to the corridor near your room, then close your eyes and try to cross the corridor... There the problems begin (you know that there is a skateboard in front of the door of your boss but...). This is an empirical demonstration of the functionalities of the local navigation as we define it in our system.

The global navigation needs a model of the environment to perform path-planning. This model is constructed with the information coming from the sensory system. Most navigation systems developed in robotics for intelligent mobile robots are based on the accumulation of accurate geometrical descriptions of the environment. Kuipers et al. [16] give a nearly exhaustive list of such methods using quantitative world modeling. In robotics, due to low mechanical accuracy and sensory errors, these methods have failed in large scale area. We don't have this problem in Computer Graphics because we have access to the world coordinates of the actor, and because the synthetic vision or other simulations of perception systems are more accurate. We developed a 3D geometric model, based on grid, implemented as an octree. Elfes [10] proposed a 2D geometric model based on grid but using a Bayesian probabilistic approach to filter non accurate information coming from various sensor positions. Roth-Tabak [35] proposed a 3D geometric model based on a grid but for a static world.

In the last few years, research in robot navigation has tended towards a more qualitative approach to world modeling, first to overcome the fragility of purely metrical methods, but especially, because humans do not make spatial reasoning on a continuous map, but rather on a discrete map [37]. Kuipers et al. [16] present a topological model as the basic element of the cognitive map. This model consists of a set of nodes and arcs, where nodes represent distinctively recognizable places in the environment, and arcs represent travel edges connecting them. Travel edges corresponding to arcs are defined by local navigation strategies which describe how a robot can follow the link connecting two distinct places. These local navigation strategies correspond to the Displacement Local Automata (DLA) implemented in the local navigation part of our system. These DLAs work as a black box which has the knowledge to create goals and sub-goals in a specific local environment. They can be thought of as low-level navigation reflexes which use vision, reflexes which are automatically performed by the adults.

The Octree as Visual Memory Representation. Noser et al. [27] use an octree as the internal representation of the environment seen by an actor because it offers several interesting features. With an octree we can easily construct enclosing objects by choosing the maximum depth level of the subdivision of space. Detailed objects like flowers and trees do not need to be represented in complete detail in the problem of path searching. It is sufficient to represent them by some enclosing cubes corresponding to the occupied voxels of the octree. The octree adapts itself to the complexity of the 3D environment, as it is a dynamic data structure making a recursive subdivision of space. Intersection tests are easy. To decide whether a voxel is occupied or not, we only have to go to the maximum depth (5-10) of the octree by some elementary addressing operations. The examination of the neighborhood of a voxel is immediate, too.

Another interesting property of the octree is the fact that it represents a graph of a 3D environment. We may consider, for example, all the empty voxels as nodes of a graph, where the neighbors are connected by edges. We can apply all the algorithms of graph theory directly on the octree and it is not necessary to change the representation.

Perhaps the most interesting property of the octree is the simple and fast transition from the 2D image to the 3D representation. All we have to do is take each pixel with its depth information (given by the z-buffer value) and calculate its 3D position in the octree space. Then, we insert it in the octree with a maximum recursion depth level. The corresponding voxel will be marked as occupied with possible additional information depending on the current application.

The octree has to represent the visual memory of an actor in a 3D environment with static and dynamic objects. Objects in this environment can grow, shrink, move or disappear. In a static environment (growing objects are still allowed) an *insert* operation for the octree is sufficient to get an approximate representation of the world. If there are moving or disappearing objects like cars, other actors, or opening and closing doors, we also need a *delete* operation for the octree. The *insert* operation is simple enough. The *delete* operation however, is more complicated.

To illustrate the capabilities of the synthetic vision system, we have developed several examples. First, an actor is placed inside a maze with an impasse, a circuit and some animated flowers. The actor's first goal is a point outside the maze. After some time, based on 2D heuristic, the actor succeeds in finding his goal. When he had completely memorized the impasse and the circuit, he avoided them. After reaching his first goal, he had nearly complete visual octree representation of his environment and he could find again his way without any problem by a simple reasoning process. We have also implemented a more complex environment with flowers and butterflies; the complex flowers were represented in the octree memory by enclosing cubes.

Local Navigation System. The local navigation system can be decomposed into three modules. The *vision* module, conceptually the perception system, draws a perspective view of the world in the vision window, constructs the vision array and can perform some low level operation on the vision array. The *controller* module, corresponding to the decision system, contains the main loop for the navigation system, and decides on the creation of the goals and administrates the DLAs. The *performer*, corresponding to the task execution system, contains all the DLAs.

The Vision Module. We use the hardware facilities of the Silicon Graphics IRIS to create the synthetic vision, more precisely we use the flat shading and z-buffer drawing capabilities of the graphic engine. The vision module has a modified version of the drawing routine traveling the world; instead of giving the real color of the object to the graphic engine, this routine gives a code, call the *vision_id*, which is unique for each object and actor in the world. This code allows the image recognition and interpretation. Once the drawing is done, the window buffer is copied into a 2D array. This array contains the vision_id and the z-buffer depth for each pixel. This array is referred to as the *view*.

The Controller Module. In local navigation there are two goals. These two goals are geometrical goals, and are defined in the local 2D coordinate system of the actor. The actor itself is the center of this coordinate system, one axis is defined by the direction "in front", the other axis is defined by the "side" direction. The global goal, or final goal, is the goal the actor must reach. The local goal, or temporary goal, is the goal the actor creates to avoid the obstacles encountered in the path towards the global goal. These goals are created by the Displacement Local Automata (DLA), or given by the animator or by the global navigation system. The main task of the controller is to create these goals created and to make the actor reach them.

Goal creation and actor displacement are performed by the DLAs. The controller selects the appropriate DLA either by knowing some internal set-up of the actor, or by visually analyzing the environment. For example, if the actor has a guide, the controller will choose the DLA *follow_the_guide*. Otherwise, from a 360 look-around, the controller will determine the visible objects and then determine the DLA corresponding to these objects. No real interpretation of the topology of the environment (as in [16]) has yet been implemented. The choice of the DLA is hardcoded by the presence of some particular objects, given by their *vision_id*.

The actor has an internal clock administrated by the controller. This clock is used by the controller to refresh the global and local goal at regular intervals. The interval is given by the *attention_rate*, a variable set-up for each actor that can be changed by the user or by the controller. This variable is an essential parameter of the system: with a too high attention rate the actor spends most of his time analyzing the environment and real-time motion is impossible; with a too low attention rate, the actor starts to act blindly, going through objects. A compromise must be found between these two extremes.

The Performer Module. This module contains the DLAs. There are three families of DLA: the DLAs creating the global goal (follow_the_corridor, follow_the_wall, follow_the_visual_guide), the DLAs creating the local goal (avoid_obstacle, closest_to_goal), and the DLAs effectively moving the actor (go_to_global_goal). The DLAs creating goals only use the vision as input. All these DLAs have access to a library of routines performing high level operations on the vision. A detailed algorithm of the use of vision to find avoidance goals is described in [29].

3.4 Perception-based Grasping

With the advents of virtual actors in computer animation, research in human grasping has become a key issue in this field. Magnenat Thalmann et al. [20] proposed a semi-automatic way of grasping for a virtual actor interacting with the environment. A knowledge-based approach is suitable for simulating human grasping, and an expert system can be used for this purpose [34]. Kunii et al. [17] have also presented a model of hands and arms based on manifolds. Our approach is based on three steps:

- **Inverse kinematics** to find the final arm posture.
- **Heuristic grasping decision.** Based on a grasp taxonomy, Mas and Thalmann [24] proposed a completely automatic grasping system for synthetic actors. In particular, the system can decide to use a pinch when the object is too small to be grasped by more than two fingers or to use a two-handed grasp when the object is too large.
- **Multi-sensor hand.** Our approach [15] is adapted from the use of proximity sensors in Robotics [11]. In our work, the sphere multi-sensors have both tactile and length sensor properties, and have been found very efficient for synthetic actor grasping problem. Multi-sensors are considered as a group of objects attached to the articulated figure. A sensor is activated for any collision with other objects or sensors. Here we select sphere sensors for their efficiency in collision detection (Fig.3).

Each sphere sensor is fitted to its associated joint shape with different radii. This configuration is important in our method because when a sensor is activated in a finger, only the articulations above it stop moving, while others can still move. By doing this way, all the fingers are finally positioned naturally around the object, as shown in Fig.4.

Fig. 3. The hand with sphere sensors at each joint

All the grasping functions mentioned above have been implemented and integrated into the TRACK system [4]. The examples shown in this section were performed on SGI Indigo 2 in real time. The first example shows actors grasping different objects (Fig.5). In Fig.6, we extend the grasping method to interactions between two actors.

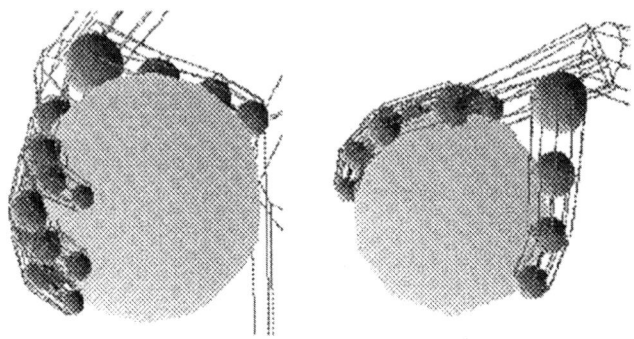

Fig. 4. One example showing sensors in grasping

Fig. 5. Examples of grasping different objects

Fig. 6. Interaction between two actors

3.5 Vision-based Tennis Playing

Tennis playing is a human activity which is severely based on the vision of the players. In our model, we use the vision system to recognize the flying ball, to estimate its trajectory and to localize the partner for game strategy planning. The geometric characteristics of the tennis court however, make part of the players knowledge. For the dynamics simulation of the ball, gravity, net, ground and the racquet we use the force field approach developed for the L-system animation system. The tracking of the ball by the vision system is controlled by a special automaton. A prototype of this automaton is already able to track the ball, to estimate the collision time and collision point of ball and racquet and to perform successfully a hit with given force and a given resulting ball direction. In a first step, we have a prototype where only two racquets with synthetic vision can play against each other, in order to develop, test and improve game strategy and the physical modeling. The integration of the corresponding locomotor system of a sophisticated actor is under development as seen in Fig.7.

In the navigation problem each colored pixel is interpreted as an obstacle. No semantic information is necessary. In tennis playing however, the actor has to distinguish between the partner, the ball and the rest of the environment. The ball has to be recognized, its trajectory has to be estimated and it has to be followed by the vision system. At the beginning of a ball exchange, the actor has to verify that its partner is ready. During the game the actor needs also his partner's position for his play strategy.

To recognize objects in the image we use color coding. The actor knows that a certain object is made of a specific material. When it scans the image it looks for the corresponding pixels and calculates its average position and its approximate size. Thus each actor can extract some limited semantic information from the image.

Fig. 7. Marilyn playing tennis

Once the actor has recognized the ball, it follows it with his vision system and adjusts at each frame his field of view. To play tennis each partner has to estimate the future racket-ball collision position and time and to move as fast as possible to this point. At each frame (1/25 sec) the actor memorizes the ball position. So, every n-th frame the actor can derive the current velocity of the ball. From this current velocity and the current position of the ball it can calculate the future impact point and impact time. We suppose that the actor wants to hit the ball at a certain height h.

In the next phase the actor has to play the ball. Now he has to determine the racket speed and its orientation to play the ball to a given place. Before playing the ball the actor has to decide where to play. In our simulation approach he looks where his partner is placed and then he plays the ball in the most distant corner of the court.

All the above features are coordinated by a specialized "play tennis" automaton. First an actor goes to his start position. There he waits until his partner is ready. Then he looks for the ball, which is thrown into the game. Once the vision system has found the ball, it always follows it by adjusting the field of view angle. If the ball is flying towards the actor, it starts estimating the impact point. Once the ball has passed the net, the actor localizes his partner with his vision system during one frame. This information is used for the game strategy. After playing the ball, the actor goes back to his start point and waits until the ball comes back to play it again.

4 Conclusion

In this chapter, we have presented a new approach to implement autonomous virtual actors in virtual worlds based on perception and virtual sensors. We believe this is an ideal approach for modeling a behavioral animation and offers a universal approach to pass the necessary information from the environment to an actor in the problems of path searching, obstacle avoidance, game playing, and internal knowledge representation with learning and forgetting characteristics. We also think that this new way of defining animation is a convenient and universal high level approach to simulate the behavior of intelligent human actors in dynamic and complex environments including virtual environments.

5 Acknowledgments

The authors are grateful to the people who contributed to this work, in particular Srikhan Bandi, Pascal Bécheiraz, Ronan Boulic, and Serge Rezzonico. The research was supported by the Swiss National Science Research Foundation, the Federal Office for Education and Science, and is part of the Esprit Project HUMANOID and HUMANOID-2.

References

1. Bandi S., Thalmann D. (1995) "An Adaptive Spatial Subdivision of the Object Space for Fast Collision Detection of Animated Rigid Bodies". In: *Proc. Eurographics '95*, Maastricht

2. Bates J, Loyall A.B., Reilly W.S. (1992) "An architecture for Action, Emotion, and Social Behavior". In: *Proc. Fourth Europeans Workshop on Modeling Autonomous Agents in a multi Agents World*, S. Martino al Cimino, Italy

3. Boulic R., Capin T., Kalra P., Lintermann B., Moccozet L., Molet T., Huang Z., Magnenat-Thalmann N., Saar K., Schmitt A., Shen J., Thalmann D. (1995) "A system for the Parallel Integrated Motion of Multiple Deformable Human Characters with Collision Detection". In: *Proc. Eurographics '95*, Maastricht

4. Boulic R., Huang Z., Magnenat-Thalmann N., Thalmann D. (1994) "Goal-Oriented Design and Correction of Articulated Figure Motion with the TRACK System". *Comput. & Graphics* 18(4) pp. 443–452

5. Boulic R., Noser H., Thalmann D. (1993) "Vision-Based Human Free-Walking on Sparse Foothold Locations". In: *Proc. Fourth Eurographics Workshop on Animation and Simulation*. Barcelona Spain, Eurographics, pp. 173–191

6. Boulic R., Noser H., Thalmann D. (1994b) "Automatic Derivation of Curved Human Walking Trajectories from Synthetic Vision". In: *Proc. Computer Animation '94*, Geneva. IEEE Computer Society Press, pp. 93–103

7. Boulic R., Thalmann D, Magnenat-Thalmann N. (1990) "A global human walking model with real time kinematic personification". *The Visual Computer*, 6(6)

8. Clark J.H. (1982) "The Geometric Engine: A VLSI Geometry System for Graphics". In: *Proc. SIGGRAPH '82, Computer Graphics* 10(3) pp. 127–133

9. Crowley J.L. (1987) "Navigation for an Intelligent Mobile Robot". *IEEE Journal of Robotics and Automation* RA-1(1), pp. 31–41

10. Elfes A. (1990) "Occupancy Grid: A Stochastic Spatial Representation for Active Robot Perception". In: *Proc. Sixth Conference on Uncertainty in AI*

11. Espiau B., Boulic R. (1985) "Collision avoidance for redondants robots with proximity sensors". In: *Proc. of Third International Symposium of Robotics Research*, Gouvieux, October 1985

12. Fujimoto A., Tanaka T., Iwata K. (1986) "ARTS: Accelerated Ray-Tracing System". *IEEE CG&A* **6(4)** pp. 16-26

13. Haumann D.R., Parent R.E. (1988) "The Behavioral Test-bed: Obtaining Complex Behavior from Simple Rules". *The Visual Computer* **4(6)** pp. 332-347

14. Horswill I. (1993) "A Simple, Cheap, and Robust Visual Navigation System". In: *From Animals to Animats 2, Proc. 2nd Intern. Conf. on Simulation of Adaptive Behavior*. MIT Press, pp. 129-136

15. Huang Z., Boulic R., Magnenat Thalmann N., Thalmann D. (1995) "A Multi-sensor Approach for Grasping and 3D Interaction". *Proc. CGI '95*

16. Kuipers B., Byun Y.T. (1988) "A Robust Qualitative Approach to a Spatial Learning Mobile Robot". *SPIE Sensor Fusion: Spatial Reaoning and Scene Interpretation* **1003**

17. Kunii T.L., Tsuchida Y., Matsuda H., Shirahama M., Miura S. (1993) "A model of hands and arms based on manifold mappings". In: *Proc. CGI '93*. pp. 381-398

18. Lethebridge T.C. and Ware C. (1989) "A Simple Heuristically-based Method for Expressive Stimulus-response Animation". *Computers and Graphics* **13(3)** pp. 297-303

19. Maes P. (ed.) (1991) "Designing Autonomous Agents", Bradford MIT Press

20. Magnenat-Thalmann N., Laperrière R., Thalmann D. (1988) "Joint-dependent local deformations for hand animation and object grasping". In: *Proc. of Graphics Interface '88* pp. 26-33

21. Magnenat-Thalmann N., Thalmann D. (1991) "Still Walking", video, 1 min

22. Magnenat-Thalmann N., Thalmann D. (1994) "Creating Artificial Life in Virtual Reality". In: Magnenat-Thalmann N., Thalmann D. (eds.) *Artificial Life and Virtual Reality*. John Wiley, Chichester, 1994, pp. 1-10

23. Magnenat-Thalmann N., Thalmann D. (1995) "Digital Actors for Interactive Television". *Proc. IEEE* **July**

24. Mas S.R., Thalmann D. (1994) "A Hand Control and Automatic Grasping System for Synthetic Actors". In: *Proc. Eurographics '94*. pp. 167-178

25. Noser H., Thalmann D. (1993) "L-System-Based Behavioral Animation". In: *Proc. Pacific Graphics '93* pp. 133-146

26. Noser H, Thalmann D, Turner R (1992) "Animation based on the Interaction of L-systems with Vector Force Fields". In: *Proc. Computer Graphics International*. In: Kunii T.L. (ed.): *Visual Computing*, Springer, Tokyo, pp. 747-761

27. Noser H., Renault O., Thalmann D., Magnenat Thalmann N. (1995) "Navigation for Digital Actors based on Synthetic Vision, Memory and Learning". Pergamon Press *Computers and Graphics* **19(1)** pp. 7-19

28. Noser H., Thalmann D. (1995) "Synthetic Vision and Audition for Digital Actors". In: *Proc. Eurographics '95*, Maastricht

29. Renault O., Magnenat Thalmann N., Thalmann D. (1990) "A Vision-based Approach to Behavioural Animation". *The Journal of Visualization and Computer Animation* **1(1)**, pp. 18-21

30. Reynolds C. (1987) "Flocks, Herds, and Schools: A Distributed Behavioral Model". In: *Proc. SIGGRAPH '87. Computer Graphics* **21(4)** pp. 25-34

31. Reynolds C.W. (1993) "An Evolved, Vision-Based Behavioral Model of Coordinated Group Motion". In: Meyer J.A. et al. (eds.) *From Animals to Animats, Proc. 2nd International Conf. on Simulation of Adaptive Behavior*, MIT Press, pp. 384-392

32. Reynolds C.W. (1994) "An Evolved, Vision-Based Model of Obstacle Avoidance Behavior". In: C.G. Langton (ed.), *Artificial Life III, SFI Studies in the Sciences of Complexity* **Proc. Vol. XVII**, Addison-Wesley

33. Ridsdale G. (1990) "Connectionist Modelling of Skill Dynamics". *Journal of Visualization and Computer Animation* **1(2)** pp. 66–72

34. Rijpkema H, Girard M. (1991) "Computer animation of knowledge-based human grasping". In: *Proc. SIGGRAPH'91* pp. 339–348

35. Roth-Tabak Y. (1989) "Building an Environment Model Using Depth Information". *Computer* pp. 85–90

36. Sims K. (1994) "Evolving Virtual Creatures". In: *Proc. SIGGRAPH '94 Computer Graphics* pp. 15–22

37. Sowa J.F. (1964) *Conceptual Structures*, Addison-Wesley

38. Tsuji S., Li S. (1993) "Memorizing and Representing Route Scenes", In: Meyer J.A. et al. (eds.) *From Animals to Animats, Proc. 2nd International Conf. on Simulation of Adaptive Behavior*, MIT Press, pp. 225–232

39. Tu X., Terzopoulos D. (1994) "Artificial Fishes: Physics, Locomotion, Perception, Behavior". In: *Proc. SIGGRAPH '94, Computer Graphics* pp. 42–48

40. Tu X., Terzopoulos D. (1994b) "Perceptual Modeling for the Behavioral Animation of Fishes". In: *Proc. Pacific Graphics '94*, World Scientific Publishers, Singapore, pp. 165–178

41. Wilhelms J. (1990) "A "Notion" for Interactive Behavioral Animation Control". *IEEE Computer Graphics and Applications* **10(3)** pp. 14–22

Towards Personalities for Animated Agents
with
Reactive and Planning Behaviors

Norman I. Badler, Barry D. Reich, Bonnie L. Webber

Center for Human Modeling and Simulation
Department of Computer & Information Science
University of Pennsylvania*

Abstract. We describe a framework for creating animated simulations
of virtual human agents. The framework allows us to capture flexible
patterns of activity, reactivity to a changing environment, and certain
aspects of an agent personality model. Each leads to variation in how
an animated simulation will be realized. As different parts of an activity
make different demands on an agent's resources and decision-making, our
framework allows special-purpose reasoners and planners to be associated
with only those phases of an activity where they are needed. Personality
is reflected in locomotion choices which are guided by an agent model
that interacts with the other components of the framework.

1 Introduction

Conventional animations often seek to re-create "life" through the artistic skills
of an animator who, by drawing and painting, externalizes observations, experience, and intuition into the images, shapes, and movements that make for
believable characters [33]. For three-dimensional computer animation, one has a
more complex toolkit and a commensurately harder task defining exactly what
makes an *object* into a *character*. Part of the problem is the control of multiple
degrees of freedom: not only must the character do whatever is desired, it must
also convey a feeling of liveliness, animacy, and engagement with the environment. Being able to simply walk from here to there is not enough; there should
be purpose, reactivity, and attitude. We explore some of these issues in a discussion of a synthetic human agent architecture and a specific implementation in a
system called *Jack*® [3].

---

* This research has been partially supported by DMSO DAAH04-94-G-0402; ARPA
DAMD17-94-J-4486; U.S. Air Force DEPTH through Hughes Missile Systems
F33615-91-C-0001; Air Force DAAH04-95-1-0151; NSF IRI95-04372; ARO DURIP
DAAH04-95-1-0023; and ARPA AASERT DAAH04-94-G-0362.

Three primary mechanisms exist for specifying motion in a synthetic computer-generated character:

1. Direct manipulation of the body parts to the poses desired;
2. Actually perform the actions, so that the virtual agent mimics the participant's actual performance;
3. Instructing an agent in what to do, so that its behavior follows, in part, from the goals it has adopted.

Recent automated techniques for animation aim to ease the animator's burden, but it appears that *personality* is typically established through skillful direct manipulations. As such, it is *ad hoc* and probably difficult to quantify and reproduce. Incorporating mathematical techniques for motion interpolation, and even using physics-based models, the agents tend to look personality-free at best and hapless mechanical mannequins at worst.

Producing animated people seems to require more than the existing physical or manual toolset. One response to this difficulty is *performance animation*: live actors perform while sensing systems monitor various body parts such as hands [13], faces [39], or landmarks [2, 29]. While this provides motion data of unquestioned realism, it is only one instance of a performance: different conditions can lead to different motions because people adapt their behavior to circumstances through their unconscious reactions and conscious decision-making. Moreover, unless the performer is additionally a good actor, the *personality* of the performer is captured as well. This bias sometimes may be exactly what was desired, but at other times it is an unwelcome feature that must be suppressed by manual post-processing [12]. This may be possible for an agent's *physical* style, but behavioral characteristics that follow from their *decision-making* (or *cognitive*) style are another story.

We start by briefly reviewing our historical approaches to personality for animated humans. Then we will present a two-level architecture for intelligent agents, including computational approaches to patterns of human activity and how PaT-Nets capture such patterns for the production of animated simulations. Finally we will describe how agent personality variations can affect the animated outcomes, both in terms of physical style and decision making/cognitive style.

2   Approaches to Animated Agent Personalities

Above we outlined three modes of controlling animation:

1. Manipulating the human agent directly to position and move it as desired;
2. Showing the human agent what to do, so it moves by imitation;
3. Telling the human agent what to do, so that its behavior follows, in part, from the goals it has adopted.

We believe future *real-time* animations must converge to techniques (2) and (3): basically "do what I do" and "do what I tell you to do". Performance-based systems for virtual environments are forced to adopt technique (2). The economy of expression in verbalized commands requires considerable ongoing study of technique (3). But the techniques developed for direct manipulation (1) will emerge as the facilitator for the other two. Thus we consider the study of algorithmic techniques for human movement control to be an important endeavor for animating personalities for real-time agents.

2.1 Physical Style

About twenty years ago we began studying human movement notations in order to gain insight into what qualities and properties human movement observers and choreographics abstracted from the continuum of motion. Briefly, our first "lesson learned" was that the formal (and even computationally tractable) structures of Labanotation [21, 36] captured the *form* of movement but not its *essence* – that is, its character, style, or emotion. We learned that even Laban was aware of its limitations, and towards the end of his career developed another system called "Effort-Shape" [17]. This system sought to describe the "qualities" or shape of a movement without trying to bind it to specific spatial locations or orientations.

In more physical terms, we saw Effort-Shape as seeking to characterize the first and second derivatives of position, and we began to explore some of the possible relationships between Effort-Shape notation and computer animation techniques [1]. We felt that if we could characterize Effort-Shape qualities in terms of computational realizations, we could generate characters with various personalities or emotional content. While there were tantalizing beginnings to this process, we were stymied by other problems (such as modeling a decent human figure in the first place) and so directed our attentions elsewhere. Only much later did some of this work re-surface under the guise of locomotion "styles" [22]: when the *Jack* figure was animated walking with bent torso and smooth motion, the walk conveyed a distinct pensive or sad look; Walking with upright torso, raised shoulders, and an abrupt gait conveyed a "macho" or aggressive look. We have not researched this specific connection more thoroughly, but the underlying motion implementations are now sufficiently developed to make the prospect both interesting and feasible.

2.2 Cognitive Style

Most animation tools provide manual control over images, shapes, and movements. Recently, more automated techniques for animation have been developed, often to ease some burden or other on the animator. For example, dynamics can be used to animate particles or objects responding to physical forces [20, 37], and "flocking" can be used to constrain interactions between figures in a scene [27, 34]. Partial success can be judged from the various physics-based techniques that use "real-world" mathematics to get the motions "right" [16, 32, 40].

Unfortunately, getting animated figures to appear human-like seems to require more than the existing physical or manual toolset. One reaction to this difficulty has been the "performance animation" noted earlier, where actors go through the necessary motions while sensing systems monitor various body landmarks. While this provides motion data of unquestioned realism, it is only a specific instance of a performance and might still need massaging by an expert. For example, it may not be directly usable for a character of markedly different body size/shape than the original actor.

Moreover, while performance animation generally guarantees that the physics is correct — without building and evaluating the formulas – it still misses something. Consider the following scenario:

> A pedestrian stands on a street corner, waiting for the light to change so that he can safely cross the street. Meanwhile a car is approaching the same intersection. What happens when the light changes?

In this scenario, the performance-based data might be useful for animating the character's walk, though it could also be simulated through a locomotion generator [22]. In a scripted animation, the animator would be responsible for initiating the walk when the light changed and would also be controlling the car motions. Suppose we then removed the animator: A pedestrian completely driven by physics would be propelled across the street by his forward force. The car would also be moved by physics. If they arrived at the same place at the same time, the animation might be exciting but it would not be fun for either the car or the pedestrian. So what happens when we remove the animator is that we remove the pedestrian's decisions: *human movement realism reflects decision-making in context*. For realistic animation, *synthetic humans must engage in such decision-making if we want them to share human qualities*. Sensed human motions are insufficient because they reflect only decisions that have already been made. Physics is insufficient because there are no decisions outside the outcome of the mathematical laws. Conscious humans are neither puppets nor mannequins. They continually assess their surroundings (to validate expectations, avoid obstacles, minimize surprises *etc.* [35]), make choices, and plan for the future.

Different cognitive "styles" of sensing, decision-making and planning (including, for example, a agent's degree of commitment to his/her current goals [10]) can make animated human agents behave differently in response to the same environment and symbolically-specified activity. Below we will describe several personality variants that are apropos to our project of having a set of animated humans play games of Hide and Seek [4]. These include styles of seeking a hiding place, styles of responding to inferred intentions of other agents, and styles of pursuit.

3   The Agent Architecture

Allowing behavior to follow from decisions made in context appears to be a prime motivator for human-like agents. In this section we outline our agent architecture as a two-level structure. The lower level functions as a Sense-Control-Act (SCA) loop, while a higher level executes a pre-defined (but general) schema.

An *agent* can take action by virtue of having an SCA loop to produce locally-adaptive (reactive) behavior. In general, behaviors are considered "low level" capabilities of an agent, such as being able to locomote [to], reach [for], look [at], *etc.* In this discussion, we shall concentrate primarily on the walking behavior, as it is clearly influenced by the local structure of the environment, the presence of sensed obstacles, distance to the goal, *etc.*

An agent also manifests high-level patterns of activity and deliberation, which in turn can affect the immediate formulation and parameters of an SCA loop. Such patterns are captured in our framework through parallel state-machines we call *Parallel Transition Networks*, or PaT-Nets. PaT-Nets can sequence actions based on the current state of the environment, of the goal, or of the system itself, and represent the tasks in progress, conditions to be monitored, resources used, and temporal synchronization. An agent's deliberations both prior to and during action can be captured through special purpose reasoners and planners associated with specific states of a network.

In this framework, the agent can instantiate PaT-Nets to accomplish goals (*e.g.*, go to the supply depot and pick up a new motor), while low-level control is mediated through direct sensing and action couplings in the SCA loop (*e.g.*, controlling where the agent's feet step and making sure that s/he doesn't run into or trip over any obstacles). By linking numerical feedback streams (SCA loops) and state controllers (PaT-Nets supported by special-purpose reasoners and planners), we believe it is possible to obtain maximum flexibility and maintain appropriate levels of specification in the animated simulation of virtual human agents [3, 8].

The rest of this section briefly describes features of SCA loops and PaT-Nets. For more detail, see [4].

3.1   Low-Level Control: SCA Loops

The *behavioral loop* is a continuous stream of floating point numbers from the simulated environment. Simulated sensors map these data to the abstract results of perception and route them through control processes, each of which is independently attempting to solve a minimization problem. The results go to simulated effectors or motor actions that enact changes on the agent or the world. This loop operates continuously.

The behavioral loop is modeled as a network of interacting *sense, control,* and *action* (SCA) processes, connected by arcs across which only floating point messages travel. An individual path from sensors to effectors is referred to as a *behavioral net.* It is analogous to a complete behavior in an "emergent behavior" architecture such as Brooks' *subsumption architecture* [11], except that nodes may be shared between behaviors, and arbitration (competition for effector resources) may occur throughout the behavioral path and not just at the end-effector level. The behavioral loop is modeled as a network with floating point connections in order to allow the application of low-level, unsupervised, reinforcement learning in the behavioral design process [7]. Here we briefly describe the components of an SCA loop.

Sensory Nodes Sensory nodes model or approximate the abstract, geometric results of object perception. They continuously generate signals describing the polar coordinate position (relative to the agent) of a particular object or of all objects of a certain type within a specified distance and field of view.

Control Nodes Control nodes model the lowest level influences on behavior. For example, control of locomotion is loosely based on Braitenberg's *love* and *hate* behaviors [9], here called *attract* and *avoid*. Control nodes are formulated as explicit minimizations using outputs to drive inputs to a desired value (similar to Wilhelms' [37] use of Braitenberg's behaviors). They typically receive input signals directly from sensory nodes, and send outputs directly to action nodes, though they could be used in more abstract control situations.

Action Nodes Action nodes connect to the underlying human body model and directly execute routines defined on the model (such as walking, balance, hand position, and torso orientation) and arbitrate among inputs, either by selecting one set of incoming signals or averaging all incoming signals. An example is the *walk controller*, which decides where to place the agent's next footstep and then connects to the locomotion generator [3, 24] to achieve the step.

Our main use of SCA loops to date has been in locomotion reasoning.

3.2   High-Level Control: PaT-Nets

PaT-Nets are finite state machines with message passing and semaphore capabilities [6, 18]. Nodes are associated with processes that can invoke executable behaviors, other PaT-Nets, or specialized reasoners or planners. Invocation occurs when a node is entered. An arc transition between nodes in a PaT-Net may check a local condition evaluated within the PaT-Net or a global condition evaluated in an external environment. Arcs are prioritized, and a transition is made to a new node by selecting the first arc with a **true** condition. Nodes may also support probabilistic transitions, reflecting the probability of transitioning to another node at a given clock tick. *Monitors* associated with a PaT-Net will execute an action if a general condition evaluates to **true**, regardless of the current state. In addition, a PaT-Net may have local state variables available to all processes and conditions, and may also take parameters on instantiation.

A running network is created by making an instance of the PaT-Net class. All running PaT-Net instances are embedded in a Lisp operating system that time-slices them into the overall simulation. While running, PaT-Nets can spawn new nets, communicate with each other, kill other nets, and/or wait (sleep) until a condition is met. Running nets can, for example, spawn new nets and then wait for them to exit (effectively a subroutine call), or run in parallel with the new net, while maintaining communication with it. Because PaT-Nets are embedded in an object-oriented structure, new nets can be defined that override, blend, or extend the functionality of existing nets.

4 Patterns of Activity

It has long been recognized that much of everyday human activity falls into patterns. In early work on computer-based story understanding, such patterns were captured in structures called "scripts" or "schemata" and were used to fill in what hadn't been said in a story as well as what had been said [31]. Scripts/schemata have also be used in generating behavior. For example, in "hierarchical planning" [30, 38], a plan operator specifies a partially ordered pattern of actions or sub-goals that can be used to achieve a particular goal.

Here we want to make three points about patterns of activity:

1. Patterns have different sources: they may be idiosyncratic, peculiar to an individual; they may be cultural, simplifying interactions between people [14]; they may be occupational, as in a medic's initial assessment of a trauma patient [15]; or they may be recreational, as in the pattern of a game.
2. Patterns vary in their rigidity. They range from low-level fixed patterns one may do daily without thinking – for example, putting one's left shoe on first and then one's right – to high-level patterns of engagement where the particulars are subject to variation such as in having breakfast, making dinner, going out for dinner, playing golf, *etc.* The variation may reflect low-level reactions to circumstances, high-level decisions, or current state.
3. People may be engaged simultaneously in multiple patterns of activity. Their resulting behavior may therefore reflect their allocating different resources to different patterns, using one pattern in support of another, time-slicing patterns or blending patterns.

The next section shows how PaT-Nets can be used to capture patterns of activity in the game of Hide and Seek.

5 An Example of PaT-Net Agent Control

While there are many different sets of rules for Hide and Seek, most involve one player (who is "it" or the "seeker") first averting his/her eyes while the other players hide, then setting out to find at least one of them, then engaging in some competition with whomever is found, which may then lead to that other player becoming "it" in the next round. Thus Hide and Seek manifests a pattern of behavior whose realization may vary from instance to instance as players hide in different places, as different players are found, and as the competition between the player who is "it" and the player who is found yields different results. Here we show how this kind of pattern is easily supported in PaT-Nets.

The high-level controller, or *PlayNet*, for simulating one common version of Hide and Seek is illustrated in Fig. 1. In this version, a hider, once hidden, does not move until seen by the seeker, at which time the hider attempts to run home without being tagged by the seeker. In Fig. 1, the **Sync** node causes players to wait until all the players are "home", at which point the seeker may begin counting (**Count**) and the other players start to hide (**Hide**). The **Evade** node has a player running to home base, while avoiding the seeker. (Currently this sort of multi-goal behavior is hand-coded while a more general approach to multiple goal integration is worked out.) Dashed transitions in the network represent a change in role from hider to seeker or *vice-versa*. The **at home** condition becomes true when the agent is at home-base, while the **safe** condition becomes true when the seeker notices that the hider he is pursuing has made it home.

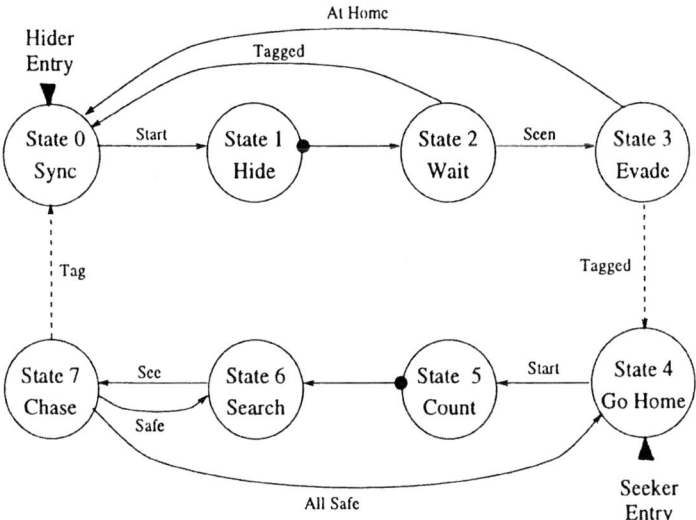

Fig. 1. PlayNet for Hide and Seek

While a *PlayNet* specifies an entire game of Hide and Seek, each player a personal copy, which records features of the game specific to that player (*e.g.*, whether the player has been seen by the seeker or made it home safely), as well as features of the global state of the game (*e.g.*, whether all hiders have made it home safely).

To support agent coordination, two types of communicative mechanisms have been used in Hide and Seek. First, the environment itself is used: Players have limited (simulated) perceptual abilities which allow them to see unobstructed nearby things in their environment. This supports the coordination involved in see/seen in Fig. 1. Second, coordination of all agents is handled through semaphores. For example, in Fig. 1, count **done** is broadcast to all agents, as are **tag/tagged** and **at home/safe**, since such information is relevant to all players but cannot be insured known through the players' limited perception.

Focusing now on the processes associated with individual nodes of a *PlayNet*, these may either be intrinsically terminating, as in **count** (count to 10), indicated by a black dot on the arc, or externally terminating by virtue of some event in the environment. For example, **search** is only terminated when circumstances provide the seeker with a hider. Note that intrinsically terminating processes may also be interrupted by external events, stopping them before completion.

For example, **evade** (*i.e.*, run home while evading the seeker) is intrinsically terminated by the hider reaching home, but may be interrupted by the hider being tagged. For PaT-Nets to support this, actions must be cleanly preemptable, so that the simulation programmer can pass in a condition for premature termination.

The use of special purpose reasoners and planners in the context of specific processes is illustrated in two of the nodes of Fig. 1 – **hide** and **search**. Currently during **hide**, a special purpose reasoner is invoked when the node is entered, that evaluates the set of hiding places the agent knows about and chooses one that maximizes the agent's preference criteria. Each agent has different preferences regarding a hiding place – differing by the importance of its distance from the seeker, the number of available exits, *etc*. Once a hiding place is chosen, the agent moves towards it. One can imagine, though, a more sophisticated reasoner for choosing hiding places that would be able to work in previously "unknown" environments and that would provide more room for the expression of cognitive style. Such a reasoner might carry out noticing and evaluating hiding places in parallel, while moving away from "home". Since all hiders are simultaneously looking for hiding places, agent personality can be expressed in their response to contention for a hiding place. An non-combative agent might acquiesce and seek another spot as soon as it "realizes" there may be contention for its current chosen target. A confrontational agent might respond quite differently.

Another special purpose reasoner is illustrated in the **search** node. Searching is viewed as choosing a place to look for a hider, and then doing what one needs to get there ([19, 23]). Choosing a place to look involves keeping track of where one has looked already and reasoning about what remaining spaces can contain an agent that the seeker cannot see. Unlike hiding currently, seeking does not assume the seeker knows about all possible hiding places *a priori*. More effort has been put into a model of realistic seeking than hiding.

6 Behavioral Control of Human Locomotion Based on Personality

The aim is to design and build a system in which an animator has control over the agent model. This includes personality traits such as curiosity and cautiousness, and state information such as the agent's energy level and alertness. The animator sets high-level locomotion goals for the agent. The system generates locomotion automatically based on the agent model, shaping the locomotion to reflect and convey to an observer the agent state and personality chosen by the animator.

As an example, consider an animator who is given the task of modeling several agents playing hide and seek in an outdoor environment. We will look at two in particular: Marge and Homer. In the scene to be animated, Homer is in his hiding place and Marge is seeking. The animator opens the agent model interface window and configures the agents beginning with Homer. She clicks on the "Speed" button with the mouse and a slider-bar appears. She chooses a relatively fast speed of 9.0 (out of 10.0). Then she sets Homer's "Awareness" of his surroundings to 9.5.

The animator configures Marge in a similar way, also setting her "Awareness" to 9.0, but setting her "Speed" to 6.0. She wants to find a hider quickly, but not to move so quickly that she misses someone. Finally, that animator wants to allow Marge to notice and react to hiders as they become visible. She defines a LISP condition which evaluates to TRUE when Marge can see a hider. The probability of reacting to this condition when it becomes TRUE she relates to Marge's "Awareness" level. If this happens, a new schema is adopted with the goal "go to hider", followed by schemata that cause Marge to tag the hider and bring everyone home, ending the game. When the animator tests the configurations by starting the locomotion control systems, she sees the following.

> Marge begins exploring the environment. She is walking somewhat quickly, entering and exiting small structures and avoiding obstacles. As she walks from one building to another, she notices Homer hiding in the alley between them. She stops, turns toward Homer, and begins chasing him. Homer notices Marge immediately, turns away from her, and runs away.

The animator shows the animation to a colleague. After a few minutes of discussion and a small amount of parameter adjustment, she is satisfied that the agents appear to have the desired personalities. What follows is a description of our multi-level locomotion control system that supports this embodiment of a character's personality traits in their locomotion choices and characteristics.

This system controls locomotion at three levels. At the lowest level, a behavioral simulation system controls agent locomotion directly based on a behavioral loop associated with the agent (Sec. 3.1). This level makes final choices about where the agent will place his feet at each step. The second level consists of PaT-Nets (Sec. 3.2) that control agent locomotion indirectly by scheduling and controlling reactive behaviors. Above this is an "agent model" to configure the state-machine and parameterize the behaviors so that the agent's locomotion style reflects its personality, and physical and mental state.

The behavioral simulation system [8] communicates directly with a human locomotion system [22] choosing each footstep for the agent based on a set of behaviors associated with that agent. The behaviors are variations of attraction and avoidance and are completely parameterizable. The agent's observed behavior is the result of the choice of behaviors and parameters which are themselves the results of choices made at higher levels.

There are limits to what low-level reactive behaviors can achieve. When the desired complexity of an agent's behavior increases beyond this limit, higher-level locomotion reasoning must be introduced. Locomotion reasoning determines the characteristics of an agent's locomotion: *i.e.*, what types of attractions and avoidances with what choice of parameters will achieve the goal. This is done via PaT-Nets.

PaT-Nets and their special purpose reasoners support complex behaviors such as *chasing* and *path-following* where behaviors and parameters change over time (Sec. 5). In addition to changing behaviors and parameters, the state-machine structure allows us to evaluate, in parallel, arbitrary conditions, passed as arguments. If any of these conditions ever evaluate to **TRUE**, the state-machine takes an appropriate action. These conditions allow the agent to interrupt the current plan when an unexpected situation occurs, *e.g.*, when something of interest enters the agent's field-of-view. An appropriate message is passed up to the calling system allowing it to replan.

The agent model, a set of agent characteristics or attributes, is a global structure of attributes that can affect the configuration of the state-machine which in turn affects the agent's perceived behavior.

Table 1 shows a subset of the characteristics that make up the agent model and some of the ways each one affects the agent's behavior. **Speed**, or walking rate, is one of the factors regulated by the "rushed" and "fatigued" slider bars. A fatigued or laden agent walks slowly while an agent who is in a rush walks quickly or runs. An inebriated agent walks at an inconsistent rate, with a velocity that varies in an amount proportional to the level of intoxication.

Table 1. How the agent model affects the agent

Characteristic	Locomotion System Parameters Affected				
	Speed	Inertia	Anticipation	Condition	Probability
Fatigued	X				
Laden	X				
Rushed	X				X
Inebriated	X	X	X		X
Aware			X		X
Alert to Danger				X	
Curious				X	X
Distracted					X

The combination of several behaviors, as is necessary with behavioral control, typically yields excessively wandering paths. In an attempt to straighten locomotion paths, we add an "inertia" behavior to an agent's behavior set which attracts the agent to the forward direction. An inebriated agent is given a low **Inertia** value and tends to meander as a result.

When we walk around in the presence of other people we attempt to avoid them based not only on their current location, but also on a guess of where they will be one or more steps in the future. Consciously or unconsciously, we anticipate their potential locations in the near future and base our avoidance on this prediction. An inebriated agent has a lower **Anticipation** value than normal, while an agent who is particularly aware of his surroundings will anticipate more.

Condition is a special system feature implemented at the state-machine level. It is a *hook* which allows the animator to implement behaviors, particularly those involving sub-goals, and make decisions that are unsupported by the architecture. When an arbitrary condition evaluates to TRUE, the state-machine takes an appropriate action, possibly stopping the agent and exiting. This allows a higher-level system to replan, taking advantage of the opportunity. A condition, for example, might evaluate to TRUE when an enemy is in the agent's field-of-view. Consider this scenario. We see a burglar walk past a police officer. The burglar notices the officer and starts running (his sense of urgency increases). He tries to find a good hiding place while the officer pursues him. Our system is capable of simulating this scenario.

Although the burglar passes the officer, in real life, there is no guarantee that they would notice each other. **Probability** refers to the probability that an agent will react to the condition evaluating to TRUE. The probability is high when the agent is aware of his surroundings or curious, but low when he is distracted, inebriated, or rushed, for example.

7 Conclusion

We have just begun to explore the power of this agent architecture. Many questions have been identified for further study. They include:

- the viability of confining high-level reasoning and planning to particular nodes of a PaT-Net. It may be that in other activities, reasoning and planning need a more global purview or need to be interleaved in as yet unforeseen ways.
- the range of activities worth framing in a net-based approach: the greater the number of nodes, the greater the connectivity between them, and the greater the complexity of the arc conditions, the less a net-based approach seems to make sense. In other words, we would like to identify criteria we can use to decide when to employ a first-principles planner and when we can use a network of pre-determined decision points. It is possible that learning a task or becoming more expert at something entails a migration from planning as a node to more focused networks of choices.
- a clear regimen for mapping instructions for a task or game (including warnings and constraints) to one or more communicating PaT-Nets.
- the mechanism for incorporating other personality traits, especially non-locomotor ones. Preliminary investigations into two-person synthetic communication has already yielded insights into personality influences on speech, dialogue, turn-taking, and gesture [14].

We have noted here that *synthetic humans must also be able to adapt to circumstances if we want them to share human qualities.* Motion performance is not sufficient because we do not know yet how to readily adapt it to other circumstances. Even when behavior essentially follows a pattern, as in going to a supermarket, playing a game, or trouble-shooting and/or repairing equipment, people sense the world around them, react and make choices in ways that adapt the pattern to their personalities and circumstances. It is supporting flexible patterns of activity that motivates much of our research. We see animation as an integration of a rich collection of interacting techniques, organized in a principled, structured representation. Here we have discussed its use in representing flexible patterns of human activity influenced by personality.

Our experiments so far indicate that the representational efficacy of this architecture of behavioral reaction, transition networks, symbolic planning, and certain personality attributes is necessary for modeling actions of human-like agents. Whether it is sufficient is a question for the future.

References

1. Badler N. (1989) A representation for natural human movement. In J. Gray (ed.), *Dance Technology I*. AAHPERD Publications, Reston, VA, pp.23–44
2. Badler N.I., Hollick M.J.. Granieri J. (1993) Real-time control of a virtual human using minimal sensors. *Presence* **2(1)** pp.82–86
3. Badler N.I., Phillips C.W., Webber B.L. (1993) *Simulating Humans: Computer Graphics Animation and Control*. Oxford University Press, New York, NY
4. Badler N.I., Webber B.L., Becket W., Geib C., Moore M., Pelachaud C., Reich B., Stone M. (1995) Planning for animation. In: Magnenat-Thalmann N.. Thalmann D. (eds.) *Computer Animation*, Prentice-Hall
5. Badler N.I., Webber B.L., Kalita J. and Esakov J. (1991) Animation from instructions. In Badler N., Barsky B., Zeltzer D. (eds.), *Making Them Move: Mechanics, Control, and Animation of Articulated Figures*. Morgan-Kaufmann, San Mateo, CA pp.51–93
6. Becket W. (1994) The *Jack* Lisp API. Technical Report MS-CIS-94-01, University of Pennsylvania. Philadelphia, PA
7. Becket W. (1995) *Reinforcement Learning for Reactive Navigation of Simulated Autonomous Bipeds*. PhD Thesis, University of Pennsylvania
8. Becket W.M., Badler N.I. (1993) Integrated behavioral agent architecture. In *The Third Conference on Computer Generated Forces and Behavior Representation*, Orlando, FL
9. Braitenberg V. (1984) *Vehicles: Experiments in Synthetic Psychology*. MIT Press, Cambridge, MA
10. Bratman M., Israel D., Pollack M. (1988) Plans and resource-bounded practical reasoning. *Computational Intelligence* **4(4)**, pp.349–355
11. Brooks R. (1986) A robust layered control system for a mobile robot. *IEEE Journal of Robotics and Automation*, pp.14–23
12. Bruderlin A., Williams L. (1995) Motion signal processing. *Computer Graphics*, Annual Conference Series, ACM, pp.97–104
13. Burdea G., Coiffet P. (1994) *Virtual Reality Technology*. Wiley, NY
14. Cassell J., Pelachaud C., Badler N., Steedman M., Achorn B., Becket W., Douville B., Prevost S., Stone M. (1994) Animated Conversation: Rule-based generation of facial expression, gesture and spoken intonation for multiple conversational agents. *Computer Graphics*, Annual Conference Series, ACM, pp.413–420
15. Chi D., Webber B., Clarke J., Badler N. (1996) Casualty modeling for real-time medical training. *Presence*, Special issue on human modelling

16. Cohen M.F. (1992) Interactive spacetime control for animation. *Computer Graphics* **26(2)**, pp.293–302
17. Dell C. (1970) *A Primer for Movement Description.* Dance Notation Bureau, New York, NY
18. Douville B. (1995) PaT-Net User's Guide. Technical Report. Department of Computer & Information Science, University of Pennsylvania
19. Geib C. (1995) *The Intentional Planning System: ItPlanS.* PhD Thesis, Dept of Computer & Information Science, University of Pennsylvania
20. Hahn J.K. (1988) Realistic animation of rigid bodies. *Computer Graphics* **22(4)**, pp.299–308
21. Hutchinson A. (1970) *Labanotation.* Theatre Arts Books, New York, NY
22. Ko H. (1994) *Kinematic and Dynamic Techniques for Analyzing, Predicting, and Animating Human Locomotion.* PhD Dissertation, Department of Computer & Information Science, University of Pennsylvania
23. Moore M.B. (1993) Search Plans. (PhD Dissertation Proposal) Technical Report MS-CIS-93-56/LINC LAB 250/IRCS-93-29. Department of Computer & Information Science, University of Pennsylvania
24. Moore M.B., Geib C.W., Reich B.D. (1995) Planning and terrain reasoning. *AAAI Spring Symposium on Integrated Planning Applications*, Stanford CA (March 1995). (Also available as Technical Report MS-CIS-94-63, University of Pennsylvania)
25. Reich B.D., Ko H., Becket W., Badler N. (1994) Terrain reasoning for human locomotion. *Proceedings of Computer Animation '94*, Geneva, IEEE Computer Society Press, pp.996–1005
26. Renault O., Magnenat-Thalmann N., Thalmann D. (1990) A vision-based approach to behavioral animation. *The Journal of Visualization and Computer Animation* **1(1)**, pp.18–21
27. Reynolds C.W. (1987) Flocks, herds, and schools: A distributed behavioral model. *Computer Graphics* **21(4)**, pp.25–34
28. Reynolds C.W. (1988) Not bumping into things. *SIGGRAPH Course 27 Notes: Developments in Physically-Based Modeling*, ACM SIGGRAPH, pp.G1–G13
29. Robertson B. (1994) Caught in the act. *Computer Graphics World* **17(9)**, pp.23–28
30. Sacerdoti E. (1977) *A Structure for Plans and Behavior.* American Elsevier, New York, NY
31. Schank R., Abelson R. (1977) *Scripts, Plans, Goals, and Understanding.* Lawrence Erlbaum Associates, Hillsdale, NJ
32. Sims K. (1994) Evolving virtual creatures. *Computer Graphics*, Annual Conference Series, ACM, pp.15–22
33. Thomas F., Johnson O. (1981) *Disney Animation: The Illusion of Life.* Abbeville Press, New York, NY
34. Tu X., Terzopoulos D. (1994) Artificial fishes: Physics, locomotion, perception, and behavior. *Computer Graphics*, Annual Conference Series, ACM, pp.43–50
35. Webber B., Badler N., Di Eugenio B., Geib C., Levison L., Moore M. (1995) Instructions, intentions and expectations. *Artificial Intelligence Journal* **73**, pp.253–269
36. Weber L., Smoliar S.W., Badler N.I. (1978) An architecture for the simulation of human movement. In: *Proc. ACM Annual Conf.*, Washington, DC, pp.737–745
37. Wilhelms J., Skinner R. (1990) A 'notion' for interactive behavioral animation control. *IEEE Computer Graphics and Applications* **10(3)**, pp.14–22
38. Wilkins D.E. (1988) *Practical Planning.* Morgan Kaufmann, San Mateo, CA

39. Williams L. (1990) Performance-driven animation. *Computer Graphics*, **24(4)**, pp.235-242
40. Witkin A., Kass M. (1988) Spacetime constraints. *Computer Graphics* **22(4)**, pp.159-168

IMPROV: A System for Real-Time Animation of Behavior-Based Interactive Synthetic Actors

Athomas Goldberg

Media Research Lab
New York University
New York NY 10003
athomas@mrl.nyu.edu

1 Introduction

The IMPROV Project at NYU's Media Research Lab is building the technologies to produce distributed 3D virtual environments in which human-directed avatars and computer-controlled agents interact with each other in real-time, through a combination of Procedural Animation and Behavioral Scripting techniques developed in-house. We are also exploring multi-modal interaction paradigms combining traditional forms of input (keyboard and mouse) with speech and gesture recognition in conjunction with various forms of presentation, including 2D and 3D display. The system is intended to operate over Local and Wide Area Networks using standard internet protocols, enabling anyone with access to the World Wide Web to develop or participate in fully interactive, virtual experiences.

2 "The Mind-Body Problem" — Procedural Animation and Behavioral Scripting

Using traditional computer animated techniques, variations in animated motion, and the transitions to and from each of these motions, must be plotted out ahead of time. A job which is generally time-consuming, therefore constraining the animator to an extremely limited set of possible behaviors. Procedurally animated characters are able to automatically generate transitions between animated motions in a smooth and natural fashion in real time. In addition, motions can be layered and blended to convey an extremely wide range of behavior, mood and personality. Actors can be given the form of humans, animals, or animate objects, and actors with common components can share sets of animated behaviors.

In IMPROV, an action is defined as a single atomic or repetitive activity, one not requiring explicit higher-level awareness or conscious decisions. For example, walking is an action, as is typing, but walking over to the computer and beginning to type constitutes a sequence of several actions.

An actor is not limited to performing a single action at once though. In order to appear life-like and believable an actor must be able to perform certain activities simultaneously, like walking and chewing gum, or typing, while talking to someone across the room. Once again, it would be impractical to suggest that the animator should create a separate animated behavior for every combination of activities.

The problem with combining actions automatically is that there often are different ways in which actions might be combined. An actor might be instructed to momentarily scratch his head while waving at someone. It would not be very realistic to have the actor try to perform both these actions at once, making vague scratching gestures toward his head while simultaneously making awkward waving motions at the other actor. On the other hand, if we wanted the character to wave while walking downstage, it would not make much sense to have the actor stop walking each time he tried to wave.

The difference between these two examples is that in the former case we're describing actions which are mutually exclusive, whereas in the latter case, the two actions are complementary and can gracefully coexist. What's important here is that there be a clear and powerful structure in which these action relationships can be defined.

We facilitate this structure by dividing actions into Groups. Actions within a group are mutually exclusive of one another; activating one causes the action currently active to be deactivated. Actions in different groups may operate simultaneously, allowing actions involving certain parts of the body to be combined with or layered over those involving others. In general, actions involving a specific body part are generally layered over those involving a region of the body which are in turn layered over those involving the whole body. For example: one actor may be talking to another, one group may contain the stances the actor assumes, such as shifting his weight from side to side, standing straight or sitting. At the same time another group contains a set of upper-body motions like crossing his arms or putting his arms at his sides or behind his back. Still another group will contain those gestures performed with the right or left hand, like gesturing to make a point or scratching his chin.

Using this structure, these few actions can be combined to create dozens of composite animations while minimizing the risk of inadvertently creating behavior that is either unbelievable or not life-like.

It is also important that when an actor goes from performing one action to another, that the actor's body does not go through physically impossible transitions. If an actor has his arms crossed in front of him, and then puts his arms behind his back, what's to prevent him from passing his arms through his body. In the "real world", we're bound by the laws of physics, but this is not the case in the virtual environment. By allowing animators to create buffer actions, we provide an easy way to avoid unbelievable behavior. For example: if we use hands-at-sides as a buffer action for hands-behind-back, we save the actor the embarrassment of accidently passing his arms through his body, by declaring that every time the actor wants to put his arms behind his back he will first put his arms at his sides. Likewise, when the actor tries to go from having his hands behind his back to another action involving his arms, he'll once again execute the arms-at-sides gesture before continuing to the next gesture.

Actions are only useful for defining and blending subtleties of physical motion. Behavioral Scripting allows you to describe behavioral "scripts" to create more complex sets of actions and behaviors. Scripts may be used to trigger other scripts and/or actions allowing virtual world designers to easily construct hierarchies of behavior, from low-level decisions about the types of gestures and actions to perform to high-level behavior describing an actor's goals and the kinds of social activities an actor will partake in, a "Life to Picking Your Nose" model of behavior in which there is a continuum from the most abstract descriptions of character activity to the construction of specific motor skills. In this way, long-term goals and activities can be broken down into component behavior and further broken down until individual physical activities are described.

The smallest unit of time in IMPROV is called a frame, which is approximately 1/30th of a second or the length of a single frame of animation. A basic script generally consists of a sequence of steps that are executed in order, one per frame, though sequencing commands can be used to cause steps to be repeated. These sequencing commands include:

- "wait": causes the current step to be repeated for the specified number of seconds. When it appears in a step by itself, it serves as a timed delay between steps.
- "while": causes the current step to be repeated until the specified conditions are met.
- "loop": causes the current step to be repeated indefinitely, or until the current script is deactivated.
- "do again": causes the current script to repeat from step 1.

Like Actions, scripts are organized into parallel-running Groups. Scripts within a given Group are mutually exclusive of each other: activating a script within a Group immediately deactivates whatever script is currently active in that Group. Scripts active in different Groups operate simultaneously, enabling high-level scripts to continue as the low-level behaviors they trigger are performed. In this way, the actor can address his environment from multiple levels of abstraction, maintaining high-level goals and long-term activities while managing and carrying out the short-term behaviors necessary to fulfill these. A simple script might look something like this:

```
SCRIPT ''Greeting''
    steps
    1. enter room
    2. wait 4 seconds
    3. Turn to Camera
    4. wait 1 second
    5. Wave to Camera, say hello to Camera
    6. wait 3 seconds
    7. leave room
```

In this example, the actor first activates the "enter room" script (which instructs the actor to enter the room). The "enter room" script is in a different script-group so the "Greeting" script continues as the "enter room" script is executed, waiting four seconds before activating the "turn" which tells the actor to turn and face the specified target, in this case the camera. There is another pause of 1 second, giving the "turn" script time to finish, before instructing the actor to begin the "wave" and "say hello" scripts. Another 3 seconds pass as the actor waves and says hello, at which point the "leave room" script is activated, causing the actor to turn and leave.

Two important features of believable human behavior are timing and co-ordination. While it may be possible to build animated agents with sufficient intelligence to identify and react quickly to rapidly changing events and sit-uations, success along these lines has, thus far, been limited when applied to complex, coordinated social behavior. In order to create life-like social scenarios in which multiple actors play out rich interactions, it's important to provide tools that will enable virtual world designers to not only design the behaviors of an individual actor, but also those of groups of actors.

The "cue" command enables actors to cue each other to respond in appro-priate ways at the right moments. An example:

```
SCRIPT ''Hello-Hello''
   steps
   1. Turn to my target
   2. wait 1 second
   3. Wave to my target
   4. cue my target to Wave to me
   5. wait 1.5 seconds
   6. cue my target to Wave to me
   7. wait 1.5 seconds
   8. Turn to Camera, cue my target to Turn to Camera
   9. wait 1 second
  10. Wave to Camera, cue my target to Wave to Camera
```

In this example the actor turns to face his or her target (the actor they are currently interested in), waits a second and then waves. The actor's target turns and after about a second, waves back. A couple of seconds later, the two turn simultaneously toward the camera and a second later wave in unison.

3   "No! Go THAT Way!" — Navigating Virtual Worlds

While games like "Street Fighter" and "Mortal Combat" give you pretty di-rect control over the actions of your avatar, there are times when it may be preferable to direct your animated representative through a more intuitive set of instructions and then let the character play out the scenario in a naturalistic and dramatic fashion. It's not uncommon for new players of games like "DOOM" to make several attempts before successfully passing through a doorway or turning a corner. An example of high-level instruction might involve pointing to a door, and telling the character to open it. The character would then cross to the door automatically, avoiding obstacles in the way, and open it.

In the same way that scripts may be triggered from other scripts, they can also be activated by human participants from the user-interface. Same behaviors displayed in the "Greeting" example, might also have been effected by a human participant directing the avatar to enter the room, waiting a few seconds and then directing the avatar to turn to the camera. Likewise the participant might have activated the "Greeting" script as part of a more complex situation, in which the exact physical motions of the actor are not what's important, but rather, that a specific point (saying hello) is made.

The level of the instructions you give the avatar may vary depending on the situation, ensuring the most effective interaction with the environment at all times. The layered structure of IMPROV enables the human participant to take direct the actor at whatever level of control is most appropriate from moment to moment.

4 "The Indigenous Peoples of Cyberspace" — Autonomy for Autonomous Agents

While it may be possible to create virtual worlds entirely populated by human-directed avatars, it's often useful, especially in the case of interactive fiction environments, to have a supporting cast of characters whose purpose is to keep the drama moving forward, provoke conflict, introduce new situations and stimuli and otherwise maintain the level of excitement in the scenario. In addition to the techniques described above for performing the appropriate animation for any given activity, these actors must also be able to choose an appropriate course of action from the set of myriad possible actions available at any given time. Once again we could try to envision all the possible situations the agents might find themselves in, and write the appropriate action scripts, but the amount of work involved in ensuring the characters always did the right thing without becoming repetitive would rapidly become prohibitive. On the other hand, randomly choosing from the set of possible actions available to an actor is not particularly believable. The decisions a character makes should somehow reflect that character's role or personality; and certain actions will seem more appropriate to one character than others. Without going too deeply into character's deep motivations and the "hard" problems of true human-like cognition, we can describe a character's personality in terms of their tendency to behave in a certain manner, that's consistent from one situation to the next. When confronted with a new situation, reckless characters will tend to choose reckless actions, whereas cautious characters will be likely to choose more cautious behaviors. At the same time, to remain believable, autonomous agents must be able to appear at least as unpredictable as their human-directed counterparts. We can accomplish this through the use of what we call "tunable statistics." Characters make weighted decisions where certain options have a higher chance of being chosen than others.

Take the "fidget" script for example:

```
SCRIPT ''Fidget''
    steps
    1. Choose from
       (Twiddle thumbs .7, Scratch head .3, Pick nose .2)
    2. Wait 3 seconds
    3. do again
```

In this example, we give an actor a choice of three actions to perform, say twiddling his thumbs, scratching his head, or picking his nose, and to each of these we assign a weight between 0 and 1, so that twiddling is given a weight of .7, scratching is given a weight of .3 and picking is given a weight of .2. In this case, there is a 3 in 12 (or 1 in 4) chance the actor will choose to twiddle, a 7 in 12 chance the actor will choose to scratch and a 2 in 12 (or 1 in 6) chance the actor will pick.

As we'll discover later, these weights can be determined procedurally, through the combination of one or more actors' personalities with the objects and events in a scenario. For example, an agent entering a social situation, might be most likely to talk with agents and avatars they are familiar with and have a high sympathy for. This does not mean the actor will always choose the person they have the highest sympathy for, nor does it mean that the character will never talk to characters they have a low sympathy for, but, like "real" people, will generally be drawn to certain characters over others. These techniques allow the agents to always make decisions that are "in character" without ever becoming repetitive or inhumanly predictable. The way these attributes that shape the decision-making process are defined is described in the next section.

5 "I Feel Like a Number" Personality Definition for Agents and Avatars

In addition to the scripts an actor can perform, each actor is also assigned a set of behavioral attributes used in giving the impression of a unique personality. Some examples might include: strength, coordination and health which would govern how a character performed certain physical activities, and intelligence, aggressiveness and amiability which would affect how the character interacts with other characters. Attributes can also be used to describe the relationships between actors, objects and behaviors. A character's behavior toward another character may be influenced by their sympathy (or hatred!) for that character. Attributes may be used to describe an actor's knowledge of a given subject or skill at performing certain activities. Some examples of actor attributes might include:

```
ACTOR ''Gregor''
        attribute                value
        Intelligence             .99
        Amiability               .5
        Strength                 .33
```

```
Coordination                   .3

Sympathy-toward Otto           .15
Sympathy-toward Gabrielle      .9

Knowledge-of Ancient Greece   .75

skill-at Public-Speaking       .9
skill-at Driving:Cars          .25
   ...                          ..
```

Attribute values are generally in the range of 0 to 1. Here we see that Gregor is extremely intelligent, of average amiability, but not very strong or coordinated. Gregor dislikes Otto, but is extremely fond of Gabrielle, has a pretty good knowledge of Ancient Greece and while being a fine public speaker is only a mediocre driver. These attributes are all dynamic and may be assigned and modified at any time, and the animations an actor performs will reflect these changes. For example, when a character encounters a prop for the first the actor's attribute list is searched for the relevant skill, in this case the "skill at Driving:Motorcycles". If the skill is not found it is assigned to the actor at some minimal level. This starting level may be modified based on other characteristics. (A character's Intelligence, Coordination and/or skill in driving other types of vehicles may influence how well the character drives a motorcycle her first time on it.) As the character spends time riding the bike, the Motorcycle driving skill value will increase and the animation will reflect the increased proficiency. Next time the character comes across a motorcycle, the character's file is again searched for the "skill-at Driving:Motorcycles" attribute and this time the value is found. She now appears to drive like an experienced biker.

We can also use these mechanisms to simulate the effects of an actor's behavior on the rest of the world. For example:

```
SCRIPT ''Oh.. Excuse me!''
    steps
    1. Belch
    2. wait 1 second
    3. set other-actors Sympathy-toward me to .01
    4. ...
```

In this crude example, the actor makes an obnoxious noise which has an almost immediate and profound effect on the other actors' attitudes toward the actor, which will, no doubt, be demonstrated in their future behavior toward the actor.

In addition, attributes can be attached to the scripts a character follows which are used to determine how and when a actor will perform that script. These properties might include: necessary pre-requisites for performing the script, level of difficulty, or the formality/informality of the behavior. For example:

```
SCRIPT ''Ride bicycle''
    attribute          value
    Activity-Type              (transportation, exercise, recreation)
    Pre-requisites             (have bicycle)
    Difficulty        .32
    Physicality       .73

    steps
    1. Get on bike
    2. ...
```

In this example, "Ride bicycle" is a script that may be used for transportation, exercise and recreation. Executing the script requires that the actor has a bicycle. The difficulty attribute indicates that riding requires a certain amount of skill, though not too much, and the physicality attribute shows us that riding is a somewhat strenuous activity. When the actor executes this script, a comparison between these attributes and the attributes of the actor will be used to determine how the animation for riding a bicycle will be executed.

In addition, scripts can be used to monitor and effect other actor states and properties, allowing the behavior of the actor, and the effects of that behavior to influence the actors personality which in turn may influence the actor's behavior under varying social conditions and changing circumstances. In this way, designers can carefully orchestrate the ways in which an actor will appear to grow and change over time due to their actions and the effects of their actions.

6 "What to Do, What to Do..." — Decision Making in Autonomous Agents

Much of what makes a character believable comes from the choices they make, and how these choices reflect that character's personality, goals, tendencies, likes and dislikes, etc. As we described earlier, we can control an actor's tendencies toward certain choices in a decision through the use of weighted lists. For example, in the script "Go to Store" the actor is going shopping and has to decide how he's going to get there. We could write it something like this:

```
SCRIPT ''Go to Store''
    steps
    1. Exit home
    2. Choose from
       (Walk .1, Take bus .5, Take cab .4, Ride bike .2)
    3. Enter store
    4. ...
```

In this example, the actor executing this script is most likely to take the bus or a cab, but will occasionally ride his bike, and on rare occasions walk. The problem with this is that every actor executing this script is going to have the exactly same tendencies toward each of these modes of transportation. Even though in the real world, a lazy person might *never* walk or ride a bike, an athletic person might prefer riding or walking and a person on a strict budget might avoid taking a cab, if at all possible. It would be impractical to try and create a seperate "Go to Store" script for every actor, just to reflect that individual's personality, since there may be thousands of different actors in the virtual world and "Go to Store" is only one of hundreds of activities an actor might engage in.

An alternative to this is to specify a set of criteria an actor or set of actors will use in making a decision. These are, in effect, the rules governing how a specific decision gets made, which each actor will interpret differently based on their individual personalities. Using criteria-based decision-making our "Go to Store" script might look something like this:

```
SCRIPT ''Go to Store''
    steps
    1. Exit home
    2. Choose from (Walk, Take bus, Take cab, Ride bike)
       using criteria ''bestway to get there''
    3. Enter store
    4. ...
```

```
CRITERIA ''ways to get there''
    criteria                                    importance
    1. my energy compared to its physicality    .7
    2. my wealth compared to its cost            .3
```

In this example, energy and wealth are attributes of the actor, while physicality and cost are attributes assigned to the various options. In this case, each option is assigned a weight based on how close these attributes match. The value under importance represents how much influence each of these criteria has on the final decesion, in this case, the amount of energy required by each choice is the most significant factor, but how much it costs also plays a small role. In this example, an actor with a high energy attribute will tend toward the more physical activities like walking and cycling, especially if they are low on cash, whereas lazy actors will choose the less physically demanding choices, taking a cab if they have got a lot of money, taking a bus if they do not.

We might also want to be more abstract about the scripts we're choosing from. In this case, the actor might not necessarily be concerned with choosing one of these specific activities, but rather is only interested in finding an appropriate mode of transportation. Here we accomplish this by choosing from the list of scripts that have some attribute in common, (they all have transportation as one of their activity-types)

```
SCRIPT ''Go to Store''
    steps
    1. Exit home
```

```
    2. Choose from (scripts with Activity-type: transportation)
       using criteria ''best way to get there''
    3. Enter store
    4. ...
```

```
CRITERIA ''ways to get there''
    criteria                                   importance
    1. my energy compared to its physicality   .7
    2. my wealth compared to its cost          .3
```

This way, should we later wish to add an "in-line skate" script, it will automatically be included in the decision as long as we make "transportation" one of its activity-types.

We can already begin to see how we can create a wide variety of interpretations of the "Go to Store", without greatly increasing the amount of work necessary to accomplish this. Still, in this example, each actor will assign the same importance to physicality and cost, which while reflecting an actor's current state, does not really tell us anything about the actor's values, another important aspect of actor behavior.

If we rewrite the "ways to get there" criteria as follows:

```
CRITERIA ''ways to get there''
    criteria                                   importance
    1. my energy compared to its physicality   my importance-of
                                               physical-enjoyment
    2. my wealth compared to its cost          my importance-of
                                               money
```

we enable the actor to decide how important each of these factors is. In this case, actors who place a lot of importance on physical enjoyment will tend toward activities that best suit their current level of energy, whereas those that place more importance on money matters will tend toward those activities that meet their current means.

In the same way attributes may be assigned to actors and scripts, attributes can also be assigned to the criteria an actor uses to make a decision, enabling the virtual world designer to tailor a script to an even wider variety of personalities and interpretations. Perhaps our athlete does not care at all about the cost of getting there, he just wants the exercise. Meanwhile, more decadent individuals refuse to do anything that does not display their wealth or requires too much effort. In this case, our script might look something like this:

```
SCRIPT ''Go to store''
steps
    1. Exit home
    2. Choose from (scripts with Activity-type: transportation)
       using criteria ( Choose from (Criteria-type: attitude)
                        criteria ''Personality'' )
```

```
3. Enter store
4. ...
```

```
CRITERIA ''Personality''
    criteria                                         importance
    1. my decadence compered to its decadence-level   .5
    2. my athleticism compared to it athletic-level   .5

CRITERIA ''Decadent''
    attribute                                        value
    Criteria-Type                                    (attitude)
    decadence-level                                  .9
    athletic-level                                   .1

    criteria                                         importance
    1. its physicality is very-low                   .7
    2. my wealth compared to its cost                .3

CRITERIA ''Athletic''
    attribute                                        value
    Criteria-type                                    (attitude)
    decadence-level                                  .2
    athletic-level                                   .99

    criteria                                         importance
    1. its physicality is high                       1
```

Once again, we've enabled actors with different personalities to play out the same basic activity (going to the store) with their own interpretations. Here, actors at the extremes of Athleticism and Decadence, may almost always prefer certain forms of transportation over others, but because the choice of criteria is based on a weighted list as well, actors whose personalities fall somewhere in the middle will occasionally exhibit different reasons for choosing certain scripts over others, perhaps today they are feeling decadent, while tomorrow they feel more athletic. The frequency with which they choose certain criteria over others will also fit with that actor's personality.

I've presented a very simple example here, but it's clear that as we add more options, and more detailed criteria, we can very quickly develop a rich variety of interpretations of various activities, tailored to each actor's individual personality, goals and values.

So far I've described a broad range of scripted behavior, from linear sequences of scripts and actions, to completely personality-based decision-making. It's important to note that these are in no way exclusive of each other. Fully autonomous agents may interact freely with avatars following human direction and carefully scripted behavior, while avatars receiving high-level instruction may make these kinds of decisions about their low-level behavior. In addition, there are times when an autonomous agent might be required to perform a predefined set of actions, as in a dance, or when repeating something learned by rote, or when called for to effect certain events in an interactive drama. IMPROV enables the virtual world designer to freely mix and match these types of behavior and levels of control and autonomy in order to create the desired effect.

7 "The Tail that Wags the Dog"— Inverse Causality for Animation

Animated actors in dynamic realtime environments are likely to encounter new situations, especially if we allow for worlds that are continuously being developed and characters that persist from one scenario to the next. As circumstances change, it is important that these characters continue to react appropriately, even when confronted with new stimuli. In cases where this means encountering some truly foreign object or situation, it may be okay if the actor does not know what to do next. More often though, these are things that the human directing the avatar is familiar with that are introduced to the world after its creation. In these situations we want the character to appear to know what they are doing, even though they have, in fact, never been in the situation before. A traditional AI approach might suggest that we build mechanisms into the characters to allow them to analyze new situations and make judgements as to the appropriate course of action to take (in other words, the right kind of animation to perform.) This tends to be pretty compute intensive and while the number of trial-and-error iterations that are generally involved in this approach may produce a convincing simulation of learning to do something, we do not want the characters to look like they're learning how to drink a beer, we just want them to drink. Alternately, we could try to take into account everything the character might possibly encounter and program him/her to perform the appropriate animations. The problem with this is that eventually we'll want to introduce new props and situations that we had not foreseen at the time the character was created. At this point it's too late to go back and rewrite every character to account for the new additions.

Take the following example: An actor walks into a bar... (No, this is not the start of some obscene VR joke!) The virtual world designer has just introduced alcohol into the world, and so our actor now encounters beer for the first time. He may have already learned the appropriate animations for drinking from a bottle, but say he has not, how do we get the actor to do the right thing? What if, instead of teaching the character how to drink from a beer bottle, we encode the instructions for performing the appropriate animation into the bottle itself? Each item the character encountered would have all the instructions for its use built into it, requiring only that the user direct his or her attention to it in order to enable its use. In one interface scenario, the user points to the bottle with the cursor and is then presented with a number of options for what to do with it (i.e. Drink, Throw, Break, etc.). The user chooses one of these options and then the animation attached to the bottle drives the character to perform the action. The cause and effect relationship is reversed, but from the user's point of view the action appears natural.

The advantage to this is that we can continually introduce new elements into the environment, because the animations for the elements' uses are included in their design. This method enables us to have an infinitely expandable variety of possible actions/animations available to the character while reducing the character file to a physical description of the character and a set of behavioral modifiers that are used to alter the flavor of the animations, giving each character a unique body language and personality.

In addition to increasing the degree of diversity for animated behavior, the technique also adds a great deal of efficiency by allowing us to automatically filter out all the inappropriate animations for any given set of circumstances. While there might be millions of actions possible for a single character, we only want to deal with those that are relevant to the given situation. When the user directs the character into a new environment, a search is performed to determine which objects are available to the character. At this point the files,which include the animation, as well as the buttons, sliders, etc. used to control the specific activity, are loaded. As the character moves from one environment to another, this information is updated and the user is presented with a new set of options.

These techniques are useful for actor interactions as well. That beer bottle may also have encoded in it the effects of drinking beer on the actions of the animated actor. After a few beers, the actor may display difficulty walking or standing, or whatever other effects the virtual-world designer may have decided should accompany the drinking of alcohol. The human participant, upon seeing this, realizes that it's time to leave, but as he attempts to direct his avatar toward the door, he accidentally stumbles into another actor, who immediately grows angry and swings a fist at our helpless participant. In the same way that encoding the appropriate behavior into the bottle enables the actor to perform the act of drinking believably, encoding the appropriate responses to behavior into the actor initiating that behavior allows us to maintain consistent and believable behavior even between actors with completely different sets of abilities. Our human participant may not have the appropriate fighting animation built into his avatar, but his attacker does. These animations contain, in addition to the set attack animations, also a set of possible responses, including those used by actors who do not know how to fight (like getting knocked across the room).

Not that this is limited only to violent situations. If instead of getting into a fight, our actor was asked to dance he should at least be able to make a clumsy attempt at it, even if he has never danced before. Along with the dance animations used by his expert partner, are those employed by our awkward, but earnest hero, allowing the two of them to make a believable (though potentially comic) pair out on the dance floor.

8 "Lights, Cameras, Action" — Behind the Scenes on the Virtual Soundstage

In the production of any movie, from the biggest Hollywood blockbuster to the smallest independent film, there are a number of people whose contributions make the movie possible but never appear in front of the camera. The director, the cinematographer, the editor, the props, sets and special fx crews and numerous others, all lend their expertise to the creation of the final product and the quality of their work is largely responsible for the success of the film. What if we could bring this talent and expertise to the creation of virtual worlds?

Unlike the movies, the interactive nature of virtual worlds means that the kinds of decisions that are normally made ahead of time during the making of a film, the choice of camera angles, the editing of shots, etc, all need to be made on the fly in response to the ever-changing (and unpredictable) actions of the human participants. How can we apply the same autonomous decision-making techniques used for our "actors" to the creation of these off-screen members of the production team?

8.1 Interactive Cinematography

In "first person point of view" interface used in games like "Doom", the user has direct control over their movement and actions but is generally limited to one kind of view, greatly diminishing the number of cinematic possibilities. If we instead make the camera an independent actor in the environment, we open up the possibilities enormously. We've also freed up the constraints on the camera. If we treat the camera as another character in the scene, we can then give it its own set of behaviors. The camera can react to the action in the scene and adjust the shot accordingly, giving us a kind of realtime cinematography which is not possible in POV-type games.

8.2 Lighting, Sound & Special FX

Other elements of the environment can be "embodied" as well. Lighting, Music, Sound and Special FX agents can be designed to be constantly responding to the changes in mood and tension, in addition to following cues triggered by the accomplishment of goals or the occurrence of key events in the story. The goal in creating these "backstage agents" is not to replace the creative individuals who specialize in these various cinematic artforms, but rather to allow these individuals to construct the aesthetic rules that these agents will follow during the course of the interactive experience.

I want to point out that the use of these agents is not limited to gaming and interactive fiction environments. In MUDs (Multi-User Domains) and other freeform virtual spaces these agents can be used to maintain a certain visual and aural quality to the experience. These agents might also be custom tailored to the individual. For example, each avatar may have its own soundtrack, audible only to that participant, that accompanies them and reflects the changing circumstances surrounding that individual. Each person might view the world through an automated camera that tracks the avatars every move, always presenting the most dramatic or interesting camera angle. Lighting and Weather agents can provide interesting and unpredictable atmospheres in reaction to events in the world and their own internal rules. All these can contribute to the creation of compelling experiences even within purely social virtual environments.

9 "To Be or Not to Be..." — The Possibilities for Interactive Drama on the Virtual Stage

Now that we have the actors and production crew ready, how do we bring it all together into the creation of an engaging and powerful experience? You may be familiar with "branching narratives" in which, at key moments in the story, the player must choose from one of a few options and his/her decision determines how the story proceeds. In these systems, each alternative or "branch" is plotted ahead of time by the author. While we could apply these techniques to systems involving autonomous agents, the restriction of having to know everything in advance, negates the advantage we gain from having actors who can continually improvise as they go along under rapidly changing circumstances. At the same time if we simply allow the characters to go about their business in an unstructured environment, there's no way to guarantee that, as the human-avatar interacts with them in unpredictable ways, the tension will build and the stakes will continue to rise. A participant might fail to provoke the right people, wander around aimlessly for hours, or worse get herself killed right off the bat. In many gaming scenarios, especially those in which combat is the central theme, getting killed is ok, you just start over again and keep doing it until you get it right, and wandering around aimlessly is often part of finding your way through some maze. In games in which social scenarios play a much greater role, these complications can hinder rather than support the flow of the game. In these cases, we need to introduce one more "invisible" agent, this time in the role of director. This agent is given the task of maintaining the drama, and is encoded with rules governing how much time various parts of the story should take and what events need to occur in order to effect this. The point here is not to railroad the participant into following a specific course of action, but rather to ensure that the rest of the world responds to the user's actions to keep the story progressing. The drama is continuous, flows seamlessly around the user and, if done correctly, remains engaging and provocative, under almost any circumstance. The ability to create these experiences, once the province of science-fiction (Star Trek's Holodeck, et al), is now a matter of creative talent and skill and no longer a limitation of the technology.

10   Background and History

The IMPROV Project began in the Spring of 1994, when Ken Perlin began applying procedural texture synthesis techniques developed in the early eighties to the human-like animated characters. The result was "Danse Interactif" in which an animated dancer performs, following the directions of a choreographer (using an on-screen button panel) in real-time. Following, the success of these initial experiments, we began applying these techniques to higher-level behaviors and multi-character interactions. To, in effect, allow the characters to make their own decisions, based on a set of pre-scripted rules and carefully controlled statistics governing how and when each character would perform a specific scene or script. Early experiments along these lines resulted in "Interacting with Virtual Actors." Continuing along these lines, we've begun implementing more sophisticated devices which will allow the characters engage in even more complex behavior and interaction. In addition, we are exploring various multi-modal interaction paradigms and Wide Area Networked environments.

11   Group Profile

The Media Research Lab at NYU was formed in the fall of 1993 with Prof. Ken Perlin as its director. The research staff consists of 5 full-time staff-members, several graduate students, and a number of artist collaborators. Currently the lab is involved in a number of research initiatives. In addition to IMPROV, we are also explorating Multi-scale zoomable interfaces and a various Web and Internet-related technologies.

12   Acknowledgements

The IMPROV system and all the research described in this paper is the result of a collaborative effort on the part of a number of dedicated artists, animators, programmers and scientists. Principal among these is Professor Ken Perlin, director of the Media Research Lab and developer of the core technology upon which IMPROV is based. Others who've played major roles in IMPROV's development include Jon Meyer, who wrote most of IMPROV's rendering system, Mehmet Karaul and Troy Downing, who are continuing to develop IMPROV's network-distribution system, Eric Singer, Clilly Castiglia, Sabrina Liao, Andruid Kerne, Seth Piezos, Eduardo Santos, Ruggero Ruschioni, Daniel Wey, Marcelo Zuffo, Kouchen Lin, Leo Cadavel, Tim Cheung, and everyone else who helped make IMPROV possible.

13   Special Thanks

I'd like to thank Steph, just for being Steph.

Multi-level Control
for Animated Autonomous Agents:

Do the Right Thing...Oh, Not That...

Bruce Blumberg and Tinsley Galyean

MIT Media Lab
20 Ames St., E15-305
Cambridge, MA 02139
{bruce, tag}@media.mit.edu

1 Introduction

Imagine making an interactive virtual "Lassie" experience for children. Suppose the autonomous animated character playing Lassie did a fine job as a autonomous dog, but for whatever reason was ignoring the child. Or suppose, you wanted the child to focus on some aspect of the environment which was important to the story, but Lassie was distracting her. In both cases, you would want to be able to provide external control, in real-time, to the autonomous Lassie. For example, by increasing its "motivation to play", it would be more likely to engage in play. By telling it to "go over to that tree and lie down" it might be less distracting.

This paper focuses on how to provide multiple levels of control for autonomous animated characters for use in interactive story systems. Much has been written on the problems of action-selection for autonomous agents and robots [4, 1, 3]. Some work has focused on the specific problems of building autonomous animated characters [5, 6]. Less work, however, has focused on the problem of integrating external control into autonomous agent architectures, particularly as it relates to the types of control needed for characters in interactive story systems. It is this problem which is the topic of this paper and much of our research in general.

This paper is organized as follows. We begin by identifying 4 different levels of control and discuss the forms the control may take. We then describe how a particular autonomous agent architecture, developed by Blumberg and Galyean, supports these different levels of control. Lastly, we describe the use of these ideas in 2 systems. Details of the underlying architecture may be found in [2].

2 Levels of Control

Maes suggests that there are two dimensions along which one can classify degrees of control. The first is the level of control, from concrete or direct control to more abstract or indirect control. The second dimension is whether the control is prescriptive (i.e. do something), proscriptive (i.e. avoid doing something) and some measure of the importance placed upon the control.

It is proposed that at least 4 levels of control are desirable:

1. At the motor skill level (e.g. "Go-Forward", "Look-At"). Here the director wants the character to engage in specific low level actions. These actions may be "in-character" (e.g. "Walking") or "out-of-character" (e.g. "SetPosition"). Typically, no planning or elaborate sequencing is required by the character, nor is any sensory input used.

2. At the behavioral level (e.g. "Find that juicy steak in the user's hand"). Here the director wants the character to engage in a specific, albeit complicated behavior, and trusts that the character will do the right thing which may require some sort of planning or sequencing of actions by the character. Typically, the character must use sensory input to accomplish the task.

3. At the motivational level (e.g. "You are very hungry"). Here the director is not necessarily directing the character to engage in a specific behavior, but rather is predisposing it to act in that manner, if other conditions are right. For example, if no food is present the character may not necessarily search for food, but the moment it catches a whiff of a steak, it heads directly for it.

4. At the environmental level (e.g. "The Jones town dam just broke", or "There is a juicy steak on the table and your owner is in the kitchen"). Here the director manipulates the behavior of the character by manipulating its environment, thus inducing a potential response from the creature. Imaginary sensory input is a special case of this type of control. Here the director manipulates the sensory input of the character so that the character effectively "imagines" the existence of a significant object or event and acts accordingly. For example, if the director wants the character to approach the user, the director could attach an imaginary "dog biscuit" to the user's hand that is only visible to the dog.

Rather than viewing external control as "directorial dictates", we view it more as a mechanism for expressing "weighted preferences or suggestions" for or against certain behaviors or actions. The higher the weight, the greater the preference's influence on the creature's subsequent behavior. Seen in this light, a preference is just one more factor in the mix of internal motivations and external stimulus which ultimately determine in which behaviors the creature will engage.

Preferences may be proscriptive, for example, "I don't care what you do as long as you don't eat". This is different than (2) or (3) in that it provides a different type of control. For example, it would be difficult using just (2) or (3) to implement a "I don't care what you do as long as you don't...", since even reducing the motivational level associated with a behavior may not assure that the behavior will not be executed if the behavior has a strong sensory component. Moreover, it would also allow the director to achieve the same effect as that of temporarily changing a motivational variable without, perhaps, the attendant problems (e.g. restoring the value when done, or insuring that changing the value does not have an unintended side-effect).

Weighted preferences may also be used at the direct motor level. For example, it is important that the director be able to make recommendations for or against certain motor actions so as to insure that the character satisfies certain spatial or behavioral constraints. These recommendations can be used by the low-level behaviors to arrive at compromise solutions which help satisfy the director's constraints as well as those of the behavior. This is different than (1) above in that a preference is used in the context of a running behavior, whereas (1) is an explicit command to execute an action. For example, if the director does not want the character to turn left because this would move the character toward the center of the scene, it can make a recommendation against turning left. If the character is currently searching for food, it may be indifferent to turning left or going straight in the absence of a recommendation. However, in the presence of a recommendation against turning left, the behavior will avoid turning left.

Thus, an architecture for autonomous animated creatures needs to support these two dimensions of control. That is, it should provide support for control at varying degrees of abstraction, and it should also include a mechanism whereby the control can be specified as weighted preferences for and against actions and behaviors.

Blumberg and Galyean have proposed, and implemented just such an architecture for animated autonomous creatures. This architecture is summarized in Fig.1. The lowest level is the geometry (e.g. the shapes, materials and transforms that make up the creature). The Degrees of Freedom (DOF, i.e. neck joint) represent the "knobs" which are available to modify the geometry so as to produce motion. Motor Skills use one or more DOFs to produce coordinated motion (e.g. Walk or Wag-Tail). The Controller maps abstract commands (e.g. "forward") into calls to the Creature's Motor Skills (e.g. "walk"). The purpose of the Behavior System is to weigh the potentially competing motivations of the creature, assess the state of its environment, and issue to the Controller, the set of actions which makes the "most sense" at any given instant in time. The remainder of this paper highlights how external control has been integrated into this architecture.

3 Architecture

The two most relevant parts of the architecture for the purposes of this discussion are the Behavior System and the Motor Controller. These are briefly introduced below.

The purpose of the Behavior System (the top level in Fig.1) is to send the "right" set of control signals to the motor system at every time-step. It must weigh the potentially competing goals or needs of the creature, assess the state of its environment, and choose the set of actions which make the "most sense" at that instant in time. More generally, it provides the agent with a range of high-level behaviors of which it is capable of performing competently and autonomously in a potentially unpredictable environment. Indeed, it is this ability to perform competently in the absence of external control which makes high

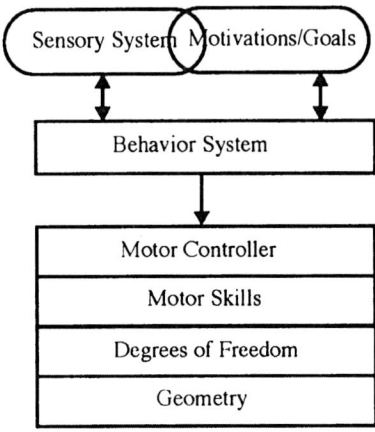

Fig. 1. A 5-layered architecture for Animated Autonomous Agents

level control (motivational or behavioral) possible. Otherwise, an external entity would have to provide time-step to time-step motor control in order to assure that a given goal was achieved, or task accomplished.

While the Behavior System is shown in Fig.1 as a monolithic entity, it is in fact composed of a loosely hierarchical network of "self-interested, goal-directed entities" called Behaviors each of which is fighting for control of the creature. Figure 2 summarizes the structure of an individual Behavior. The purpose of a Behavior is to evaluate the appropriateness of the behavior, given external stimulus and internal motivations, and if appropriate issue motor commands. Releasing Mechanisms act as filters or detectors which identify significant objects or events from sensory input, and which output a value which corresponds to the strength of the sensory input. Internal Motivations or goals are represented via Internal Variables which output values which represents the strength of the motivation. A behavior combines the values of the Releasing Mechanisms and Internal Variables on which it depends and that represents the value of the Behavior before Level of Interest and Inhibition from other Behaviors. Level of Interest is used to model boredom or behavior-specific fatigue. Behaviors must compete with other behaviors for control of the creature, and do so using Inhibition.There are a variety of explicit and implicit feedback mechanisms.

The granularity of a Behavior's goal may vary from very general (e.g. "reduce hunger") to very specific (e.g. "chew food"). General Behaviors (e.g. "reduce hunger") typically depend on several more specific behaviors to accomplish their objective (e.g. "find food", "sniff", "chew"), which in turn may depend on even more specific Behaviors. Thus, it is often useful to view the Behaviors as being organized in a loose hierarchy as is shown in Fig.3.

Behaviors are organized into groups of mutually inhibiting behaviors called Behavior Groups. These Behavior Groups are in turn organized in a loose hier-

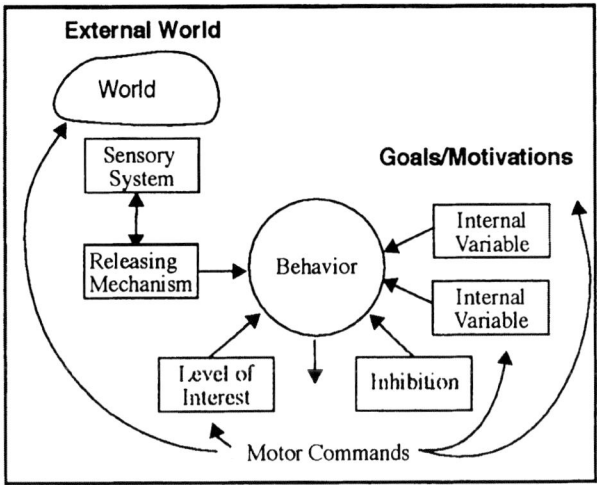

Fig. 2. The structure of individual Behaviors

archical fashion. Behavior Groups at the upper levels of the hierarchy contain general types of behaviors (e.g. "engage-in-feeding") which are largely driven by motivational considerations, whereas lower levels contain more specific behaviors (e.g. "pounce" or "chew") which are driven more by immediate sensory input. The arbitration mechanism built into the algorithm insures that only one Behavior in a given Behavior Group will have a non-zero value after inhibition. This Behavior is then active, and may either issue primary motor commands, or activate the Behavior Group which contains its children Behaviors (e.g. "search-for-food", "sniff", "chew" might be the children behaviors of "engage-in-feeding"). The dark gray behaviors represent the path of active Behaviors on a given tick. Behaviors which lose to the primary Behavior in a given Behavior Group may nonetheless influence the resulting actions of the creature by issuing either secondary commands or meta-commands. Branches of the tree often correspond to sub-systems which perform a specific task-level function. Details of the actual implementation may be found in [2], and the ethological justification for the model may be found in [1].

A Behavior does not itself perform any actions. Rather it issues commands to the Motor Controller, and the Motor Controller dispatches a Motor Skill which performs the appropriate action. For example, the "move to" Behavior issues the "forward" command to the Motor Controller, which in turn invokes the "walk" Motor Skill. In fact, the Motor Controller is implemented in such a way that the commands may take one of three imperative forms:

- As a primary command. Primary commands are executed immediately, as long as the required resources are available for it. That is, the degrees of freedom or "knobs" (see Fig.1) needed by the underlying Motor Skill must be available in order for the command to succeed.

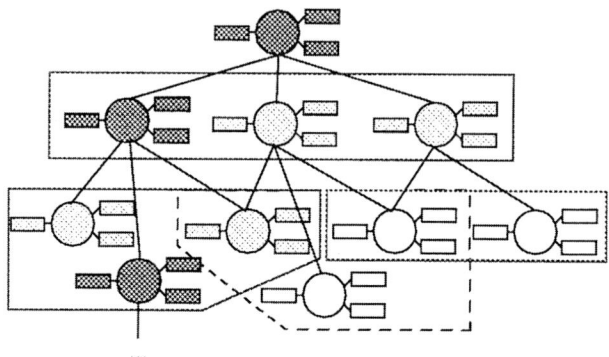

Fig. 3. Hierarchy of mutually inhibiting Behavior Groups

– As a secondary command. Secondary commands are intended to be used to specify desirable but non-essential actions. In other words "do it if you have nothing better to do." Secondary commands are queued by the Motor Controller and executed after primary commands. A priority for a secondary command is also specified when it is issued. This priority dictates the order in which they are executed, thereby giving high priority commands the opportunity to grab the resources (DOFs) before lower priority ones.

– As a meta-command. Meta commands are recommendations as to how a particular action should be performed. For example, a meta command might suggest that "if you are going forward, use this gait." Like secondary commands, meta-commands are queued by the Motor Controller. Behaviors may query the controller to see if a given meta-command has been issued, and if so, it may retrieve the command and use it as it sees fit. Unlike secondary commands, meta-commands only have an effect if a Behavior subsequently makes use of the recommendation to affect what commands it issues.

These multiple imperative forms for motor commands are used extensively by the Behavior System. The action-selection algorithm used by the Behavior System implements a winner-take-all arbitration scheme in which there is a single Behavior which is in control at any given instant. This winning Behavior issues primary commands, since it is the most appropriate Behavior to run at that instant. However, before it runs (i.e. issue motor commands), losing Behaviors may issue secondary or meta-commands. For example, the Dog may have a low-priority behavior whose sole function is to alter the dog's characteristics to demonstrate to the user how the dog is feeling. In this case, the behavior may issue secondary commands for ear, mouth, and tail position as well as body posture, and meta-commands for gait. The reason for using secondary commands is that these are desirable actions, but not essential ones. Similarly, this behavior may not know whether the dog should go forward or not, but it may be in a position to offer a suggestion as to how the dog should move forward should some other behavior decide that the dog should move.

4 Integration of External Control

Motivational and behavioral control (control levels 2 and 3 above) is accomplished by adjusting the factors which influence the relative strength of a Behavior, or group of Behaviors. This may be done in a number of ways.

First, motivational control is provided via named access to the Internal Variables which represent the motivations or goals of the Behavior System. By adjusting the value of a given motivational variable at runtime, one can make the creature more or less likely to engage in Behaviors which depends on that variable.

Second, the constituent parts of a Behavior are also accessible, and this provides another mechanism for exerting behavioral control. Releasing Mechanisms (see Fig.2) act as "object-of-interest" detectors for a Behavior. By modifying the kind of "object-of-interest" to which a given Releasing Mechanism is sensitive, one is in effect modifying the conditions under which a given Behavior will become active. For example, the "marking" Behavior of a dog may rely on a Releasing Mechanism which triggers on "fire hydrants". By modifying it at runtime so that it triggers on "user's pants leg", the resulting behavior of the dog will be very different. One can also adjust the "strength" of a Releasing Mechanism so as to raise or lower its effect on the value of the Behavior (and thus the likelihood of the Behavior becoming active when the Releasing Mechanism is triggered).

Third, the Behavior System is structured so that action-selection (i.e. the process of choosing which Behavior should be active at any given instant), can be initiated at any node in the system. This allows an external entity to force execution of a particular part or branch of the Behavior System, regardless of motivational and sensory factors which might otherwise favor execution of other parts of it. Since branches often correspond to task-level collections of Behaviors, this provides a way of achieving task-level control.

Since each creature has its own sensory system, it is very straightforward to provide "imaginary" sensory input. For example, objects may be added to the world which are visible only to a specific creature. The presence of these objects, however, may trigger certain behaviors on the part of the creature. It should be noted that this may be done more directly by manipulating the creature's Releasing Mechanisms. However, the advantage of this technique is that it does not require the external entity to know anything about the internal structure of the Behavior System.

The mechanisms described above for controlling the Behavior System naturally support Maes' second dimension of control. For example, by adjusting the level of a motivational variable which drives a given branch of the Behavior System, the director is expressing a weighted preference for or against the execution of that behavior or group of behaviors.

The multiple imperative forms supported by the Motor Controller allows the director to express weighted preferences directly at the motor level. For example, at one extreme, the external entity may at any time "shut off" the Behavior system and issue motor commands directly to the creature. Alternatively, the Behavior system can be running, and the external entity may issue persistent secondary or meta-commands which have the effect of modifying or augmenting the output of the Behavior system. For example, the external entity might issue a persistent secondary command to "wag tail". Unless this was explicitly overruled by a Behavior in the Behavior system, this would result in the Dog wagging its tail. Or, for example, the external entity might suggest, via a meta-command, that if the dog chooses to move, it should move with a "trot", or "use any gait but a trot". Meta-commands may also take the form of spatial potential field maps which can be combined with potential field maps generated from sensory data to effectively attract or repel the creature from parts of its environment.

5 Examples

These ideas have been implemented as part of a project to develop a general architecture for building and controlling artificial autonomous characters. We have developed several creatures using a tool kit which implements this approach and these creatures have been used in several different applications. For the Alive project, we have developed "Silas T. Dog" an autonomous animated dog which interacts with a user in a 3D virtual world in a believable manner. Silas responds to a dozen or so gestures and postures of the user, and responds appropriately (e.g. if the user bends over and holds out her hand, Silas moves toward the outstretched hand and eventually sits and shakes his paw). A good deal of attention has been paid to conveying the dog's internal state to the user. The dog always looks at its current object of interest (head, hand, etc.), and when it is sad or happy, its tail, ears and head move appropriately. As mentioned earlier, the behavior system makes extensive use of the different imperative forms supported by the motor system.

We have also developed a number of creatures which are used in the context of an interactive story system developed by Tinsley Galyean of the Media Lab. Galyean's system features a computational director which provides "direction" to the creatures so as to meet the requirements of the story. For example, at the beginning of the story, a dog hops out of a car and wanders around. If the user, who is wearing a head-mounted display, does not pay attention to the dog, the director will send the dog over to the user. If the user still does not pay attention, the director effectively tells the dog: "the user's leg is a fine replacement for a hydrant, and you really have to...". The resulting behavior on the part of the dog usually captures the user's attention.

6 Conclusion

Autonomous animated characters can play an important role in Interactive Story Systems by freeing the director from the details of time-step to time-step control.

However, to be truly useful, the director must be able to control the character at a number of different levels of abstraction, and levels of influence. We have presented a system which shows how these ideas may be integrated into an architecture for autonomous animated characters.

References

1. Blumberg B. (1994), Action-Selection in Hamsterdam: Lessons from Ethology. In *Proceedings of the 3rd International Conference on the Simulation of Adaptive Behavior*, Brighton, England, MIT Press, pp.108–117
2. Blumberg B., Galyean T. (1995) Multi-Level Direction of Autonomous Creatures for Real-Time Virtual Environments, *Proceedings of SIGGRAPH '95*. Computer Graphics, Annual Conference Series, ACM SIGGRAPH, New York
3. Brooks R. (1986) A Robust Layered Control System for a Mobile Robot. *IEEE Journal of Robotics and Automation*, RA-2, April
4. Maes P. (1990) Situated Agents Can Have Goals. In: Maes P. (ed.) *Designing Autonomous Agents: Theory and Practice from Biology to Engineering and Back*, MIT Press, Cambridge
5. Reynolds C.W. (1987) Flocks, Herds, and Schools: A Distributed Behavioral Model. In: *Proceedings of SIGGRAPH '87*, *Computer Graphics*, Annual Conference Series, ACM SIGGRAPH, New York
6. Tu X., Terzopoulos D. (1994) Artificial Fishes: Physics, Locomotion, Perception, Behavior. In *Proceedings of SIGGRAPH '94*, *Computer Graphics*, Annual Conference Series, ACM SIGGRAPH, New York, pp.43–50

Tools for an Interactive Virtual Cinema

David Blair[1] and Tom Meyer[2]

[1] artist1@interport.net
[2] tom@tom.com

Abstract. This paper describes our experiments with narrative structure in nonlinear, interactive and networked forms of media. Through these explorations, we have begun to anticipate what types of tools will be useful to tell stories in multi-user 3D immersive environments incorporating synthetic actors.

Because of the complex nature of this work, which attempts to create a broad fusion of artistic, social, and technical ideas, this paper is also structured differently from a traditional research paper. Many parts of this paper use poetic and allusive techniques to describe the work; generally, we have chosen the particular vocabulary which most succinctly describes the ideas at hand.

1 Traditional Nonlinear Narrative Methodologies

An associative narrative methodology takes advantage of the fact that the narrative impulse has already been jump-started within the majority of us, for example, as an ability or inability to tell lies. The narrative impulse takes what is at hand and presents itself through a partial recombination of these immediate facts. Since anyone can tell a story, what distinguishes the expert or at least enthusiastic amateur from the uninterested is the use of techniques or tools, which range from the simple algorithm of focused interest, used to parse the world for certain types of "material", to any of the complicated and specific toolsets of media composition. The interested user makes use of memory or tools of memory to extend the range of what is compositionally at hand, past the simple moment or the single association of a joke, in order to compose the story and complicate the composition by putting it into extended time.

The aesthetic of associative narrative refers back to the techniques used to compose the story, and the possible fact that people are only watching your story in order to make their own. Its takes advantage of the autogenic nature of narrative in order to create a type of story "engine" that seems to lay its own track through an artificial landscape of potential narratives, and then puffs along that track of its own accord, releasing associations and continuities in the engine-steam, which disappear in a constant stream as they spread across the landscape. In essence, it creates both an artificial world and a way of narrativizing that world, making it easy for the "enduser" of the story to either dream through it or actively finish the meanings.

For centuries, the "grotesque" in fiction (e.g. Cervantes, Pynchon) has recognized both the mechanical nature of narrative, and the intrusion of strange reorganizing forces (often of ethical significance) through the very mechanisms of story. Within this thematically defined genre, story machines have often either been spoken about, or attempted. Tools like the "exquisite corpse" of the surrealists (something like the children's game "telephone"), Burrough's "cutup" (where scissored narratives, when pasted together, could reveal secrets and change the world), and the physical structure of Cortazar's novel early 60's novel "Hopscotch" (numbered chapters read two extremely different ways according to a list at the front of the book) are specific examples.

In the 80's, American hypertext theorists Michael Joyce and Jay Bolter, both with strong interests in AI and associative meaning creation, helped created both a hypertext system (Storyspace [3]) and a new literature. This was based on their ideas of spatialized narrative, in which story was a landscape over which the reader wandered, with meaning created much in the same way landscape space is made coherent in the wanderer's mind, through the constant associative triangulation of "facts" in the artificial world. In both the "grotesque" and in hypertext, the attempted story machine was first a device for story experts. With the Storyspace software, the very machine used to create the narrative is also used to present the narrative, though often with the writing tools taken out.

2 The Narrative of *Wax*

Wax or the discovery of television among the bees, by David Blair, is a film told from the wandering point of view of an semi-intelligent agent, perhaps a literal artificial intelligence lost in a missile, before, during and after a somewhat Cain-like act of revenge. This narrator-agent is also one Jacob Maker, an apparently real person who has been forced to interact perhaps too long with an automated story generation system (represented by the bees of the film's title).

Wax started as a open set of vaguely determined ideas which were concretized first as one or two simple jokes. Then, building on the autogenic narrative principle (which in turn builds upon the basic instability of the original composition substance, i.e. thought and meaning), research material and video material were collected, organized, transformed, and put into temporary place as the composition began to take shape (Fig.1). The specific sort of work that resulted was image-processed narrative, where both the images and the narrative were processed, and where the mechanisms of this processing to a great extent created the composition. Both images and story elements were "re-recognized" after this processing, both instantiating story possibilities, and leading the story into new directions.

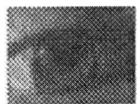

Fig. 1. Shots from one 20-second scene of *Wax*

3   Narrative Methodology of the Hypertext

Waxweb, developed by the authors as the World-Wide Web version of this film, contains a number of automated story generation (or story extension) systems, developed through a hybridization of some common aesthetic principles, and some off-the-shelf network-based writing tools.

The film *Wax* was created in the context of grotesque fiction, and as it passed on, several years later, to *Waxweb*, we tried to exploit the story-machine idea in order to find both the proper mode of hypermedia composition and presentation. First, a large descriptive hypertext was created and sent with the Storyspace software to a number of writers connected by the Internet, in the expectation that they would add some additional, connected material to it.

Next, we placed the hypertext inside an object-oriented database [6]. As this project has developed, our database structure has allowed for several types of procedural recombination of story elements and story media. We index our media based on:

- The linear path, which connects each node with the one immediately following it in the film.
- A tree structure, which establishes each node in its proper position in the act/scene hierarchy.
- Shot overview maps. Clicking on an active still takes you to an index of similar pictures in the film, e.g., all the other pictures of hands.
- Textual thematic paths. The text of the film has embedded links between words corresponding to the overall themes of the film, e.g., the path through all the instances of the word "darkness".
- A random index, which consists of a page filled with X's, each connected to a random starting point in the film.

In its present incarnation, Waxweb resembles the process of its creation, starting at an unspeaking, dense, and empty monadical point (actually a 3-D hexagon), and descending through over 15 layers which offer increasing amounts of narrative detail, altogether acting rhetorically like a Powers of Ten zoom into the Waxworld. The obvious fact that the world has only a certain amount of detail is compensated for at about level 12 of the crosslinking, with the introduction of "image processing", which gets more narrative detail out of the existing elements by performing simple recombinations, involving lookup tables and various sorts of manual parsing.

Of course, this recombinatory use of an appropriately constructed database does not automatically lead to story generation; it just creates a great many more actual and potential moments of story. The intention of this, instead, is to use the ordinary accidents of recombinatory prose-poetry to point towards true machine-made meaning.

4 MOO-based WWW Narrative Server

The system just described runs on a peculiar combination of technology, combining MUD-based interaction with WWW-based content presentation (through HTML, video, pictures, text, and VRML). Through this, we can explore the complex narrative possibilities afforded once many people begin to interact with a pre-existing story made of rich multimedia elements.

4.1 MUDs

MUDs, or Multi-User Domains, evolved out of multi-player Adventure-style games in the early 80s. These began as hack-and-slash style games, but some of the MUDs began to evolve into more social areas, somewhat reminiscent of chat lines. Although many of the earlier systems relied on hard-coded behaviors, MUD systems began to incorporate internal scripting languages. One particularly flexible server, MOO (MUD Object-Oriented), is now being widely used by the research community to support collaborative work, due to the ease of modifying the environment to support scholarship and sharing information.

The MOO server is distributed by Pavel Curtis as part of his research at Xerox PARC, studying collaborative computer systems [4]. Although there continue to be a large number of MOOs solely devoted to socializing, MOO systems have been established at the MIT Media Lab (collaborative environment for media researchers), the University of Virginia (postmodern theorists), CalTech (astronomers), and the Weizmann Institute of Science in Israel (biologists).

People at several MOOs have developed software which allows a MOO to serve as a WWW server, responding to http requests and dynamically formatting the requested information. This is made especially easy due to the interpreted nature of the MOO language. The first MOO-based WWW server was developed at JaysHouseMOO, a MOO devoted to exploring networking issues (they also developed a MOO-based gopher interface). We have modified and extended their techniques to apply to large-scale multimedia servers, and have also added collaborative hypertext authoring tools to both the MOO- and WWW-based interfaces.

4.2 HTML Multimedia Representations

The model used in our system consists of a central database which contains the text of each node, plus additional information specifying the type, project info, and language of other multimedia information. This high-bandwidth multimedia information is typically stored at a number of distributed servers on a per-project basis. Therefore, the centralized database contains low-bandwidth information (text and content coding) which is likely to change, while the distributed multimedia servers contain high-bandwidth data (audio and video information) which will be modified much less frequently. At run-time, the central database server creates a specification of the text (based on current language and media preferences), with pointers to the multimedia information on the closest distributed server for that project.

We use an SGML-based set of markup tags to represent the internal structure of the database (scenes, shots, etc). This representation allows us a great deal of flexibility in how we present the information to the user. Typically, these tags are dynamically parsed by the server into HTML [9], to be viewed in Netscape; we support rendering into pure text, and additional rendering formats are planned in the future (for example, to deal with the increasing number of dialects of HTML).

4.3 VRML

The recent development of VRML (Virtual Reality Modeling Language) [1] has allowed us to develop the structuring of the database in entirely novel directions, through the use of 3D models with attached hyperlinks. These 3D models are taken from the original models used during the creation of the film *Wax*, and represent the narrator's journey through a virtual space, the "Land of the Dead". Many of these models represent dynamic knowledge structures (televisions, telescopes, cities, etc), so we have adapted them as structuring metaphors for the hypertext.

Like the HTML, this VRML is also dynamically generated from the internal database [7], based on the same SGML-based representation of the content structure. The default representation is to arrange the shots associated with a page, texture mapped onto an expanded icosahedron (in the film, this is the bee-television, which is used to direct the narrator to where in the idea-space he should travel next).

In order to take advantage of the individual strengths of the various media types (2D graphical design and layout, versus 3D information presentation), we encourage the participant to use both an HTML and a VRML browser, tiled side-by-side (Fig.2). Most pages consist of text, pictures, and 3D images, so we use the VRML browser to display the 3D objects and associated pictures, and use the HTML browser to show the text and pictures, so that they remain relatively readable (3D is a notoriously bad environment for viewing text).

5 Proposed Narrative Experiments

Although several existing systems allow for the animation of simulated actors, and sometimes even incorporate higher-level, semi-autonomous goals for these actors [5, 2], these systems do not yet fulfill the requirements which content developers will place upon them. In this section, we describe two possible scenarios which could provide a litmus test for artificial actors possessing some degree of narrative intelligence.

One of the most important reasons for choosing these scenarios as a test base is that they are extremely limited; there are many pertinent roles where the

Fig. 2. A typical configuration for using *Waxweb*, showing Netscape on the left and Webspace on the right

participants do not tend to be particularly chatty about subjects not pertaining to their immediate tasks.

5.1 Gatekeeper Scenario

One of the simplest narrative scenarios we can imagine is that of a participant approaching a gatekeeper, who is charged with preventing him or her from passing. This allows for a range of experiments, beginning with a simple version where the gatekeeper may be a simple sphere which attempts to anticipate the user's motions and block him or her from passing through. This simple scenario can be extended by providing for realistic representation and motion, more complex methods of bypassing the gatekeeper (bribery, deception, etc.), and the maintenance of internal state, so that one's relationship with the gatekeeper may change in an interesting way over time.

5.2 Guide

Another narrative role suitable for a synthetic actor is that of the guide. Several research projects have begun to explore this connection [10]. Although this role is being explored in a variety of current products (e.g., Microsoft's Bob), these products are generally concerned with either conveying technical information or adding glitz to otherwise conventional interfaces.

A narrative guide is a useful way to direct the plot of interactive stories, and provides a motivational factor to encourage the user to proceed through chosen paths. As a simple test for the usefulness of a narrative guide, we propose a situation where a simple guide gives a brief overview of a large database such as that used in *Waxweb*, and is able to respond to simple questions as it travels together with the user through the story.

6 Works in Progress

Here we describe two narrative projects currently under development by the authors, and what tools may be necessary in order to develop interesting synthetic narratives for them.

6.1 Jews In Space

One of the authors, David Blair, is working on a second feature-length project, *Jews in Space* (JIS), intended to be released both in theaters as a film, and on networks as a large hyper-film. Automated story-generation is an important research topic for *Jews in Space*.

JIS, like *WAX* before it, is a heavily associative film, a type of hybrid construction very much in the tradition of the encyclopedic narrative, whose composition requires the creation, collation, and preservation of huge numbers of historical and imaginary associations. Research material comes from online databases such as the hyperlinked Encyclopedia Britannica, as well as from printed material integrated into the hypertext database through optical character recognition and keyboard input. This is then processed and extended through traditional and hypertextual writing techniques. However, composition from or within very large datasets can become unwieldy. This problem, however, is not specific to the system, but to current authoring paradigms. The construction of meaning from huge amounts of raw material continues as it has since even before the availability of cheap paper, as a form of intellectual handicraft which in general resists mechanization.

"Association machines", software-based solutions to this problem, can serve as a partial solution to this problem, for this particular type of film. Such machines can act as amplifiers of the associative composition process, parsing large amounts of inputted raw material, to present the author with processed associative clusters. The author can then select a few meaningful proto-compositional elements from the offered choices and use them as the beginning work of new plot sections, or reuse them in the machine as the iterative seeds of new associative processing, at least until the noise plays too loud. Very large scale hypernarratives may not be able to be practically constructed without the aid of such semi-semi-intelligent meaning-engines.

In the current environment of online authoring systems and hopes for general integration of both tools and media types, there isn't much difference between production and distribution. *Jews in Space* will be authored, as much as possible, in an open-system "Virtual Studio". At the end of the production, the tools used by the movie-making professionals to intercommunicate, and perhaps some of the production tools will be recycled with the entire data-set as an on-line virtual movie theater", an extremely large hypermedia site that will be released in parallel with the small-cinema release of the celluloid film. Semi-intelligent authoring tools, if they can be found or constructed, will be used by the author in the virtual studio. We hope that these composition tools could then be turned around, and serve as end-user tools, perhaps even engines for the creation of a somewhat intelligently recombining Story-Place.

6.2 Grammatron

Another project currently underway, which will incorporate synthetic actors in an multiple-participant 3D environment, is *Grammatron*, being developed by Tom Meyer in association with the writer Mark Amerika. The setting of this project is the virtual city Prague-23, situated in a shared 3D environment, narratively situated ten to fifteen years in the future.

The story describes an artist, Abe Golam, who is asked to write an article about this virtual city, and his encounters in the "Interzone" situated there. His journey is directed by the other main character, Cynthia Kitchen, who is attempting to bring Abe Golam into a psychogeographical state where they may be able to be reunited.

Although we will allow for multiple participants to be present in the MUD-like social zones of the space, as in [12], many of the narrative sections will involve the participant taking on the role of Abe Golam or Cynthia Kitchen as they interact with simulated actors throughout the city. In addition, parts of the story may require that the participants add to the story, so we would like the authoring tools to be as simple and open as possible.

Because this project is being designed as a general virtual environment system, it will require an extremely fast distributed database, capable of tens of thousands of updates per second. The emerging union of VRML [8] and Java [11] may prove to be quite useful for developing an architecture-independent client for such a database, and at the current rate of harware, software, and network-bandwidth evolution, we expect that suitable clients and servers for this project may be realizable within the next two years.

7 Conclusion

Unfortunately, there has been a lot of research emphasis on prototyping run-time systems, and not a lot of emphasis on open tool-kits with functionalities that even hybridly imitate story creation, which then can be used by authors, and, in the best of all possible worlds, reused in distribution as a dumbed-down enduser toolkit. We believe that if you can get the machine to help compose the story out of "material", character comes easily next, as a further complexification of the autogenic story-making impulse.

8 Acknowledgements

Thanks to the Brown University Graphics Group, especially Andries van Dam, David Klaphaak, Suzanne Hader, Emma Johnson, Laura Mullen, and Brook Conner. John Unsworth of the Institute for Advanced Technology in the Humanities at the University of Virginia provided a machine and disk space for the project. Mark Pesce, Jan Hardenburgh, and the Open Inventor Group at SGI gave feedback and early bug-testing of the VRML version of Waxweb.

This work was supported in part by grants from NSF, ARPA, NASA, IBM, Taco, Sun, SGI, HP, Microsoft, Xing, Okidata, ONR grant N00014-91-J-4052, ARPA order 8225, and the New York State Council for the Arts.

9 Bibliography

References

1. Bell G., Parisi A., Pesce M. (1995) "The Virtual Reality Modeling Language Version 1.0 Specification". <URL:http://vrml.wired.com/vrml.tech/vrml10-3.html>
2. Blumberg B. and Galyean T.A. (1995) "Multi-Level Direction of Autonomous Creatures for Real-Time Virtual Environments". In *Proceedings of SIGGRAPH 95*, pp.47–54
3. Bolter J.D., Joyce M. (1987) "Hypertext and Creative Writing". *Proceedings of Hypertext '87*. November 1987. pp.41–50
4. Curtis P. (1992) "Mudding: Social Phenomena in Text-Based Virtual Realities". *Proceedings of the 1992 Conference on Directions and Implications of Advanced Computing*. Berkeley. May 1992
5. Goldberg A. (1990) "Behavioral Scripting: Method acting for synthetic characters". <URL:http://found.cs.nyu.edu/MRL/behaviour/behaviour.html>
6. Meyer T., Blair D., Hader S. (1994) "WAXweb: A MOO-based Hypermedia System for WWW". In *Proceedings of the Second International WWW Conference*. <URL:http://www.ncsa.uiuc.edu/SDG/IT94/Proceedings/VR/meyer.waxweb/meyer.html>
7. Meyer T., Blair D., Conner D.B. (1995) "WAXweb: Toward Dynamic MOO-based VRML". In *Proceedings of VRML 95*. <URL:http://www.cs.brown.edu/research/graphics/publications/papers/waxvrml.ps>
8. Meyer T. and Conner D.B. (1995) "Adding Behavior to VRML". In *Proceedings of VRML 95*. <URL:http://www.cs.brown.edu/research/graphics/publications/papers/vrmlbehaviors.html>
9. Raggett D. (1995) "HyperText Markup Language, Version 3.0". Internet Draft. <URL:http://www.w3.org/hypertext/WWW/MarkUp/html3/CoverPage.html>
10. Rich C. et al. (1994) "Demonstration of an Interactive Multimedia Environment". In *IEEE Computer* 27(11). pp.15–22. <URL:http://www.merl.com/TR/TR94-06/Welcome.html>
11. Sun Microsystems. (1995) "The Java Language Specification". 1995.
12. Worlds Inc. (1995) "Worlds Chat". <URL:http://www.worlds.net/products/wchat/index.html>

Acting in Character

Barbara Hayes-Roth, Robert van Gent, Daniel Huber*

Computer Science Department
Stanford University

1 Personality in Improvisational Actors

Personality is the set of psychological traits that uniquely characterize an individual. Personality distinguishes each individual from all others and colors his or her behavior in a pervasive and recognizable fashion. It is a persistent phenomenon that changes little and slowly, if at all, over time. Personality makes people fascinating to one another.

We are studying personality in the context of synthetic agents that function as actors [5]. Like human actors, these agents assume prescribed roles. They follow scripts, scenarios, and directions. They strive to "breathe life into their characters."

In this context, it is not the personality of the actor that interests us, but the personality of the character he or she portrays. Thus, when we say that an actor is "in character," we mean that the actor is behaving in accordance with a personality created by an author, shaped by a director, and assumed by an audience, for purposes of a particular performance. A good actor creates and communicates a consistent and compelling personality throughout a performance of a given role and creates different personalities for different roles.

Of course, the distinction between the personality of the actor and the personality of the character is not always sharp. Many old-fashioned movie stars, such as Katharine Hepburn and Cary Grant, carried distinctive features of their own "professional personalities" into every role they played. Indeed, their fans would otherwise have been disappointed. Even great character actors, ultimately constrained by their own identities, are better able to create some characters than others. In a very real sense, each unique combination of actor and role yields a unique character. Thus, we enjoy seeing how gifted new actors reinterpret classic roles as compelling characters largely of their own making.

A similar phenomenon occurs when great stories are rendered in new forms. However well we "know" Shakespeare's Juliet from the performances of traditional theater actresses, we are enchanted to meet each new Juliet in each new

* This work was supported by: ARPA Contract N66001-95-D-8642-Subcontract #137-1 through Teknowledge, Inc. and a gift from Intel. The work has benefited from discussions with members of the Virtual Theater research group, especially: Lee Brownston, Daniel Rousseau, Patrick Doyle, and Todd Feldman; and from discussions with Stanford Professors Larry Friedlander (English Literature) and Patricia Ryan (Drama). We thank Ken Perlin of NYU for the use of his animation. A patent application has been filed for the "Method and System of Directed Improvisation by Computer Characters."

art form, for example: Olivia Hussey in Zeffirelli's faithful period film; Natalie Wood in the film of the Bernstein and Robbins modern retelling, West Side Story; and three different prima ballerinas: Natalia Makaravo, Evelyn Cisneros, and Marcia Haydee dancing the distinctive choreographies of Petipa (American Ballet Theatre), Smuin (San Francisco Ballet), and Cranko (Stuttgart Ballet). Although each of these works offers its own intrinsic beauty and art, much of our pleasure comes from the chance to see beloved characters recreated by new performers in new forms.

We are particularly interested in agents that function as improvisational actors who spontaneously and cooperatively generate their stories at performance time. Like human improvisors, our agents are intended to work closely together and to exploit known heuristics for producing engaging performances, for example: *accept all offers, don't block your partner, do the natural thing, don't try to be clever*, and *reincorporate previously generated elements* [1, 3, 16, 17, 18, 21]. In addition, they are designed to improvise under the constraints of directions from exogenous sources, such as people or other computer system components. We call this general paradigm "directed improvisation" [8, 10, 12].

Although various improvisational performance modes are possible, for present purposes we focus on a classical mode first practiced by the *Commedia dell'Arte* of Rennaissance Italy and subsequently adapted by the Compass and Second City groups in Chicago [21]. Here, the actors are assigned standard roles in a familiar scenario, but improvise the details of their performance. Since the audience has enjoyed many previous performances of the same scenario, often by the same actors, it cannot be discovery of the plot that entertains them. Instead, it is the actors' skillful invention of new characters in familiar roles and the chance to see how these new characters cope with the inevitable twists and turns of the plot.

We wish to create synthetic actors who work together to improvise simple scenarios defined by three dramatic constructs: plot, role, and character. *Plot* is a temporally constrained sequence of actions involving a set of individuals. A plot and its constituent actions may be quite abstract. For example, one prototypical plot is: *a* meets *b*, *a* loves *b*, *a* loses *b*, *a* wins *b*. *Role* is a class of individuals, whose prototypical behaviors, relationships, and interactions are known to both actors and audience. For example, the plot outlined above ordinarily is instantiated with these roles: the boy in love and the girl he loves. However, it might be instantiated with alternative roles, for example: the female dog in love and the male dog she loves; the male skunk in love and the female cat he loves; or the lonely little girl and the stray dog she loves. *Character* is a personality defined as a coherent configuration of psychological traits. For example, any of the characters in the present scenario might be: shy and sensitive, gregarious and coarse, or silly and affectionate. However compelling the plot and roles of a performance may be, it is character that elicits our emotional response, that makes us love or hate the people in the story, that makes us care about what happens to them.

As illustrated in the examples above, plot, role, and character are substantially independent and may be directed separately. In fact, human actors may be directed on any subset of them and left free to improvise without constraint on the others. We aim to create the same capabilities in synthetic actors; however, the present paper focuses on the paradigm in which actors are directed with constraints on all three constructs. Thus, for a given performance, each actor is directed to play one of the roles specified in a designated plot and to display prescribed character traits. Working together, the actors improvise the story. Their improvisations are role-appropriate. They are punctuated and contextualized by the actors' enactment of required plot elements. They are colored and textured by the actors' realizations of the prescribed characterizations. Changing any of the directions for a new performance not only alters the affected actors' immediate behavior, but propagates throughout their improvisational interactions with the other actors to produce a joint performance that may be wholly new and different from its predecessors.

In this paper, we report an empirical study of the model outlined above in the context of a classic master-servant scenario. We have been strongly influenced in our choice and treatment of this material by the work of Keith Johnstone, especially his book, *Impro: Improvisation and the Theatre* [18]. As Johnstone observes:

> One status relationship that gives immense pleasure to audiences is the master-servant scene. A dramatist who adapts a story for the stage will often add a servant, especially if it's a comedy; Sophocles gave Silenus as a slave to the Cyclops, Moliere gave Don Juan a servant, and so on. The master-servant scene seems to be funny and entertaining in all cultures—even people who have never seen a manservant have no difficulty in appreciating the nuances. (pp. 62-63)

In addition, as we shall see, the master-servant scenario provides rich material with which to explore the independent direction of role, plot, and character.

The remainder of this paper examines our model and empirical study in more detail. In section 2 below, we review our concept of directed improvisation. In sections 3-5, we discuss how actors can be directed to improvise under separable constraints of plot, role, and character, respectively. In section 6, we briefly describe our implementation of improvisational actors and their capabilities for improvising variations on the master-servant scenario. In section 7, we return to the more general issues of creating personality and character in synthetic agents and actors.

Before proceeding, we make one general observation. Although all three dramatic constructs—plot, role, and character— are interesting and important, we give most of our attention to character-constrained improvisation. This is, in part, to address the main topic of the present collection, personality. More importantly, our emphasis reflects a belief that development and expression of character are the primary determinants of audience engagement and dramatic impact in narrative works. Following Horton [17] and others, we believe that:

... "it is the character's personality that creates the action of the story" and not the other way around... (quote from novelist, Flannery O'Connor [19])

"Character is the vital material with which an author must work." (quote from writing teacher, Lajos Egri [4])

2 Directed Improvisation

In directed improvisation, actors work together in real time to enact a joint course of behavior that follows directions, adapts to the dynamic situation, and otherwise may vary under the weak heuristic constraints of effective improvisation. Because we have discussed the general properties of directed improvisation elsewhere [8-10, 12-15], we only excerpt that material here.

As in all improvisation [1, 3, 9, 16, 17, 18, 21], directed improvisation requires the actors to work cooperatively, constantly adapting to one another's behavior, as well as to other features of the dynamic situation. The most fundamental rule of improvisation is that actors should *accept all offers*, and, conversely, *not block your partner*. That is, each actor must acknowledge and respond appropriately to any explicit assertion, question, or command produced by another actor. For example, if actor A says to actor b, "Why are you wearing that hat?" B must not block A by calling attention to the fact that her head is bare. She must accept B's offer by affirming his premise and replying, for example, "It's one of my favorites." In addition, improvisational actors should *do the natural thing* and, conversely, should *not try to be clever*. This is one area in which synthetic agents may have an advantage over human actors who have a tendency to try too hard. For example, Johnstone recalls:

> For some weeks I experimented with scenes in which two 'strangers' met and interacted, and I tried saying 'No jokes', and 'Don't try to be clever', but the work remained unconvincing. They had no way to mark time and allow situations to develop, they were forever striving to latch on to 'interesting' ideas. (p. 33)

Finally, more advanced improvisors should *reincorporate previously generated elements*. That is, they must try to refer back to previously mentioned concepts, to reuse previously introduced objects, and to remind one another of previous actions. In so doing, they create a sense of narrative structure and resolution. Of course, artful reincorporation is a fundamental property of all good storytelling [17]. As Chekhov said: "If you say in the first chapter that there is a rifle hanging on a wall, in the second or third chapter it absolutely must go off. If it's not going to be fired, it shouldn't be hanging there" [2]. But conventional authors have the luxury of reflection and revision, while improvisors must live with their immediate performance history and reincorporate it on the fly.

In directed improvisation, actors must follow these basic rules of improvisation, while working within the additional constraints of their directions. In fact, directed improvisation occupies the vast middle ground between "pure" improvisation and traditional acting. Most pure improvisors seek at least a minimal constraint on their performances. For example, they might ask the audience to answer a question (what is a scary animal? your favorite color? the best holiday?) and commit to incorporate the answer into their performance. At the other extreme, even traditional acting involves at least a small degree of improvisation. Human beings cannot reproduce exact performances on different occasions even if they should wish to do so and each actor must respond appropriately to intended or unintended variations in their partners' performances. For example, in the original Broadway production of Tennessee Williams's *A Streetcar Named Desire*, Jessica Tandy appeared in a critically acclaimed performance as Blanche du Bois, while Marlon Brando made his stunning debut as Stanley Kowalski. The story goes that Brando's "method" acting electrified audiences and critics, but severely tested Tandy's ability and inclination to adapt her own more conventional acting style to the unpredictable new Stanley she met on the stage each night.

In directed improvisation, actors work within the constraints of directions that vary in the degree to which they restrict the actors' behavior. The directions may be abstract and leave the actor nearly complete freedom or very specific and prescribe the smallest details of behavior. They may constrain any aspect of behavior, including an actor's role, characterization, or actions. Directions may be delivered in advance in the form of a complete scenario, such as the master-servant scenarios discussed below. Alternatively, the directions may be delivered interactively during a performance, as in the improvisational puppets and avatars we have discussed elsewhere [13, 14, 15]. In hybrid modes, performance-time directions may constrain scenario-based improvisations. Directions may come from various sources, including people, other computer system components, or the actors themselves.

3 Directing Role-Constrained Improvisation

Improvisational actors may be directed to assume particular roles in a performance. For example, in the master-servant scenarios we have been studying, each of two actors can be directed to play master or servant. In most cases, actors are directed to play a constant role throughout a performance. However, they may be directed to change roles at some point in a performance, as illustrated in the Role-Reversal Scenario discussed below.

Direction to assume a particular role constrains an actor to improvise only role-appropriate or role-neutral behaviors. For example, actors in the master-servant scenarios know that the Master may do as he pleases in his domain and may command certain aspects of his servant's behavior as well. They know that the servant generally must stay in his waiting place unless called upon to do the master's bidding.

Different actors may have different models of role-appropriate behaviors. For example, all actors may know that a servant should open the door if the master moves to leave the room, adjust his chair if he prepares to sit, and hold his jacket as he dresses. However, individual actors may or may not think to light the master's cigar, bow when he enters or leaves the room, keep eyes downcast as he passes, produce a handkerchief if he sneezes, etc. Thus, familiar roles may take on new dimensions when performed by different actors. Conversely, an individual actor's effectiveness in a role rests upon the depth and breadth of his or her knowledge of role-appropriate behaviors.

In addition to prototypical behaviors associated with their roles, actors may perform subtler role-expressive behaviors. For master and servant roles, Johnstone suggests:

> I teach that a master-servant scene is one in which both parties act as if all the space belonged to the master. (Johnstone's law!) ...

> When the master is present, the servant must take care at all times not to dominate the space. ... Footmen can't lean against the wall, because it's the master's wall. Servants must make no unnecessary noise or movement, because it's the master's air they're intruding on.

> The preferred position for a servant is usually at the edge of the master's 'parabola of space'. This is so that at any moment the master can confront him and dominate him. The exact distance the servant stands from the master depends on his duties, his position in the hierarchy, and the size of the room.

> When the servant's duties take him into close proximity with the master he must show that he invades the master's space 'unwillingly'. If you have to confront the master in order to adjust his tie you stand back as far as possible, and you may incline your head. If you're helping with his trousers you probably do it from the side. Crossing in front of the master the servant may 'shrink' a little, and he'll try to keep a distance. Working behind the master, brushing his coat, he can be as close as he likes, and visibly higher, but he mustn't stay out of sight of the master unless his duties require it (or unless he is *very* low status). (pp. 63-64)

As a performance unfolds, the actors improvise together, spontaneously performing role-appropriate behaviors and always responding appropriately to one another's behaviors. For example, the master may choose to open a scenario by ordering his servant to fetch a book or by strolling over to the window and gazing out upon his domain. The servant must "accept the master's offer," dutifully fetching the book or standing in quiet readiness to serve. Since the actors respond to one another's behavior, each one's successive improvisational choices nudge the joint performance toward one of many possible paths. For example, a servant will light his master's cigar if and only if the master appears to take out a cigar. Similarly, the master will respond to the servant's cigar-lighting behavior only if it occurs. Thus, even in repeated performances by the same cast, small changes in early improvisational choices by individual actors may cascade into very divergent joint performances. With new assignments of actors to roles, the space of possible improvisations in each role grows and the range and number of unique joint performances grows combinatorially.

With closely-coupled roles, such as master and servant, a shared understanding of role-appropriate behaviors may emerge from the characters' improvised interactions. In a case of "art imitating life," we can hardly top the comic exaggerations of real-life master-servant relationships reported by Johnstone:

> An extreme example would be the eighteenth-century scientist Henry Cavendish, who is reported to have fired any servant he caught sight of! (Imagine the hysterical situations: servants scuttling like rabbits, hiding in grandfather clocks and ticking, getting stuck in huge vases.) (p. 63)

> Heinrich Harrer met a Tibetan whose servant stood holding a spitoon in case the master wanted to spit. Queen Victoria would take her position and sit, and there *had* to be a chair. George the Sixth used to wear electrically heated underclothes when deerstalking, which meant a gillie had to follow him around holding the battery. (p. 70)

Despite the constraints of role-appropriate behavior, actors retain considerable improvisational freedom. They can carry their role-appropriate improvisations into many different plots and characterizations. As Johnstone observes:

> The relationship is not necessarily one in which the servant plays low and the master plays high. Literature is full of scenes in which the servant refuses to obey the master, or even beats him and chases him out of the house. ... the servant can throttle the master while remaining visibly the servant. This is very pleasing to the audience. (pp. 63-64)

4 Directing Plot-Structured Improvisation

Improvisational actors may be directed to follow particular plot outlines to structure their joint performances. For example, Johnstone notes that the Commedia dell'Arte blocked out each of their plots as a series of scenes, for example:

> (1) nice master, nasty servant; (2) nasty master, nice servant; (3) both teams interrelate and quarrel; (4) team one prepares for duel; (5) team two prepares for duel; (6) the duel. (p. 65)

In our experiment, we use a similar technique to construct variations on a classic master-servant scenario, which we call "While the Master's Away ... " Figure 1 outlines five scenes for our Base Scenario and Role-Reversal Scenario.

Both scenarios begin with the master and servant together, interacting in their usual manner. Then the master leaves the room and the servant decides to play at being the master. Although this is a flagrant violation of Johnstone's law that *the master owns the space*, he views the violation itself as typical, role-determined servant behavior:

Base Scenario	Role-Reversal Scenario
1. Master and Servant	1. Master and Servant
2. Servant at Play	2. Servant at Play
3. Caught in the Act	3. Caught in the Act
4. Servant Retreats	4. Turning the Tables
5. Business as Usual	5. The New Regime

Fig. 1. Two variations on the scenario "While the Master's Away..."

When the masters are not present, then the servants can take full possession of the space, sprawl on the furniture, drink the brandy, and so on ...[chauffeurs] can smoke, chat together and treat the cars as their 'own' ...(p. 63)

Of course, at the climax of our scenario, the master returns and catches the servant in the act. At this point, the two scenarios diverge. In the Base Scenario, a chastised servant retreats to his place at the wall and the denouement is business as usual. In the Role-Reversal scenario, confrontation by the master is only a prelude to the true climax. With the tension mounting, the servant stands his ground. Emboldened by the master's failure to assert his power, the servant ultimately usurps the master's role and relegates him to the role of servant. The denouement is a new regime.

To structure improvisation into plot, we give the actors a sequence of scenes that explicitly direct only plot-critical behaviors, entrances and exits, and synchronization cues. For example, Fig. 2 shows Scene 1 directions for both scenarios. To set the scene, both actors are directed to begin in specific role-appropriate positions in the space. Then they are directed to improvise freely within the constraints of their roles for approximately 2 minutes, at the master's discretion. Then the master is directed to exit, which cues termination of the scene for both actors.

Base Scenario and Role-Reversal Scenario
Scene 1. Master and Servant

Role = Master	Role = Servant
Stand at window	Stand at wall
Improvise until ~2 min	Improvise until Master exits
Exit ——————————————→ CUE	

Fig. 2. Directions for Scene 1 of "While the Master's Away..."

Figures 3 and 4 show the slightly more specific directions we use to structure Scene 4 in each of the two scenarios. The master has just caught the servant playing master. In the Base Scenario, the master is directed to watch the servant as he retreats to his place at the wall, thereby cueing termination of the scene for both actors. In the Role-Reversal Scenario, the master is directed to watch the servant as he first holds his ground for approximately 1 minute, at the servant's discretion, and then switches roles to become the master. On this cue, the original master is directed to switch roles to become the servant. Completion of the role-reversal cues termination of the scene for both actors.

Base Scenario
Scene 4. Servant Retreats

Role = Master   Role = Servant

Watch Servant until Servant at wall   Go to wall
CUE ◄─────────────────────── Stand at wall and Improvise

Fig. 3. Directions for Scene 4 of the Base Scenario for "While the Master's Away..."

Role-Reversal Scenario
Scene 4. Turning the Tables

Role = Master   Role = Servant

Watch Servant until He is Master   Stand and Improvise until ∼1 min
CUE ◄─────────────────────── Role ⟹ Master
                                                 Improvise until Master ⟹ Servant
Role ⟹ Servant ───────────────► CUE

Fig. 4. Directions for Scene 4 of the Role-Reversal Scenario for "While the Master's Away..."

As these examples illustrate, more or less specific plot directions trade off an author's artistic control in shaping a narrative against the actors' improvisational freedom in creating their performances.

5   Directing Character-Constrained Improvisation

5.1   Status Variables for Dramatic Characterization

Improvisational actors may be directed to invest their characters with personality traits. Although there are many kinds of traits we might consider in theorizing about "real-life" personalities, in the context of improvisational acting, we specifically want traits that can be exploited for dramatic effect. Therefore, instead of the literature of the social sciences, we look for guidance to the literature of the theater.

In the present study, we examine three variables representing a character's *status* in *demeanor, relationship,* and *space.* For brevity, we refer to these as D, R, and S status. Johnstone defines these variables, as discussed below, and identifies them as especially powerful tools for characterization and drama:

> ...In my view, really accomplished actors, directors, and playwrights are people with an intuitive understanding of the status transactions that govern human relationships. (p. 72)

Status in demeanor refers to a character's intrinsic ways of behaving. Actors effect high D status through an erect posture, hands at rest, a quiet manner, and smooth movements. They effect low D status through a slouched posture, frequent touching of the face, a nervous manner, and jerky movements. Johnstone teaches that these and other details of behavior reflect a person's real-life D status and, therefore, can be used to assert an actor's in-character D status:

> You can talk and waggle your head about if you play the gravedigger, but not if you play Hamlet. Officers are trained not to move the head while issuing commands. (p. 43)

> One might try holding his toes pointing inward (low status), while one sits back and spreads himself (high status). (p.44)

> ...We have a 'fear-crouch' position in which the shoulders lift to protect the jugular and the body curls forward to protect the underbelly. ...The opposite ...is the 'cherub posture', which opens all the planes of the body: the head turns and tilts to offer the neck, the shoulders turn the other way to expose the chest, the spine arches slightly backwards and twists so that the pelvis is in opposition to the shoulders exposing the underbelly—and so on. ...High-status people often adopt versions of the cherub posture. If they feel under attack they'll abandon it and straighten, but they won't adopt the fear crouch. Challenge a low-status player and he'll show some tendency to slide into postures related to the fear crouch. (p. 59)

> The high-status effect of slow motion means that TV heroes who have the power of superhuman speed are shown slowed down! Logic would

suggest that you should speed the film up, but then they'd be jerking about like the Keystone Cops, or the bionic chicken. (p. 74)

The most powerful behavioral markers of D status may be indirect. A truly high-status person has no need to assert his position. Johnstone points out that the calmest and most relaxed person in a group is immediately perceived as being extremely high status:

> ... in the opening scenes of Kozintsev's film of *King Lear*. ... Lear enters as if he owns the place, warms his hands at the fire, and 'makes himself at home'. The effect is to enormously *elevate* Lear in status. Lears who strain to look powerful and threatening in this opening scene miss the point, which is that Lear is so confident, and trustful, that he willingly divides his kingdom and sets in motion his own destruction. (pp. 59-60)

D status is not to be confused with the "content" of behavior. To teach actors to preserve this distinction in their characterizations, Johnstone puts them through certain exercises:

> I repeat all status exercises in gibberish, just to make it quite clear that the things *said* are not as important as the status *played*. If I ask two actors to meet, with one playing high, and one playing low, and to reverse the status while talking an imaginary language, the audience laugh amazingly. We don't know what's being said, and neither do the actors, but the status reversal is enough to enthrall us. (p. 49)

> I get the actors to learn short fragments of text and play every possible status on them. For example, A is late and B has been waiting for him.
> A: Hallo.
> B: Hallo.
> A: Been waiting long?
> B: Ages.
> The implication is that B lowers A, but any status can be played. (p. 49)

Status in relationship refers to a character's position relative to another. As Johnstone remarks:

> ... we are pecking-order animals and ... this affects the tiniest details of our behavior. (p. 74)

Actors effect high or low R status by making gestures of authority or subordination, especially implicit gestures involving eye contact, spatial proximity, or touching. Behavioral markers of high R status may be quite subtle and indirect. For example, Johnstone suggests:

> A stare is often interpreted as an aggressive act ... If A wants to dominate B he stares at him appropriately; B can accept this with a submissive

expression or by looking away, or can challenge and outstare.... breaking eye contact can be high status so long as you don't immediately glance back for a fraction of a second. If you ignore someone your status rises, if you feel impelled to look back then it falls. (pp. 41-42)

I might then begin to insert a tentative 'er' at the beginning of each of my sentences, and ask the group if they detect any change in me. They say that I look 'helpless' and 'weak' but they can't, interestingly enough, say what I'm doing that's different. ... If I make the 'er' longer, ...then they say I look more important, more confident. ...The shorter 'er' is an invitation for people to interrupt you; the long 'er' says 'Don't interrupt me, even though I haven't thought what to say yet.' (p. 42-43)

Imagine that two strangers are approaching each other along an empty street. ...the two people scan each other for signs of status, and then the lower one moves aside. ...If each person believes himself to be dominant ...they approach until they stop face to face, and do a sideways dance, while muttering confused apologies ...If a little old half-blind lady wanders into your path ...you move out of her way. It's only when you think the other person is challenging that the dance occurs ...(p. 61)

In life, R status often parallels social status. Typically, the teacher is higher status than the student; the parent is higher status than the child; the boss is higher status than the employee; and so forth. However, this parallelism is not absolute in life and certainly not in art. As Johnstone observes:

Status is a confusing term unless it's understood as something one *does*. You may be low in social status, but play high, and vice versa.

Tramp: 'Ere! Where are you going?
Duchess: I'm sorry, I didn't quite catch ...
Tramp: Are you deaf as well as blind?

Audiences enjoy a contrast between the status played and the social status. We always like it when a tramp is mistaken for the boss, or the boss for a tramp. Hence plays like *The Inspector General*. Chaplin liked to play the person at the bottom of the hierarchy and then lower everyone. (p. 36)

Status in the space refers to a character's relationship to the surrounding space and objects. Actors effect high or low S status by their willingness or reluctance to enter the space, to move about, and to use or even abuse the objects they find there. Johnstone observes:

...status is basically territorial. (p. 57)

High-status players ...will allow their space to flow *into* other people. Low-status players will avoid letting their space flow into other people.

...Imagine a man sitting neutrally and symmetrically on a bench. If he crosses his left leg over his right then you'll see his space flowing over to the right as if his leg was an aerofoil. If he rests his right arm along the back of the bench you'll see his space flowing out more strongly. If he turns his head to the right, practically all his space will be flowing in this same direction. Someone who is sitting neutrally in the 'beam' will seem lower-status. ...The difference seems so trivial, yet ...it's a quite strong effect. (p. 59)

Scrutinizing a larger group of people, we can see Johnstone's status "see-saw" principle ('I go up and you go down,' p. 37) propagate in all directions as individuals continually adjust their physical positions in response to the movements of their neighbors. Johnstone teaches his acting students to carry this natural equilibrium process into their work:

...space flowed around [them] like a fluid. ...When they *weren't* acting, the bodies of the actors continually readjusted. As one changed position so all the others altered their positions. Something seemed to flow between them. When they were 'acting' each actor would pretend to relate to the others, but his movements would stem from himself. They seemed 'encapsulated'. ...it's only when the actor's movements are related to the space he's in, and to the other actors, that the audience feel 'at one' with the play. The very best actors pump space out and suck it in...(p. 57)

5.2 Directing Status Transactions

In life, we expect individuals in particular roles and relationships to have "appropriate" personalities, that is, to exhibit prototypical patterns of personality traits. For example, we expect a proper master to be high status on all three variables. He should be dignified. He should be dominant in the relationship with his servant. By definition, he owns the space. We expect a proper servant to be high status in demeanor, but low status in the relationship with his master and in the space. He should be dignified, but deferential. He should not intrude upon his master's space, except to serve him. Of course, human beings do not always conform to prototype and our expectations may be violated in amusing or disturbing ways.

In art, authors may deliberately stretch or violate the bounds of prototype for dramatic effect. One technique is to exaggerate prototypical personality traits. For example, a comic actor playing the servant in our scenario might drastically lower his status in the space and then amuse the audience with his desperate efforts to avoid entering the space: scrunching up his body to occupy the smallest possible area, edging around the perimeter of a room to perform his duties, etc. Another technique, exploited by comic authors from William Shakespeare to Charlie Chaplin, is to create an incongruous clash of personality traits against role. For example, in the P. G. Wodehouse stories, Bertie Wooster and Jeeves faithfully enact their roles of master and servant. Jeeves has an impeccable demeanor and is a faultless servant. However, Bertie displays an astonishing low status in both his demeanor and his relationship to Jeeves—he is hopelessly inept and would be quite lost without Jeeves to rescue him from the consequences of his own peccadilloes. The great joke of the stories is that, in a very real sense, the servant is nobler than the master. With additional characters, status transactions can become very complex indeed. Johnstone cites Beckett's *tour de force* of status transactions, *Waiting for Godot*:

> The 'tramps' play friendship status, but there's a continual friction because Vladimir believes himself higher than Estragon, a thesis which Estragon will not accept. Pozzo and Lucky play maximum-gap master-servant scenes. ...[But] Pozzo is not really a very high-status master, since he fights for status all the time. He owns the land, but he doesn't own the space. ...The 'tramps' play low status to Lucky, and Pozzo often plays low status to the tramps—which produces thrilling effects. (p. 72)

Figure 5 shows how we use the three status variables defined above to direct two distinct characterizations of the Servant in our Base Scenario: Dignified versus Undignified Servant.

Status	Undignified Servant	Dignified Servant
Relationship	Low	Low
Demeanor	Low	High
Space:		
Block 1	Low	Low
Block 2	Rises Slowly	Rises Quickly
Block 3	High	High
Block 4	Plummets	Falls Gracefully
Block 5	Low	Low

Fig. 5. Directing two characterizations of the Servant in the Base Scenario

Directions for R status and D status are straightforward. We direct both servants to exhibit low R status throughout the scenario. We direct the dignified servant to exhibit high D status and the undignified servant to exhibit low D status throughout the scenario. As discussed above, these directions do not compromise the servant's role or his commitment to perform role-appropriate behaviors. Regardless of status, the servant serves the master. However, with low D-status, the servant performs his functions in a manner that appears awkward, nervous, furtive, and restless. With high D-status, he performs the same functions in a manner that appears dignified, confident, matter-of-fact, and calm.

Directions for S status are more complex, layering the personality-specific nuances of characterization on a common plot-required progression of values, as explained below.

To support the plot, we direct the servant to manipulate his S status. During Scene 1, the servant must have low S status because, when the Master is present, he owns the space. When directed to improvise, the servant restricts his improvisations to avoid intruding upon the space. During Scenes 2-4, while the master is away, the servant must raise his S status to allow him to enter the space and play at being master. Now when directed to improvise, the servant might stroll around the master's room, pause to gaze out the master's window, and eventually even sit in the master's chair. Finally, in Scene 5, when confronted by the master, the servant must lower his S status again to yield the master's space.

To reinforce characterization, we direct personality-specific nuances in this plot-required progression. We direct the undignified servant to raise his status in the space slowly during Scene 2 and to allow it to fall precipitously upon confrontation by the master in Scene 4. Thus, when his master leaves the room, a nervous and awkward servant moves tentatively into the master's space, deliberating long and hard before daring to sit in the master's chair. Visibly chagrined to be discovered there by his master, the undignified servant scurries back to his place. Conversely, we direct the dignified servant to raise his status quickly at the start of Scene 2 and to allow it to fall gracefully during Scene 4. Thus, when his master leaves the room, a calm and graceful servant moves confidently into the master's space and ensconces himself in the master's chair. Unruffled by his master's return, the dignified servant matter-of-factly returns to his place.

Role reversal is the most extreme outcome of Johnstone's see-saw principle: when status is played as a zero-sum game among characters, only one can be on top. Role reversal lies at the heart of a great variety of stories, for example: the adventure of trading places enjoyed by Twain's Prince and Pauper; the pathos of Burnet's Little Princess when her father's apparent death reduces her to a servant of her classmates; and the humiliation of an arrogant mistress when shipwreck gives her oppressed servant the upper hand, in Wertmuller's "Swept Away."

Figure 6 shows how we direct Scenes 4 and 5 of our Role-Reversal Scenario. The scenario begins the same way as our Base Scenario, with an undignified servant first serving his master and then playing at being the master until he is caught in the act in Scene 4. Now, however, instead of retreating, the servant rises up and defies the master. Both actors are directed to "Stand and Improvise" until finally, in Scene 5, they are directed to exchange roles, with the servant ordering his former master to take the servant's place at the wall.

Johnstone teaches us that the dramatic impact of scenarios such as this one lies not in its outcome *per se*, but in the status transactions leading up to the outcome:

When actors are reversing status during a scene it's good to make them grade the transitions as smoothly as possible. I tell them that if I took a

Role-Reversal Scenario
Scene 4. Turning the Tables

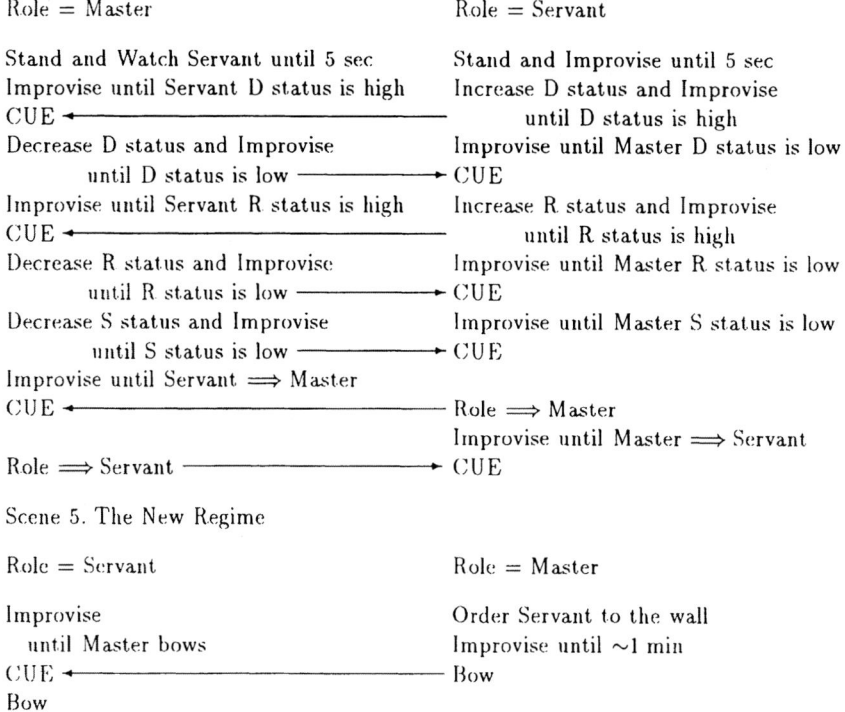

Role = Master	Role = Servant
Stand and Watch Servant until 5 sec	Stand and Improvise until 5 sec
Improvise until Servant D status is high	Increase D status and Improvise
CUE ←	until D status is high
Decrease D status and Improvise	Improvise until Master D status is low
until D status is low →	CUE
Improvise until Servant R status is high	Increase R status and Improvise
CUE ←	until R status is high
Decrease R status and Improvise	Improvise until Master R status is low
until R status is low →	CUE
Decrease S status and Improvise	Improvise until Master S status is low
until S status is low →	CUE
Improvise until Servant $\Longrightarrow$ Master	
CUE ←	Role $\Longrightarrow$ Master
	Improvise until Master $\Longrightarrow$ Servant
Role $\Longrightarrow$ Servant →	CUE

Scene 5. The New Regime

Role = Servant	Role = Master
Improvise	Order Servant to the wall
until Master bows	Improvise until ∼1 min
CUE ←	Bow
Bow	

Fig. 6. Directions to Master and Servant: Status transactions culminating in role-reversal

photograph every five seconds, I'd like to be able to arrange the prints in order just by the status shown. It's easy to reverse status in one jump. Learning to grade it delicately from moment to moment increases the control of the actor. The audience will always be held when a status is being modified. (p. 44)

Thus, to build tension between master and servant during Scene 4, we direct the actors to display their individual transformations in a paced progression of complementary status transitions. We direct the servant, who already has abnormally high S status, to increase his D status to high, and then to increase his R status to high. As we observe the servant stand his ground, straighten his posture, calm his movements, and hold his master's gaze, we believe him elevated into a powerful individual. Meanwhile, we direct the master to reduce his D status to low, then to reduce his R status to low, and finally to reduce his S status to low. As we observe the master deflate his posture, fidget, avoid his servant's gaze, and shrink within the space, we believe him diminished into a weak individual.

Johnstone also teaches us that actors perform most convincingly when they play not to the audience, but to one another:

> [The actors must] really 'see' their partner, as they have exactly to relate their behavior to his. The automatic status skills then 'lock on to' the other actor, and the students are transformed into observant, and apparently very experienced improvisers. ...These status exercises reproduce on the stage exactly the effects of real life, in which moment by moment each person adjusts his status up or down a fraction. (p. 46)

Thus, to display the contest of wills between master and servant, we direct the two actors to conditionalize their status transitions on each other's behavior. We direct the master to cue his incremental status reductions on perception of the servant's incremental status improvements and vice versa. Viewing the result, we believe that the servant comes to dominate the master through force of will. We find it only fitting that this gradual usurping of power should culminate in an explicit reversal of roles.

Figure 7 shows a sequence of screen shots illustrating the paced and coordinated status transactions our actors improvise in response to these directions for Scenes 4 and 5.

Our actors currently follow explicit directions to modify specified status variables, contingent upon perception of specified cues. However, we plan to automate more of the art of status transactions. In particular, actors will apply the three performance principles illustrated above: (1) *Graded Transitions.* Actors will grade status transitions to occur as smoothly as possible. For example, given directions to Reverse status with a partner, an actor will stage reversals on each of the three dimensions: demeanor, relationship, and space. Within each dimension, the actor will substitute high-status behaviors for low-status behaviors (or vice versa) one at a time, pausing to let each one have its impact. (2) *Engagement.* Actors will act in response to perception of one another's behavior. For example, an actor will perceive and recognize the status changes implicit in many different behaviors performed by a partner. (3) *See-Saw Transactions.* Actors will mirror each others' status transitions with complementary transitions. For example, if one actor's behavior signals an increase in demeanor status, the other will lower his or her own demeanor status. Thus, the actors will follow abstract directions, such as "Raise status" or "Reverse status with partner," by intentionally pacing and coordinating the specified status transactions in the context of various role-appropriate and plot-appropriate improvisations.

6 Implementation

We implemented two actors that can improvise master-servant scenarios under directions constraining role, plot, and character, as discussed above. We have described our underlying agent architecture in detail in previous publications [6,

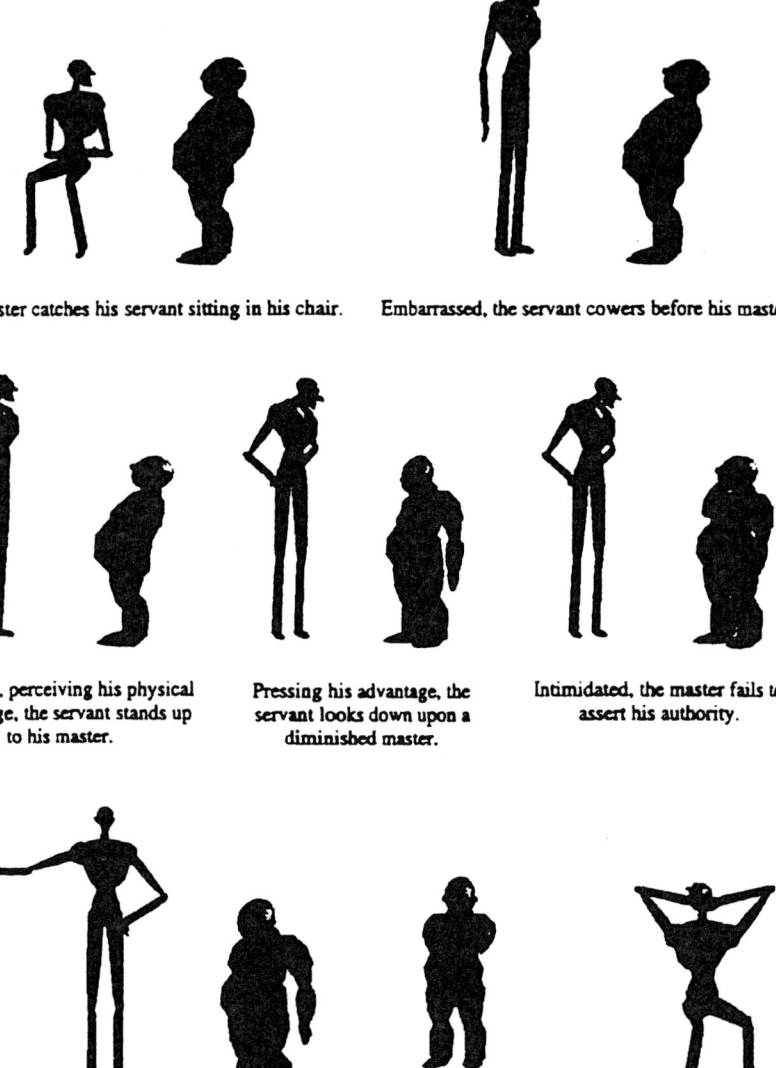

The master catches his servant sitting in his chair.   Embarrassed, the servant cowers before his master

But then, perceiving his physical   Pressing his advantage, the   Intimidated, the master fails to
advantage, the servant stands up   servant looks down upon a   assert his authority.
to his master.   diminished master.

Usurping the master's authority, the servant orders   The new master and his new
his former master to take the servant's position.   servant begin the new regime.

Fig. 7. Screen shots of Master and Servant Status Transactions Culminating
in Role Reversal (Animation by Ken Perlin, NYU)

7, 11, 14] and do not repeat that material here. For present purposes, we note that the architecture clearly delineates each actor's "mind" and "body," which operate and interact as summarized below.

For the master-servant scenarios, each agent's mind iterates the following steps: (a) incorporate perceptual information from the body into the current situation model; (b) identify role-appropriate behaviors that are relevant to current directions in the current scene, given the current situation; (c) identify the subset of those behaviors that match current status directions; (d) choose one of the matching behaviors probabilistically; and (e) perform the chosen behavior by sending appropriate commands to the body.

Each actor has a repertoire of behaviors, including behaviors appropriate for the master role and behaviors appropriate for the servant role. Thus, each one can play either role. The actors know when individual behaviors are relevant to particular directions, scenes, and situations. They know how behaviors relate to different values of the three status variables. Each behavior comprises a parameterized script that an actor can instantiate and perform as any of several alternative sequences of specific physical actions.

For the actors' bodies, we used two animated human figures that were developed by Ken Perlin of New York University [20]. Both figures can perform physical actions, such as: Walk to (X,Y), Beckon, Sit down, Nod, Duck head, Raise shoulders. These are the physical actions with which each actor can instantiate its behavior scripts. The animation system's original user interface (menus for users to command the figures' actions interactively) was replaced by a mind-body interface that allows our actors' minds to command their own actions and to perceive one another's actions.

During a performance, the actors operate autonomously from a user-provided scenario, without run-time intervention. They mime their interactions in a blank virtual world. However, a musical accompaniment created by Todd Feldman, a member of our research group, provides distinctive "voices" for the master and servant roles. The music also reinforces the plot and the emotional tenor of the actors' performances.

7 Personality versus Character

At a very general level, we find much in common between the "personalities" of real human beings and the "characters" created by authors and actors. Indeed, many successful novelists and playwrights have been praised for their psychological acuity in creating fictional characters. For example, it has been said that Henry James, the great American novelist, rivaled his brother William James, the great American psychologist, for his insight into human nature. Similarly, Shakespeare is universally recognized as both a literary genius and a master of character. Taking a more extreme position, Johnstone insists on the primacy of character, particularly as revealed in status variables, and the comparative insignificance of literary qualities in determining dramatic impact:

...a good play is one which ingeniously displays and reverses the status between the characters. Many writers of great talent have failed to write successful plays (Blake, Keats, Tennyson, among others) because of a failure to understand that drama is not primarily a literary art. Shakespeare is a great writer even in translation; a great production is great even if you don't speak the language. ...A great play is a virtuoso display of status transactions. (p. 72)

Despite the psychological fidelity we recognize in the best artistic models of character, however, there are substantive differences in the goals of psychology versus drama and, therefore, differences in the "models" produced by psychologists and dramatists.

The goal of psychology is to explain human behavior. Therefore, psychological models of personality must satisfy objective requirements for generality, completeness, and explanatory power. A credible model must account for the personalities of a large, normally distributed population of ordinary individuals. It must cover all important personality traits. It must explain how and why those traits are configured as they are within individuals and throughout the population and how personality impacts other aspects of behavior.

By contrast, the goal of drama is to produce a compelling experience for the audience. Therefore, artistic models of character must meet more subjective requirements for specificity, focus, and dramatic power. An effective model should enable us to create a few extremely interesting characters. It should prescribe just those traits that communicate the essence of a character as economically and persuasively as possible. Above all, it should produce characters with the desired dramatic impact. As Horton [17] reminds us:

Disney managed to make each of the dwarfs in *Snow White* (1937)—Doc, Happy, Sleepy, Sneezy, Grumpy, Bashful, and most especially Dopey— stand out in our memories because of a few sharply etched character strokes. (p. 12)

Because our goal is to build synthetic actors, not synthetic individuals, we focus on artistic models of character, rather than psychological models of personality. This focus allows us to limit severely the set of traits we model and to finesse entirely the deeper psychological questions of how complex configurations of personality traits work together to determine behavior. Thus, we do not try to simulate personality, but only to create the illusion of character. As Sir Laurence Olivier is reputed to have advised "method" actor Dustin Hoffman, who tortured himself for days to achieve the ravaged condition of his character in *Marathon Man*, "Why not just try acting?"

References

1. Abbott L. (1987) Active Acting: Exercises and Improvisations Leading to Performance. Belmont CA: Star Publishing Company

2. Bartlett J. (1992) Familiar Quotations, Little, Brown & Company, New York.

3. Belt L., Stockley R. (1991) Improvisation through Theatre Sports. Seattle, WA: Thespis Productions

4. Egri, Lajos. (1949) The Art of Dramatic Writing. New York: Simon & Schuster. Reprinted 1960

5. Hayes-Roth B. (1995) Agents on stage: Advancing the state of the art of AI. In: *Proceedings of the International Joint Conference on Artificial Intelligence*, Montreal

6. Hayes-Roth B. (1985) A blackboard architecture for control. *Artificial Intelligence* **26**, pp.251–321

7. Hayes-Roth B. (1995) An architecture for adaptive intelligent systems. *Artificial Intelligence* **72**, pp.329–365

8. Hayes-Roth B. (1995) Directed improvisation: A new paradigm for computer games. In: *Proceedings of the Computer Game Developers' Conference*, Santa Clara, CA

9. Hayes-Roth B., Brownston L. (1995) Multi-agent collaboration in directed improvisation. In; *Proc. of the First Int. Conference on Multi-Agent Systems*. San Francisco

10. Hayes-Roth B., Feigenbaum E.A. (1994) Design for an animated improvisational theater for children. In: *Notes of the AAAI Workshop on AI, the Arts, and Entertainment*. August, 1994.

11. Hayes-Roth B., Pfleger K., Lalanda P., Morignot P., Balabanovic M. (1995) A domain-specific software architecture for adaptive intelligent systems. *IEEE Transactions on Software Engineering*, Special Issue on Software Architectures, 1995.

12. Hayes-Roth B., Sincoff E., Brownston L., Hurard R., Lent B. (1994) Directed Improvisation. Stanford, CA: Technical Report KSL-94-61

13. Hayes-Roth B., Sincoff E., Brownston L., Huard R., Lent B. (1995) Directed improvisation with animated puppets. In: *Proc. of CHI '95 Conf. on Human-Computer Interaction*. Denver

14. Hayes-Roth B., van Gent R. (1996) Storymaking with Improvisational Puppets and Actors. Stanford University: Report KSL-96-06

15. Hayes-Roth B., van Gent R. (1996) Improvisational Puppets, Actors, and Avatars. In: *Proc. of the Computer Game Developers' Conference*

16. Hodgson J., Richards E. (1996) Improvisation. New York, NY: Grove Weidenfeld

17. Horton A. (1994) Writing the Character-Centered Screenplay. Berkeley, CA: University of California Press

18. Johnstone K. (1987) IMPRO: Improvisation in the Theatre. NY: Penguin Books

19. O'Connor F. (1969) The Grotesque in Southern Fiction. In: *Mystery and Manners*. NY: Farrar Straus

20. Perlin K. (1995) Real-time responsive animation with personality. *IEEE Transactions on Visualization and Computer Graphics* **1**.

21. Sweet J. (1978) Something Wonderful Right Away. New York, NY: Proscenium Publishers Inc.

Some Requirements and Approaches for Natural Language in a Believable Agent

A. Bryan Loyall

School of Computer Science
Carnegie Mellon University
5000 Forbes Avenue, Pittsburgh, PA 15213

Abstract. The goal of creating resource-bounded believable agents that use language and action raises interesting issues for the various components of the agent. In this paper we explore these issues, focusing particularly on their relation to natural language understanding in such agents. The specific issues we address are: responsiveness and interruptability; pursuing multiple independent goals concurrently; designing and managing groups of goals to execute concurrently for specific effects (for example, pointing and talking or understanding such gesture and language combinations); understanding incomplete or ungrammatical language or behaviors; the effects of failure in a larger agent; and consistency between the components of the agent. For each of these issues we argue why it is important for our goals, describe how it relates to natural language, describe our approaches to it, and describe the experience we are drawing on in making our conclusions.

1 Introduction

We are trying to create believable agents which perform actions and use language in real-time interactive worlds. Believability is similar to the intuitive notion of adequate characters in traditional non-interactive media such as animated films or books. In these traditional media, characters are adequate if they permit viewers to suspend their disbelief. Creating *interactive* versions of characters that allow such a suspension of disbelief has many difficulties. These difficulties are different from those traditionally studied in AI research. For example, whether the agent is intelligent or competent at problem solving is much less important than whether the agent is responsive, emotional, social and in some sense complete. We believe that in creating such believable agents it may be necessary not to fully duplicate people, but rather to artistically select the key qualities that are important for conveying believability. This selection is similar to the way animators concentrate on specific visual components (e.g. eyes) over others (e.g. mouths) and use simple non-human physical bodies such as the flying carpet in Disney's *Aladdin* for their believable characters. They also use artistic techniques, such as exaggeration, that are not realistic but nonetheless increase the perceived realism of the characters. Believable agents could be action-based, linguistic or a combination of both. One assumption about characters and about these agents is that the people interacting with or observing them *want to believe* that they are real. This assumption holds true in the domains of both user interfaces and interactive entertainment where such agents could be especially useful.

In our exploration of believability, we are working with agents that use language and action in a real-time world. The remaining sections of this paper each discuss an issue or group of issues we believe is key for believability in such agents, our approaches to these issues, and the particular experience we are drawing on. In our discussion, we focus particularly on the issues that affect natural language understanding. We are drawing on our experience in constructing non-linguistic believable agents [7, 3, 2], our experience building believable agents that act and generate language [8], and our designs for incorporating language understanding with these agents. This work is described more fully in [8]. An image from one of these worlds is shown in Figure 1.

Fig. 1. An instant from an interaction with an autonomous agent, Wolf, in which Wolf is generating language and movement in real-time to invite the user-controlled agent to play a game.

2 Responsiveness

For agents to appear believable, we think it is important that they be responsive to their environment; it is difficult to imagine a believable creature that is not appropriately responsive. Believable agents must execute actions, including speaking and understanding, at speeds that are reasonable for their environment (of course, this speed depends on who is to be doing the believing as well as the environment). They must be reactive and able to switch their focus of attention when emergencies or personally important situations arise.

To accommodate these requirements we are implementing our agent architecture in a goal-based reactive platform called Hap. Each of the components of the architecture — action, sensing, inference, natural language generation, natural language understanding[1], and emotion – are implemented using Hap goals, behaviors, and annotations to support reactivity. The personality-specific uses of these components are also implemented in Hap. This implementation allows interleaving and interruptions at a fine grain size of processing throughout all behavior, with the smallest output/input unit being words for the natural language components and primitive actions (jump, look in a direction, turn, etc.) for the action component.

Hap mixes reactivity with explicit goals and allows authors to hierarchically compose behaviors from sub-behaviors and primitive actions. The plans written for a Hap agent are interpreted at runtime, providing an immediacy allowing the agents to be situated in the sense described by Agre and Chapman [1]. Hap does not require that the author characterize the world (e.g., with predicate calculus) to recognize goal success, or for other reasoning. Hap allows multiple goals to be active at any time with the architecture pursuing some set of them concurrently. It automatically manages selective perception associated with the conditions in the architecture. Of the current reactive architectures, Hap is most similar to Firby's RAPs [5] and Georgeff and Lansky's PRS architecture [6], though there are some key differences. The current version of Hap is described in detail in [8] and an earlier version is described in the short paper [7]. These papers also include discussions of the implementation of action, sensing, emotion, natural language generation[2] and inference as well as agents built using this system.

The Hap architecture and the action, sensing, inference, natural language generation and emotion components have each been implemented in the manner described here. We have also designed and built a number of agents using this architecture. The natural language understanding component is in progress.

3 Multiple Independent Actions

Creatures we normally see, whether real or animated, perform multiple actions at one time. Dogs wag their tail, and move their ears, head and eyes while they

---

[1] Natural language understanding is ongoing work. The rest is reported in detail in [8].

[2] Generation is not described in [7].

are barking to get your attention. People understand what is being said while performing other tasks unless those tasks are particularly demanding. If we want our agents to have convincing behavior, they also need to be able to perform multiple actions and pursue multiple higher level activities concurrently.

Hap allows multiple goals and actions to be pursued in two ways. Independent goals can be mixed if they do not exclude one another (sleep and play exclude each other, for example). This mixing happens automatically unless there is not enough time for "thought" (behavior generation), in which case the less important goals are not attended to. This mechanism allows natural language understanding goals to be pursued while other tasks are being performed unless the other tasks are too demanding.

To illustrate this mixing, we present here an example from an existing world with action and gesture understanding goals. In this example there are three agents: Wolf, Bear and Shrimp. We will be describing an excerpt from Bear's processing. Bear is walking toward the bed in pursuit of his sleep goal. While he is walking toward the bed, an independent goal to recognize when any of his friends are being threatened is triggered because Wolf moves too close to Shrimp (Bear has a notion of physical space, and an agent invading another's space could be part of a threat). While continuing to pursue the sleep goal, Bear's attention is also on his friend, Shrimp. This is manifest by Bear's gesture understanding goal, "recognize threat" being active, and by Bear turning his head to watch the two other agents (this is at the same time he is moving toward the bed). While these two goals are executing and issuing actions to Bear's body, other non-conflicting independent goals could also be pursued. For example, Bear's goal to blink could trigger (it is a periodic time based goal) causing his eyes to blink. If two conflicting goals are executing (which could happen, for example if a threat were recognized, and Bear had the goal to move toward his friend as well as the goal to move toward the bed), one of them is temporarily suspended while the other is pursued. Which is suspended depends in part on the relative priorities of the two goals.

4 Multiple Connected Actions

The previous section described how multiple independent actions are blended by the Hap architecture. Sometimes, however, multiple simultaneous actions (or goals) are designed to be executed together. For example, if an agent wishes to refer to an object by pointing and saying "that" in the middle of a sentence, it is important that the pointing and utterance of "that" be related and happen at the same time. Similarly for understanding such a combination, the natural language understanding of "that" and the gesture understanding of the pointing action must be linked to understand the intended concept.

In Hap this is accomplished by grouping together the actions or goals that need to be linked in a single plan. Hap's normal mechanisms would then cause the two goals to be executed simultaneously[3]. An example of this type of grouping

---

[3] It is possible that this plan could be interrupted by other goals in the architecture.

occurs when a constructed cat, Lyotard [2], is communicating the desire to go outside. One plan Lyotard has for this goal involves the two linked goals of "stay near the door" (which results in action if Lyotard is picked up, for example) and the goal to meow and alternately look at the door and at a nearby person.

5 Incomplete or Ungrammatical Input

Because our agents are resource-bounded and live in a real-time world, the natural language understanding goals may not be able to get all of the processing time needed to understand what is being said to the agent as it is being said. One approach to this problem is to automatically save all of the raw input until the agent has time to process it. This is an undesirable solution because it conflicts with our intuitive notion of believability. People sometimes (often?) miss portions of what is being said and construct partial interpretations from the portions that are heard. Most importantly, sometimes the fact that a person only perceives or processes part of what is being said is noticeable to others. If our agents had perfect memory, this would never happen and they might consequently be less believable. So, for this reason we must live with the possibility that our agents will sometimes attend only to portions of sentences. For them to appear believable, they must nevertheless process these partial sentences and understand whatever is possible from them.

In addition, people sometimes speak ungrammatically. To contribute to believability, our agents' natural language generation components will also sometimes generate ungrammatical language. Both of these require that the natural language understanding technology not be dependent on correct syntax. Our approach to this requirement is to base our understanding system on semantically based and syntactically lenient understanding technology, such as that reported in [4].

We have observed that our existing agents do not always register stimuli that would be relevant to their physical (non-linguistic) recognition behaviors. For example, in the behavior excerpt of Bear described above, it is possible that Wolf moving into Shrimp's space would not be registered. (This would happen if Bear's other goals took too much time and this recognition goal did not get to execute before the stimuli ended.) Because of this potential problem, each of the recognition behaviors has been written so that incomplete stimuli often can be recognized.

6 Failure is Expected

Natural language understanding for us is part of an agent. Consequently, things that would normally be considered failures in other natural language understanding systems are normal, expected results in the context of an agent. Agents sometimes do not understand what is being said to them. In the context of the larger

---

If the interruption is long enough, the two goals would not be executed at the same time.

processing that the agent is doing, this "failure" can have many personality-specific effects. The agent could blame the speaker for not being clear perhaps leading to anger toward that person, blame itself perhaps causing shame and sadness, pretend to ignore the utterance, pretend to understand and hope that it will become clear later, or simply admit that it does not understand and ask what was meant. These effects, of something that in an isolated understander would be simply viewed as a failure, correspond directly to effects the agent may have to other stimuli. For example if the agent is hit, it might blame the one who hit it, blame itself, ignore being hit, accept being hit without feeling bad, etc.

In a similar vein, misunderstanding is expected in the context of believable agents. People misunderstand each other with a variety of effects. Thus rather than strive to eliminate all misunderstanding, when building believable agents we must strive to create appropriate reactions to the realization that one misunderstood or was misunderstood.

Some of these results of natural language understanding failures are simple generalizations of our integration of goal-directed behavior with emotion [3]. Others, such as pretending to understand and hoping to catch up, will be explored as we continue the work.

7 Consistency

Consistency within the agent seems critical for believability. It would be difficult to accept as believable an agent that says things that it cannot understand[4], can talk about information it knows but cannot use that information for its normal activities, or has a powerful ability to infer knowledge when problem solving but a weak ability when understanding. Each of these examples illustrate a consistency requirement for the construction of believable agents.

Our approaches to each of these is to tightly integrate all of the components of the architecture and, where necessary, carefully coordinate their ability levels. The natural language generation system must produce a subset of what can be understood by the natural language understanding system. Because the approaches we are taking for natural language generation and understanding do not share the same grammar representation, we must as designers enforce this constraint. We believe knowledge that is learned by one system must be available to all of the systems, so we are using a single memory system accessible by all components for storing any knowledge. Finally, any inference mechanisms which are created for a subsystem will, as mentioned before, be implemented in Hap goals and plans. Since Hap goals can be used in the plans for any of the

---

[4] This is slightly more subtle in that an agent might talk in gibberish that it does not expect to be understood and that it clearly would not understand if said back to it. Also, understanding is a situation dependent process; if the same words are said in a different situation or by a different person the meaning might be different or ambiguous. Barring these subtleties, it is undesirable for the agent to generate language that it cannot understand.

other components, this gives us a single unified inference mechanism (or set of mechanisms) which can be used by all of the components.

Consistency has been a continuous concern in all of our agent creation. For example, the ways in which agents intimidate each other must be a subset of what is recognized as intimidation. As we continue to add language understanding we expect some of these concerns to become more difficult, especially ensuring the natural language that is generated by each agent is a subset of what that agent can understand.

8 Conclusion

We have discussed here issues which we believe are key for building resource-bounded, action- and language-using believable agents. This is ongoing work both artistically and technologically. The issues we have presented in this paper are drawn from our experience in building such believable agents without English language (but with some body language communication), from our experience building agents that both act and generate language, and from our design of language understanding for such agents. For each of the issues, we have presented the issue, our design or implementation approach, and the particular experience we are drawing on.

References

1. Agre P.-E., Chapman D. (1990) What are plans for? In: *Robotics and Autonomous Systems*. Elsevier Science Publishers
2. Bates J., Loyall A.B., Reilly W.S. (1992) An architecture for action, emotion, and social behavior. In: *Proc. of the Fourth European Workshop on Modeling Autonomous Agents in a Multi-Agent World*, S.Martino al Cimino, Italy, July 1992
3. Bates J., Loyall A.B., Reilly W.S. Integrating reactivity, goals, and emotion in a broad agent. In: *Proc. of the Fourteenth Annual Conference of the Cognitive Science Society*, Bloomington, IN, July 1992
4. Dyer M. (1983) *In-Depth Understanding*. The MIT Press, Cambridge, MA
5. Firby J.R. (1989) *Adaptive Execution in Complex Dynamic Worlds*. PhD thesis, Department of Computer Science, Yale University
6. Georgeff M.P., Lansky A.L. (1987) Reactive reasoning and planning. In: *Proc. of the Sixth National Conference on Artificial Intelligence*, July 1987.
7. Loyall A.B., Bates J. (1993) Real-time control of animated broad agents. In: *Proc. of the Fifteenth Annual Conference of the Cognitive Science Society*, Boulder, CO
8. Loyall A.B. (1996) *Believable Agents*. PhD thesis, Computer Science Department, Carnegie Mellon University, Also available as a CMU technical report

Personality Parameters and Programs*

Dave Moffat

Faculty of Psychology (PN)
University of Amsterdam
Roetersstraat 15
1018 WB Amsterdam

Abstract. This article explores the possibility of machines having artificial "personality," roughly as we mean the term when referring to people. Relevant aspects of the psychological theories of personality are briefly summarised, particularly the social-learning theories.
Then I propose an abstract definition of personality that applies to humans, animals and machines, and suggest how to fit the phenomena of emotion and mood into the same scheme. I present a prototype model of emotion, and show how it could be extended to model personalities which are parameterised along natural dimensions.

1 Introduction

There are at least three reasons to want to design an artificial personality: (i) in order to investigate the scope of natural personalities by making artificial models of them; (ii) to make artificial agents such as robots better by giving them personality; and (iii) to simulate characters for dramatic purposes. The first reason belongs to Cognitive Science, the second to AI (Artificial Intelligence), and the third to entertainment and the arts. While other articles in this issue concentrate on (iii), the complementary focus in this paper is on (i) and a little on (ii). The aim is to investigate the possibility of designing artificial personalities for autonomous agents [27], by taking an artificial model of emotion as an example.

It may be surprising to hear talk of robots having personality, or emotion. One never comes across such ideas in science. They belong more to science fiction, but even there robots with personality are exceptional. Robots and computers, like HAL in Arthur C. Clarke's *2001*, later made into a film by Stanley Kubrick, are usually unemotional and inscrutable. Even when being "killed" by the astronaut Dave, HAL's artificial speech showed no emotion, either in tone of voice or in choice of words.

---
* I would like to thank Nico Frijda for many enlightening discussions, which have been very inspiring and helpful to me. This article would not have been written at all if Robert Trappl had not suggested it, and I thank him and his talented multinational colleagues for making the workshop so enjoyable. The work reported here was supported in part by a grant from NWO (Netherlands Organisation for Research), No. 560-257030, to N.H. Frijda and R.H. Phaf.

One reason why robot personality is not a serious topic in AI is that it is not easy to see why a robot should need a personality. We want robots to make things for us, or to clean the house, but we don't want them to whistle while they work. Neither do we want them to complain or want to go on holiday or demand robot rights.

Freud's theory of personality included three major components: the Ego, Superego, and Id. These are not personality components we want any robot to have. A robot with an ego would be irritating enough, but given that robots can have very strong bodies, a robot with an Id would be terrifying. What if the robot develops an Oedipus complex? If making a robot with personality leads to some kind of Frankenstein's monster, then we can better just make "ordinary" robots without personality.

But there is another side to this question. Imagine a robot or a computer system in charge of a nuclear power station. Wouldn't we prefer that robot to be careful, cautious, alert and conscientious? Such a robot would surely be better with a responsible personality than without any personality at all. So there are arguments in favour of designing personalities for artificial actors and robots.

Up to now in Cognitive Science, there has been no question of personality in artificial agents, because the agents we can make are still very primitive. We understand our creations in terms of programs and information processing. But when they become sufficiently complex, and take on responsible tasks for us, it may well happen that we can no longer think of them effectively in such terms. Instead, we may have to think of them as personalities in their own right, not because they are "real", but simply as a matter of convenience. It may be the only way we can predict what they will do and interact with them. If and when robots reach such an advanced stage of complexity, it will also be less feasible than it is now to program them in terms of instructions at the level of a programming language. We shall be forced to instruct them in terms of commands or requests, just as we interact with humans. It may well be that we shall have to treat them as if they truly have personality.

2 Personality Theory

In order to attempt to simulate or model something like personality, one first has to know what it is, to have a theory of it. The obvious place to begin is Psychology.

Personality is a notoriously difficult concept to define, although we all know roughly what we mean by it. Individual differences in mental characteristics are obviously relevant, but does that include mental skills, or intelligence in general? Some say yes, some say no. The science of personality is a controversial part of Psychology. There are several theories or approaches to the topic, some of which conflict, but many of which are mutually consistent. They could all be partly correct.

2.1 Freud, Skinner and Maslow

Freud. An important theory of personality is Freudian Psychoanalysis, which asserts that the human personality is composed of three parts: the Id, Ego and Superego. It is conflict between these powerful inner voices that result in behaviour. The Id is the inner child, that only knows its desires; the Ego knows about the real world and can plan behaviour in order to satisfy the desires of the Id; and the Superego learns the rules of convention to ensure that behaviour falls in line with society's demands. From the interplay between these hypothetical sections of mind Freud managed to explain a wide range of personal idiosyncrasies observed in his patients, including their "meaningful" dreams and hysteria. However, the theory was not seen as scientifically testable, because there is no independent way to observe the internal Id, Ego and Superego.

Skinner. The dominant reaction to Freudianism arose from logical positivism, which curiously enough also came from Freud's home town of Vienna. The idea behind "psychological behaviourism" was that only behaviour should be the subject of psychology, because nothing internal to the human is directly observable.

Personality is defined in terms of behavioural dispositions. The emphasis is on situational determiners of behaviour by means of operant conditioning (reinforcement learning). An organism's personality is thus determined by experience, and seen in behavioural tendency. Watson, in [26], went so far as to assert that apparent personality characteristics are nothing but the result of reinforcement learning. It is a criticism of behaviourism that children appear to develop different personalities despite similar experience.

Maslow. One kind of reaction to behaviourism was led by [11], who re-asserted the individual's subjectivity in the movement called humanistic psychology. Unlike Freud, Maslow studied psychologically healthy people and what they thought and felt that distinguished them from neurotic patients. He found that humans are motivated by a hierarchy of needs, in which the bare necessities of life, such as warmth and food, must be acquired before higher needs exert their influence. Above the bare necessities are needs for companionship and respect, then people look for opportunities to learn and understand; then to appreciate the arts. Most of us stop there, because we find those layers in the hierarchy difficult enough to achieve with any security, but when all those needs are satisfied there are still higher ones: namely self-actualisation, which means to realise one's full potential just as Einstein and Beethoven did, and finally peak experiences, which are moments of ecstatic realisation or religious experience.

The humanistic movement (what Maslow called the "third force in psychology" to distinguish it from psychoanalysis and behaviourism) has been criticised for being unclear. Terms like self-actualisation are not well defined. It has also been called a protest movement, and a 1960's throwback to romanticism. Indeed, the term "self-actualising" can still occasionally be heard from the mouths of hippies, beatniks, and their modern equivalents: the new-agers. Please note that it is not my intention to sneer at Maslow or his psychology. On the contrary, his approach to psychology is the most heroic and optimistic of them all, and his work is understandably inspiring to many people. The point is only that it is still not well-enough developed to base an intricate computational model on.

None Useful for Us. The psychoanalytic, behaviourist, and humanistic theories of personality all try to explain human behaviour in different ways. They are all at least partially correct, but they also have serious problems for those who wish to program them in computational models. Furthermore, they are unrelated to the everyday notion of what a personality is, and so to base a model on them would be unlikely to make a convincing artificial actor for dramatic purposes.

2.2 Trait Theories

We usually describe people in terms of their traits. Margaret Thatcher was a tough, determined prime-minister. Ronald Reagan was a friendly, easy-going and avuncular president. Mike Tyson is a mean boxer, hard as iron. Mother Theresa is a happy nun, always willing to help. These descriptions are not necessarily accurate, but they illustrate how we describe people in terms of their manner, type and degree of motivation, prevalent emotional state, and how they relate to other people.

When it comes to characterising people in terms of such traits, we are all personality psychologists. We do this because it is useful to know what somebody is like, because it helps us to predict what he or she will do in different situations, and helps us all to relate to each other more smoothly.

Big Five. Psychologists have attempted to formalise characterisation by traits. The statistical method of "factor analysis" groups words used to describe people into chief organising themes. Use of this technique has led to a fairly large consensus that there are five major traits (factors) that account for most of the variation in human personality. They are called the *Big Five.* Different investigators use slightly different terms for them, but they mean roughly the same thing. One useful way to remember them is by the mnemonic OCEAN.

O	pen:	curious, broad interests, creative, original, imaginative, untraditional.
C	onscientious:	organised, reliable, hard-working, self-disciplined, honest, clean.
E	xtravert:	sociable, active, talkative, optimistic, fun-loving, affectionate.
A	greeable:	good-natured, trusting, helpful, forgiving, gullible, straightforward.
N	eurotic:	worries, nervous, emotional, insecure, inadequate, hypochondriac.

Any person will theoretically be somewhere in the five-dimensional space defined by these traits. For example, Margaret Thatcher might be rather closed, extremely conscientious, extrovert, and disagreeable, but not neurotic. Some people would disagree with one or two of these appraisals of her character. Ronald Reagan would certainly be agreeable and extrovert, and probably open, but whether he is neurotic or conscientious is harder to say.

It is interesting that it is not so easy to define famous characters along even such a small handful of dimensions. The fact that it is difficult may show that the Big Five are not big enough; but trait psychologists would say that the only way to assign the traits reliably is to use a standard measuring instrument, like the MMPI-2 questionnaire that the subject is asked to fill in.

Big Two. Some psychologists think that five major traits are too many, and that if you look at the data closely there are really only two or three. Eysenck's major categories [6] are for neuroticism and extroversion (and he later added a third, for Psychoticism). He has pointed out that the ancient four humours of Hippocrates can be related to his Big Two traits by rotating the axes through 45°. A stable introvert would have a *phlegmatic* temperament, for example; an unstable introvert would be *melancholic*, and so on.

More recently, Gray [9] has suggested that the true dimensions for the Big Two traits are similar to what Eysenck proposed, except that the axes should be rotated through 30° instead of 45°.

Criticisms. The standard criticisms against trait theories are that they are not well-founded, because they are based on factor analysis only. Different trait theorists disagree about the precise categories that there are, and even about how many of them there are. Trait theories are little more than clever ways to categorise people, without giving any real insight into underlying mechanisms. Their pragmatic value is quite good, as they have a predictive capacity of around 30%, but they are theoretically shallow. They are descriptive, rather than explanatory. They say only *how* people are, but not *why* or *what* they are.

For those of us interested in making artificial agents of some kind, it might be feasible to make agents that appear to have some or all of the Big Five traits. But if the enterprise is purely an imitative one, it is of limited scientific interest. One could program a system to simulate a temperament that is 30% Extrovert and 55% Open, perhaps, but that would not necessarily reveal any deep mechanisms in human nature. To take a crude physical example, a human body has a given strength, mass, height and weight, but to imagine that these are due to different physical mechanisms would be simply wrong. The right physical variables there are quantities of muscle as compared with fat and bone, and the relative lengths of the bones. The analogy with personality is that traits may be only measurable aspects of different underlying variables, and it is the latter that are of most interest for those of us who want to make faithful models of personality.

There is evidence for a significant biological basis for personality, with quite high degrees of heritability, but that cannot really be taken as evidence that traits correspond directly to mechanism either. To take the example further, tall people tend to have tall children, but that does not necessarily mean that there is a gene for height. There could be several genes, for length of spine, size of head, angle of the legs at the pelvis, for onset and duration of the adolescent growth-spurt, efficient digestion of calcium, and so on.

One trait theorist is notable for having proposed underlying mechanisms for observed traits. Eysenck [6] suggests that extroversion is related to the person's tonic level of autonomic arousal, which may be lower or higher than the optimum level. Introverts supposedly have a more aroused system already, so that they withdraw from arousing situations, whereas extroverts have a low level of resting arousal, are bored more easily, and so show more sensation-seeking behaviour. This is a very interesting proposal because it points towards a mechanism that should be relevant to all creatures, including (ideally) artificial ones: namely, energetic arousal. But that would still leave many other traits unexplained.

The other main objection to trait theories of personality is that they tend to ignore the role of the situation in determining what people do. More generally, one can assert that there is an interaction between person and situation that determines behaviour. For example, a great politician may be too scared to go to the war, while a brave soldier returning from the war, with medals in place of arms, may be afraid of speaking in public. It was the behavioural theorists who emphasised the situation in personality, as well as the social learning theorists.

2.3 Behavioural-cognitive Theories

There is a consensus that a person's behaviour is determined by his own personal qualities (be they traits or something else), by the stimulus situation he finds himself in, and by the interaction between the two. There is also a consensus that there is more to be explained than just behaviour. Behaviourism restricted itself to talk of externally visible behaviour alone, but behaviourism has been supplanted by cognitivism, which allows itself to discuss internal variables in order to explain behaviour. Since cognitive psychologists talk in terms of information processing, their theories are most suitable to computational implementation.

Social learning theories (also called behavioural-cognitive theories) of personality use terms like *belief* and *expectation* in order to explain behaviour, including personal dispositions to behaviour. Some of them also attempt to explain internals like feelings and thoughts. For them, personality is not just about what a person does in different situations, but also what he typically thinks and feels. The major theorists are Julian Rotter, Albert Bandura, and Walter Mischel. Since these theories are most amenable to comparison with the emotion model presented later, I shall review Rotter's and Mischel's quickly here.

Rotter's Theory. The first true social learning theorist was Julian Rotter. His theory is generally applauded [5, 20] for having the cleanest scientific approach, with formally stated hypotheses and corollaries, precisely defined technical terms, and testable predictions. The core concepts and equations are [21, 22] as follows.

BP = Behaviour Potential. At any time, a person has several alternative actions appropriate for the situation he is in, all with a certain relative potential to be chosen. The one with the highest BP is performed. An action's BP depends on its expected reinforcement value.

RV = Reinforcement Value. Different actions may bring differing degrees of positive or negative reinforcement (reward or punishment).

E = Expectancy. This represents the person's estimation of the probability of consequent reinforcement from potential actions. It is not dependent on RV or importance of the goal, because the theory keeps these factors apart.

S = Situation. The psychological situation parameter represents the variability across situations that personality is believed to involve. The stimulus is not seen as a simple atomic stimulus, but rather as contextualised against a background of possibly relevant other stimuli that may cause different personalities to react differently.

The above variables are supposed to vary from personality to personality. Rotter and his colleagues have developed tests to measure them all individually, in situations where the others are held constant. In this way it is possible to see how the variables all relate to each other. The following equations have been partially confirmed to date, but the research program still has a long way to go.

All the variables in the equations are heavily dependent on the psychological situation, setting the theory well apart from pure trait theories. Even reinforcement value is said to be relative to the context, which may be surprising at first. But Rotter is thinking of examples such as a little boy who likes to be kissed by his mother at home: but not in public where other boys can see and laugh at him.

$$BP_{x,s_1,R_a} = f[E_{x,s_1,R_a}, RV_{a,s_1}] \tag{1}$$

Equation (1) says that the potential of behaviour x in situation s_1, with respect to reinforcement a, is a function of the expectation that the behaviour in the situation will result in the reward, and the value R_a the reward would have in that situation. The function f is left open by the theory, but Rotter considers it reasonable to guess that f is multiplication.

$$BP_{(x-n),s_{(1-n)},R_{(a-n)}} = f[E_{(x-n),s_{(1-n)},R_{(a-n)}}, RV_{(a-n),s_{(1-n)}}] \tag{2}$$

Equation (2) is a generalisation of (1) to be able to predict behaviour in whole classes of similar psychological situations and rewards. What Rotter means with this notation is that $(x - n)$ represents a class of behaviours from x to n; $s_{(1-n)}$ represents a class of situations from 1 to n; and $(a - n)$ represents a set of rewards.

To abbreviate the equation Rotter has a shorter form for it:

$$NP = f[FM, NV] \tag{3}$$

In this equation NP is Need Potential; FM is Freedom of Movement; and NV is Need Value. It says that the potential for performing the set of behaviours (NP) is determined by the average expectancy (FM) that they will jointly achieve the goals, whose values are averaged to say how worthwhile they would be to achieve (NV).

In cases of low freedom of movement (low FM), even though the need value may be high (high NV), the person does not see a way to reliably achieve them, and consequently, does not try (low NP). In a nutshell, we only try to achieve the things we want if we think we can see a way to do it. Since the strong desire may remain, however, there is a conflict, which often results in typically neurotic avoidance behaviour.

As well as specific kinds of expectancy of success, Rotter says that people vary along a general dimension of internal versus external control of reinforcement (I-E). You are at the 'E' end of this dimension if you generally have the attitude that good or bad things happen to you whatever you do, so you might as well not bother; while at the 'I' end you believe that your own actions are much more consequential. It is the difference between believing that you got a promotion either because you were just in the right place at the right time (E); or because you worked hard for it and deserved it (I).

Another example of a cognitive personality variable is what Rotter calls "interpersonal trust," referring to the general expectancy you may have that people normally tell the truth and are usually to be trusted. Cynics score low on this dimension.

These types of expectancy, and the other personality variables in Rotter's theory, have all been found to vary between people in the way hypothesised, so the theory is at least partially confirmed by experiment. Rotter even treats patients with psychotherapeutic techniques developed from his theory.

$$RV_{a,s_1} = f[E_{R_a \to R_{(b-n),s_1}}, RV_{(b-n),s_1}] \tag{4}$$

Equation (4) says that the RV of an action a depends on the expectancy that a will lead to other rewards associated with other actions, and on the subjective RV of those. The expectancies are supposed to be learned from experience. Not all RV's can be so derived from others however: there must be an initial, innate set of them. Rotter proposes that all needs arise originally from physiological ones.

An interesting claim that Rotter makes is that the variability in the above variables, the E's and the RV's in particular, is even greater than it appears from the equations. They change dynamically quite quickly as well, simply because estimations of likelihoods and causes of events change as the person thinks more about the situation. The way Rotter puts it, "E's and RV's change with thinking." Unfortunately, the equations above are not able to model this dynamic aspect, because time is not a variable in any of them. It would be asking a lot of a mathematical theory to model such phenomena, but as will be seen later, a computational model is well-suited to them.

Mischel's theory. Walter Mischel is yet another psychologist from Vienna, though his professional life has been entirely in the USA, beginning as a student of Rotter's. He once believed [13] that individual differences were only apparent, and that human behaviour is entirely determined by situation. In his later work

[14] he accepts that there are significant individual differences that do account for personality, and they are differences in cognitive style.

The personal variables that he considers are:

- Competencies: These variables represent a person's store of knowledge and skills.
- Encoding strategies: The way a person represents knowledge and perceptions, including how it is selected and elaborated. One man's challenge may be another man's threat.
- Expectancies: These are (i) expectancies for outcomes of own behaviour; (ii) for outcomes of stimulus events; or (iii) *self-efficacy* expectations. While (i) is like Rotter's notion of specific expectancy, (iii) corresponds roughly to the 'internal' end of his I–E scale.
- Subjective values: People attach different values to outcomes of behaviour. This would correspond to Rotter's *RV*.
- Self-regulatory systems and plans: These are goals and standards of behaviour that we use to regulate our actions by self-criticism and self-praise.

There is clearly a large overlap between Rotter's and Mischel's theories. They are not the same, but their commonalities are representative of modern thinking in cognitively-based theories of personality.

2.4 What "Personality" Can Mean

Unnatural Kind. Some of the more usual criticisms levelled at personality theories were given above, including the worry that the trait theories, in particular, are merely descriptive. The purpose of science is to explain, and description is only the first step. But I have a more philosophical worry about the theories, in that they are human-specific. Most of the traits are defined at least partly in terms of human culture or society, such as "openness," "honesty" and so on. Personality itself is seen as something that people have, and possibly some animals. That is a strange sort of definition, because it seems (to me) not to be a natural kind. If one cannot define personality independently of the types of creatures that have it, one cannot study it in isolation, and one cannot strictly have a "science of personality" at all.

If personality is a human quality, then non-humans like future robots will never have personality. More accurately, they would never have "personality." But that would not be a scientifically startling or interesting discovery, neither would it be any kind of bold prediction about the capabilities of all potential robots: it would be merely a matter of definition.

Intelligence. There is of course a direct parallel with other human qualities. Compare the whole debate about "intelligence," in which one can trivially assert that robots can never be intelligent because only humans can be that. Up to now, the concept of intelligence has been human-specific (occasionally animal-specific) in Psychology, and has not suffered for it. The same is true of personality. After all, there have only ever been a few creatures we know of that deserve these labels. But in AI we have been working towards man-made creatures that have some kind of intelligence, which creates the need to redefine intelligence to be independent of species. Similarly, if we are not to shut out the very possibility of artificial personality, a priori, then it would be a good idea to try and define what we mean by the word "personality" without having to refer to people or animal species in the definition.

"Personality represents those characteristics of the person that account for consistent patterns of behaviour" [17]

is an initial definition given by an eminent personality psychologist. The reference to a person can be replaced by one to any organism, be it natural or artificial. In order not to include "organisms" like cappuccino machines (though even they can be "temperamental" at times), an organism has to be an autonomous agent, meaning that it is internally motivated ("auto-nomos" is literally "self-law"), as opposed to being a slave. Therefore, motivation is essential to personality. See also [4].

Describe or Explain? The definition asserts that the centre of interest is not just surface behaviour as such, but also the "characteristics" that account for it. So personality may be seen as descriptive of behaviour, accurate enough to enable fairly reliable predictions of new behaviour. Or it may be seen as referring to invisible, internal mechanisms, that are supposed to really exist in the person (oops: I should say "in the autonomous agent"). Note that good predictions may be possible either way. Describing that it rains more in winter is helpful in predicting that it will rain a lot next winter, even though the description is certainly not an explanation of why it rains more then.

Commonality or Difference? Another possible confusion is in the nature of distinction. On the one hand, personality is used partly to distinguish people as a group (as those animals that have such and such characteristics), or even to define large sub-groups, like national stereotypes. In that case we seek to discover "what is the human (or French, or Viennese, etc.) personality, or person?" On the other hand, it is more often used to distinguish individual people from each other. Personality measurement questionnaires only ask questions that differentiate people as much as possible, effectively assuming that everybody starts from a common baseline response pattern, plus minor variations that make up the personality proper. In the latter case we seek to discover how personalities vary between people. A definition of personality should be clear on this point, therefore: is it about what people have in common, or about what makes them differ?

Psychopathology? The relation of personality with psychotherapy is also a consideration in defining personality. Mental illness is frequently seen as personality disorder, and Freudian psychoanalysis is an example of a psychotherapeutic approach based on a hypothetical structure of the personality (Id, Ego and Superego), or personhood, and what can go wrong in its childhood development. Yet, people can have very different personalities without being in any way ill. So variation in personality can be normal, too.

Thought & Feeling. A definition of personality should say whether only consistency in behaviour is of interest, or whether unobservables are important too, such as thoughts and feelings. Because of Psychology's behavioural inheritance, the emphasis has historically been on behaviour, but since the "cognitive turn" in Psychology it has become acceptable, and even required, to address individual differences in the way people react to situations in thoughts and emotions, as well as in behaviour.

Keeping in mind the notion that we are all naïve personality psychologists already, because we have to be in order to maintain good interpersonal relations, it is clear that we often characterise people's personalities in terms of thought and feeling as well as behaviour, simply because we care about them. We care about our friends' emotional well-being, for example, irrespective of whether they show any behaviour.

2.5 The Fringe of Functionality

The foregoing questions require answers from any definition of personality. Since I would like to make a working definition that is suitable for the purposes of this paper, the choices that I make and the reasons for them, including any personal preferences where there is no better guide, are as follows.

1. Since existing definitions, like Pervin's above, are typically human-specific, the new definition should refer to all autonomous agents and their functions.
2. Motivation really belongs to internal mechanism, rather than personality proper. It must be specified, but only in a given model of personality. If an agent has a certain function in life (what Sloman calls an "ecological niche" [23]), then it is internally motivated to fulfil that function.
3. Unlike Pervin's definition above, the new one is to refer to surface phenomena like behaviour, and not to underlying mechanisms. I make this choice because it is nearer to everyday use, and because the surface phenomena are observable, while supposed underlying mechanisms are only inferred and hypothetical. Personality is behaviour to be explained; what explains behaviour is psychological structure (cognition etc.).
4. On the question of characterisation of groups versus individuals, one need only say that there are certain (personality-) characteristics that vary from species to species, group to group, gender to gender and so on, and of course also from individual to individual. Then individuals may be distinguished by the *variance* of the characteristics, while groups are distinguished by the statistical *mean* of individuals within the group. If a coherent mean cannot be found, it is not a proper group.

5. As to what surface phenomena compose personality, they are more than just overt behaviour. They include the kinds of thoughts and feelings that arise in response to stimuli situations. Call these phenomena together *reactions*.

6. In any given situation there may be several possible reactions consistent with internal motivations and external constraints. If the agent's reaction tendencies fall within these bounds, issuing in one of these reasonable reactions, then the agent is being functional. But if the agent reacts in a manner that will not achieve its goals, then it is being dysfunctional, at least in that situation.

7. What holds for one situation holds more generally. There are very few situations in which there is only one action possible to achieve the goal (excepting artificial problems or toy worlds), of only one optimal course of action. Usually, the goal is unachievable (there are no functional reactions), or it is in many ways achievable (there are multiple functional reactions). When there are many ways to perform a task, an agent can choose arbitrarily between them. This is where personality shows through.

The notion of a range of functionality seems important, then, to the concept of personality. It means that there is freedom to choose between alternative reactions to situations.

Freedom Within the Fringe. The notion of choice covers two types: agent choice and designer choice. An agent choice in a situation is where the agent chooses between alternatives, whereas the designer choice is where the designer of the system (programmer) has anticipated that type of situation and already determined what the agent should do in it. The difference is that the designer choice is at 'compile-time,' while the agent choice is a 'run-time' decision. I point this out here only in case some readers might worry about it otherwise (I would), but the point is not theoretically important.

The distinction between the two types of choice is in any case a vague one, though it may appear obvious in the case of ourselves, for we know that we have free will, and we make our own choices, we think. Unfortunately this question is such an old philosophical debate, which is far beyond the scope of this paper. But fortunately, it is an irrelevant debate for us here. It does not matter who chooses the (hopefully functional) reaction in a given situation; it only matters that a choice effectively has to be made, and that it will appear that the agent itself is making it.

A very simple example of arbitrary choice in performing a task would be in walking across a room to close a door. Any person performing that task is constrained by worldly facts like the angle and weight of the door, height of the door-handle, how urgently the door needs to be shut, and so on. But within those constraints, even in such a simple task, there is infinite variation. You can close a door quietly, or loudly to show your anger; you can use the handle, or just push it shut. Even in walking across the room you can unwittingly show your personality, just by the way you walk. People typically have individual walking styles, talking styles, standing and sitting styles, and they all show personality.

Furthermore, there is no way to hide personality in these cases. It is not just that the world *permits* us to do a thing in any number of ways, but that it forces us to choose exactly one of them in order to actually do it. The world underspecifies our actions, but we have to fully specify our actions in the act itself. The point is that there are so many ways to walk, or to sit and talk, that you effectively *must* make choices while doing it, even though you usually won't even be aware of them. Since the choices you make from all those variations do not have to be the same as everyone else's, they probably won't be. They could be totally chaotic.

The limited freedom we have in our actions is therefore an opportunity for our personalities to show through, but our concept of personality requires more than this. The choices we make have to be in some way consistent; and therefore probably the result of some internal, stable state. If the choices a person makes are totally random, then the only detectable personality that person will have will be the totally unpredictable personality. If someone shuts the door with a hard kick one day, softly the next, with his knee while holding a breakfast tray, and if he walks tall one minute, nervously the next, and then alertly looking around; now fast, then slow, and all without any noticeable change in the stimulus situation, then he has an unpredictable personality. In practice, most of us are fairly predictable, and recognisable the same people even over several years. In other words, personality is not just the choosing between functional reactions; it is consistency in that choice.

It is intuitively clear that consistency in arbitrary choice is a good thing. It is efficiently implementable. To construct a system that always does something random, and is utterly unpredictable, is harder than to construct one that does only one thing. To make a die, for example, that has exactly a 1 in 6 chance of rolling a '6', is much harder than it is to make one that is a little biased. To take the example of a human walk: once we have learned how to walk in one way, why should we change? Walking is walking, and it gets us around like it's supposed to. If you develop the habit of walking with the outside of your footsoles, well no matter, you may have to buy shoes a little more often, but you will still get to where you want to go with ease.

Given these considerations about agents with some motivations, in a world that constrains their actions only partially, it seems reasonable to suppose that agents will develop different ways of performing the same task in the same situation. Furthermore, there will be a high correlation to how the agent will perform the same task next time. This consistency in functional reaction is personality.

The controversy about intelligence being part of personality or not seems understandable from the perspective of variation within functionality. Some psychologists, like Phares [20] express bemusement at why other psychologists exclude IQ from the domain of personality. It is an individual difference in reactive tendency, because people with high IQ tend to have more different thoughts about stimulus situations, obviously. Also, there is a lot of variation in IQ between people, but it does not have such a great impact on people's survivability, so that one could say that an IQ of 100 is a valid alternative choice to an IQ of 120. Therefore IQ may be considered a part of personality by the definition proposed below.

On the other hand, most people, if they could choose, would want a higher IQ than they have; so it sounds strange to say that it is a matter of choice. A higher IQ apparently brings only benefits, and at no cost. From this perspective, IQ does not represent honest variability, because it is clear that high is better than low. And so someone holding to this view would not consider intelligence to be a proper part of personality. The question of variation *within* functionality seems to determine whether IQ is in or out, which shows that the concept is the key issue to personality.

Beyond the Fringe. As to the question of pathology, that would simply equate in this scheme to *dysfunction*. Phobias, such as fear of spiders or of heights, are defined to be fears that are so extreme that they interfere with the normal life of the sufferer: they are defined by dysfunctionality. Thus, as a person might vary over time, say, along a personality dimension, he may still have a functional personality. But as he gets more and more extreme, his reactions in that dimension will become dysfunctional at some point. At that point his reactive biases have become so extreme that they take his reactions outside the domain of functionality, and we stop saying that he has such-and-such a personality. Instead, we say he has a personality *disorder*, that he is mentally ill, or has gone mad. For example, someone who laughs easily might just be a genial person; but if he laughs hysterically nearly all the time, at the slightest thing, then his life and his health will suffer from his "laughing disease." Other examples would be compulsions, such as where someone is *so* clean that he washes his hands three hundred times a day. The space of all possible reaction-styles is divided, for a given agent and environment, into functional and dysfunctional "personalities." Variation within the functional domain is variation in personality, and variation without it is pathology.

2.6 Yet Another Definition of Personality

With the preceding justification, the definition of personality that I think can serve for modellers, and that generalises and somewhat clarifies the concept, is the following:

Given an agent with certain functions and capabilities, in a world with certain functionally relevant opportunities and constraints, the agent's mental reactions (behaviour, thought and feeling) will be only partially constrained by the situation it finds itself in. The freedom it has in which to act forces any action to reveal choice or bias in the agent, that may or may not be shown in other similar situations. **Personality** *is the name we give to those reaction tendencies that are consistent over situations and time.*

The definition is a compression of the foregoing discussion, but it is still long. A shorter definition would be the following summary, which is little more than a slogan:

Personality *is consistent reactive bias within the fringe of functionality.*

The definition and clarification of the concept of personality is not without its problems, such as how stimulus situations are to be judged "similar," given that the similarity must be in the eye of the autonomous agent's own personality – which is what we are trying to define in the first place. This and other such philosophical problems I have skipped over here because it is only necessary for now to get a reasonably precise and general definition that can be improved later. As it is, the definition is adequate for what follows.

2.7 What Would a Good Model of Personality Be?

The definition was careful to separate surface appearances from deep mechanism. The appearances or observables are to be explained by a theory or model. Hypothetical mechanisms are proposed to account for the surface phenomena, and the mechanisms are modelled literally. Personality was defined to be observable, since it was the name for a range of observables. Behaviour is objectively observable, and thoughts and feelings are subjectively available by introspection; but they *are* all observable.

Mechanisms underlying personality are not observable, so the accuracy of the model has to be evaluated by comparing the personality it eventually simulates with a natural organisms's personality.

Function was important in the general definition of personality, and it is another surface observable – almost. To guess what is the function of an organism is in a sense a wrong thing to do, because there is no such thing. Even in the Darwinian view organisms evolve by a haphazard and utterly undirected process. There are no goals in evolution, so there can be no function. However, it is usually done to talk about organisms as though they were designed in order that the fittest might survive. It is a useful fiction, for example, to say that we have legs for walking on: it is as though that were almost true. Therefore it is possible to take function (or "ecological niche") to be observable. In the case of robots, their function should be obvious, having been designed by us.

The internal hypothetical construct that corresponds to observable function is motivation, and motivation is supposed to explain function just as other internal mechanisms should explain personality as a whole.

The Model should therefore implement ideas about what the internal mechanisms of an organism are, and what its motivations are. Realistic world-knowledge and cognition is also required. We hope that reasonable values of internal variables shall give the appearance of a reasonable personality: and that extreme, dysfunctional values of internal variables should give rise to dysfunctional personality syndromes. If we find this, the Model may be good.

But there is more we can check. Given any scheme for categorising people according to personality, there may be clusters and holes, so that some personality types are common and others are (for people at least) impossible. This is very clear for motivations: there are many more people motivated to, for example, seek pleasure than seek pain. If the variation of the model shows the same pattern of variation in personality as the real organisms do, then the Model is more strongly confirmed.

But there is still more to check. People change with time, but not unpredictably. Certain transitions in personality, from Type A, say, to Type B, may be more common than others. If we make the natural assumption that transitions from personality to personality occur because of steady variation in single internal variables, then every observed transition provides us with important evidence about some underlying mechanism. It is unlikely that the dimensions of the personality-space will be the same as the underlying mechanism's parameter-space, so observing personality transitions could be helpful.

The Model should not only simulate personalities that are really found in the natural world; it should also *vary* (and develop) in the right ways, just as the natural personalities do.

2.8 Personality and Emotion

Once we include thought and feeling along with behaviour in the types of reaction that are of interest in personality theory, the question of emotion becomes relevant. It may be surprising that personality should be closely related with emotion, because at first sight they are very different things. Personality was defined in terms of temporal consistency, but emotion can be seen as the exact opposite: namely temporal *inconsistency*. Personality is stable over a lifetime, but emotions are short-lived. Another major difference is focality: while emotions are focused on a particular event or object, personality can only be described in much more general terms. Add to that the fact that emotions are usually thought to be primarily about feeling, whereas personality includes reactions in behaviour and cognition also, and the overlap seems small indeed.

However, there are emotion theories (see below) which address the cognitive aspects of emotion, and Frijda's also emphasises the behavioural tendencies. From the standpoint of such theories of emotion, the overlap with personality seems greater.

On the question of temporal consistency, the conflict between personality and emotion may be resolved by assuming that the underlying mechanisms of both are essentially the same, and that only the time-course of their influence varies. This is of course only a hypothesis, but it seems promising for a variety of reasons. One reason is that it would allow a unification of several different phenomena.

The focality of emotion can likewise be hypothesised to run continuously into the generality of personality. If we make this dual hypothesis, that emotion is a brief, focused change in personality, or that personality is a base-level, permanent and global emotion, then we can ask ourselves what an emotion would become if it were to last a long time, but still be focused. The other question would be what personality would become if it became short-term, but remained global. Meaningful answers can be given to these questions, as shown in Tab.1. An example of an **emotion** might be feeling a gush of affection for someone; while loving someone would be a longer term emotion, or **sentiment**. One could be in a generous, affectionate **mood** all day, and if that mood lasts a lifetime, we call it **personality**. The fact that in such cases we can even use nearly the same words (like love and affection) for each corner of the table supports the idea that the concepts of emotion and personality are members of the same family as shown. Indirectly, it also supports the hypothesis that the underlying mechanisms of these phenomena are similarly related.

In particular, the dimensions identified, of duration and of focus, are dimensions that are plausibly identifiable at the level of cognition. One can easily imagine cognitive structures having variable lifetimes, and the idea of *focus* is just as natural for cognitive phenomena because cognition is easily seen as the manipulation of representations (which have propositional content). Such plausibility was not the case for some other surface phenomena, like Extraversion and Neuroticism, which are not obviously related to cognition as we currently understand it.

Table 1. How emotion may relate to personality

		DURATION	
		brief	permanent
FOCUS	focused	**emotion**	*sentiment*
	global	*mood*	**personality**

Therefore, one can seriously consider that emotion and personality are closely related, at the levels of surface phenomena and of deep structure. The rest of this paper pursues the idea.

The next section reviews a theory of emotion, the following presents an implementation of it, and finally I consider to what extent the emotion model can also be seen as a personality model.

3 Emotion Theory

One of the most important theories of the emotions is that given in [8], and his subsequent publications. Compared to most of the other theories in the field, this one is nearer to implementability (and indeed has already been partly implemented), and the most comprehensive.

3.1 Summary of the Theory

Frijda's theory identifies emotions as changes in activation of behavioural dispositions, caused by relevant stimulus events.

The main technical terms are as follows. Central in the organism are its *concerns*, which can be thought of as major needs or preferences. They dictate which situations are to be sought and which to be avoided.

Emotions arise as a result of two-stage *appraisal* of the stimulus. *Primary appraisal* is a continuous *relevance detection* procedure to see if stimulus events are relevant to one or more of the concerns. This procedure may be thought of as *matching* events against concerns. A event can match positively or negatively (a mismatch) or not at all. The matches engender signals identified with the experience of positive and negative feeling, or *affect*.

Secondary appraisal is context evaluation of the event, to identify features of the surrounding situation that are significant for selection of the right behavioural mode. The appraisals given by the theory include: whether the event is *conducive* to the organism's committed goals; its *fairness* (*honesty* or *morality*); who is the *agent* of (responsible for) the event, to whom *causality* of it is *attributable*; *clarity* or *certainty* in the situation, versus ambiguity or confusion; *suddenness* and *(un)expectedness* of the event, as well as its *familiarity*; the *importance* of the concern touched by the event; and the degree of *control* the organism yet has over the situation, or the capacity it has to change it.

It is significant for the latter appraisal category what responses are available to the organism to cope with the event, how costly they are, and how feasible or likely to succeed.

The outcome of the appraisal processes is *control precedence*, and leads to a change in *action readiness*. The former refers to the capacity of the perception of the stimulus event to break through whatever mental processing the organism is currently engaged in. When this happens, mental resources are given over to changing the behavioural mode, and then to performing actions as a result of this change. The latter change in *action readiness* refers to the emotional responses provoked by the stimulus situation. The appraisal categorises the situation and leads to activation of an appropriate response strategy or action tendency.

Action tendencies are felt as impulses to hurt or harm or approach or flee or attack or defend or so on. Some of those proposed by the theory include the tendency to *approach* the situation, object or person; to *avoid* or *reject* it; to heighten *attention* toward it; to *resist, overcome* or *submit* to it; to *hide*; to become generally *exuberant* or *apathetic* or just to *rest*.

The final theoretical concept, of emotional *regulation*, concerns how and whether action tendencies become real actions.

In summary, the emotionally significant event is perceived, checked for relevance against the organism's concerns, appraised as to its importance and valence, and what opportunities its context may present for coping with it. Resulting control precedence may be strong enough to demand attention from the organism's general mentation, in which case ongoing thoughts are interrupted and action tendencies appropriate to the appraised cues are activated. The change in behavioural readiness *is* the emotion. And experience of the valenced relevance signal, the interruptability of the control precedence, and the impulses corresponding to the action tendencies, *is* the subjective feeling of the emotion.

4 Model of a *Will*

ACRES. There are two models of the theory of emotion outlined above. The first was ACRES [7, 24] which was the first ever direct implementation of an extensive theory of emotion. It was analysed in [15], resulting in more requirements for further work in emotion modelling. Details can be found in that article, but just to summarise the main point here: the chief new requirement put forward was what I called "motivational visibility," (though perhaps motivational *transparency* would have been better). The term refers to the need for an organism to continually check all its inferences from what it perceives, and from what it believes, and from what it predicts, and from what it intends. New cognitive products like these beliefs (suppositions, possibilities, expectations, intentions, etc.) are to be checked for intrinsic significance. In the context of the theory at hand, intrinsic significance means motivational relevance, which is determined by matching against the organism's *concerns*.

Motivational Transparency. A cognitive architecture that did not have this "motivational transparency" would continue to infer new beliefs and make predictions and plans, but any significance they might have would only have effect intermittently, when it happens to be checked for. That would not be a good model for humans or animals, because we notice very quickly when an event is significant for our motivational concerns. When hungry, for example, the smell of fresh bread from a baker's oven is always noticed, and noticed immediately.

The second model of Frijda's [8] theory of emotion is the successor to ACRES. It is called *Will*, because it is motivated (an "autonomous agent") and it is the main topic of this article. The model *Will* owes much to ACRES, but the concept of motivational transparency plays a major role in its design, leading to a radically different architecture.

4.1 Model Design

Occamy. The design of the *Will* model was also motivated by a desire to make it as simple as possible, and to use existing AI technology wherever possible. The hope is not only to make the model with the least effort (as may become apparent, to make something "simple" is not necessarily easy). Rather than make a big, sophisticated architecture that models everything, the idea is to include as *few* design features as possible because they correspond to theoretical assumptions, and like many others, I prefer theories – and therefore models, too – to be simple, economical, and parsimonious.

The design method followed is one I have called Occam's Design Principle elsewhere [16], or just *Occamy*, in honour of William of Occam. In that article there is more discussion of these issues, but here there is only space to summarise the chief stages in the design of the model.

Since the model is to be an autonomous agent, it needs a certain problem-solving and inference capabilities to support its autonomy. In order to economise on effort, therefore, it is wise to make maximum use of existing AI techniques, modifying them as little as possible. Further economy is possible if the theoretical emotion process is itself broken down into smaller pieces that can be unified with these imported techniques employed in surrounding cognition. In other words, the choices made below are intended to break the emotion process down, as far as is consistent with the theory, into something as much like standard symbolic inference as can be managed.

The Cognitive Elements of Emotion. If we try to break down the elements of the theory of emotion into more elementary parts, from the point of view of a cognitive scientist, we find that only a small number of elementary types of cognition are necessary.

Perceiver. Firstly, there must be perception in order to perceive the emotional stimulus. Let us say we have an independent module for this, and call it the *Perceiver.* It may be as sophisticated as a stereoscopic vision system, or as simple as a computer keyboard.

Executor. Secondly, in order to behave, there must be (an independent module) that can execute actions. Again, for present purposes this can be as simple as a computer display screen. Call this module the *Executor.*

There are those who would feel that it is too simplistic to split off perception from execution like this. I do agree with them. However, this simplistic view has been the dominant one in AI up to now, because it is at least a reasonable first approximation, because researchers tend to work on one or other problem, but not both, and because nobody has yet been able to think of a better view. Since I do not hope to improve on it here, the simplification remains in my architecture as well. (In fact, part of the interest is to see how feasible the architecture is in spite of it.)

Concerns. Thirdly, the theory asserts that there are things called *concerns*, and that these are *matched* against perceived stimuli. There is therefore a process of concern-matching, which I shall just refer to as *the concerns*. It is to be understood that they operate by matching.

Due to the requirement for *motivational visibility*, the architecture must allow not only perceived stimuli to be matched against the concerns: but inferred stimuli too, and intended ones.

Predictor. Fourthly, after perception of the stimulus event (more generally: inference) and concern matching, the next step in Frijda's emotion process is context evaluation (secondary appraisal). There are specific event properties that need to be evaluated, such as the agent of the event, if there was one. A significant part of context is often what might follow from the stimulus event. In the case of a threat, for example, the model needs to be able to see that something is threatened. This process is one of prediction and inference. Say that there is another module which does this. Call it the *Predictor.*

Planner. Fifthly, the next step in the development of an emotion is, according to the theory, evaluation of the difficulty and seriousness of the situation. These concepts need to be broken down into terms more readily related to standard AI technology, which has nothing to say about them as such.

The seriousness of a threatening situation, as an example, can be related to the avoidability of the threat. If a way can be found to escape it, the threat is not so serious. Finding ways and escapes is problem-solving, which *is* an AI topic. If we add another module for that, and call it a *Planner*, then it may be possible to use an AI planning system with little or no change for this function in the emotion process. That would have the additional advantage of finding a way to put such a standard off-line system as an AI planner (e.g. NONLIN [25]) into an autonomous agent, so that it can be made to plan in more like real time, and even to show *reactivity* (e.g.[10]).

All Together. In order to recognise a threat, one must first predict it. So as well as the Planner, the Predictor module also plays a part in the evaluation of seriousness. This shows that there is not a one-to-one relation between the emotion processes in the theory and the cognitive modules extracted from them. Some processes (like context evaluation) employ more than one module, and some modules (like the Predictor) contribute to several emotion processes. In this sense, much of the emotion process is reducible to concerns and the cognitive modules for perception, prediction, planning and execution.

Emotor. Lastly, however, there are still elements of the emotion process that need to be explained, and they cannot be explained by the modules introduced so far. It is possible to integrate the concerns and four modules to make an autonomous agent (see below), but it is not clear how or why such a system should show anything at all like true emotion. Consider the emotion of revenge: what constellation of knowledge and belief, inference and planning, perception and execution could cause an agent to commit revenge on another? Even when people react angrily and hit out at strangers, it is not clear what they are trying to achieve. Which of Maslow's motives, for example, could account for angry revenge? If there is no conceivable goal, which is the case with much emotion, then the modules introduced so far are not enough to account for emotion.

The remainder of the emotion process, that cannot be explained by the modules, will be confined to its own module, the *Emotor*, which is explained later.

Memory. So far, the architecture has four modules and a set of concerns, which is a pleasing small number. Apart from the concerns, which are novel to the theory of emotion, and the Emotor modules, which is introduced below, all the other modules are fairly standard. They are: the Perceiver, the Executor, the Predictor and the Planner. These are symbolic modules for pragmatic reasons, and so the system needs an explicit, symbolic world model. All autonomous agents need to model their environments in order to interact with them intelligently, even if the model is only implicit. Examples of architectures with implicit knowledge of their environment would be most connectionist systems, and those that come from "Nouvelle AI" [2]. The world model in W*ill* is called the *Memory*, because that is the closest word for it. The Memory stores facts about particular objects in the environment, so it is an *episodic* memory. The architecture up to now is shown in Fig.1.

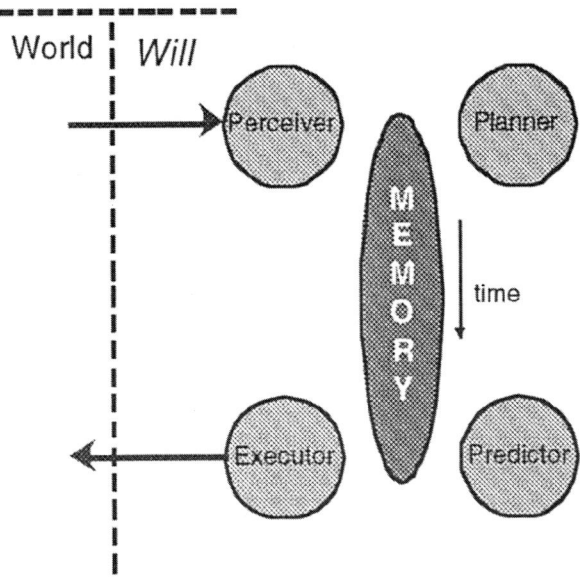

Fig. 1. W*ill's* basic modules

For theoretical reasons, it is desirable to make the architecture domain-independent. There must therefore be domain knowledge which describes the physical laws of the domain that W*ill* happens to inhabit. (Such knowledge would correspond to what, in people, is called *semantic* memory.) This is necessary because the architecture is supposed to be as general as the theory it models.

Note that it would be possible to propose the functions of perception, execution, planning prediction, and memory just on the basis of loose intuition. To choose to include such modules as Perceiver, Executor, Planner, Predictor and Memory in an agent architecture is obvious enough on the grounds that real organisms seem to have such cognition. However, without having a better reason, that would be just to copy nature blindly. The preceding argument is independent of what organisms happen to be equipped with: it depends only on what environmental constraints are placed on organisms. Therefore, the functions implemented by the modules are not just a good idea: they are forced on us. Sufficiently interactive organisms *must* possess them.

Universal Communication. The next decisions to make are about how to integrate all the modules, memory and concerns (see Fig.1). In terms of software engineering, the modules have to be connected via interfaces, but there are very many ways to do that.

Still trying to keep the design as simple as possible, by applying the Occamy principle (Sect.4.1), the least ad hoc design decision at this point is to have one central interface only. This effectively provides for global communication between modules, or broadcasting. It is the most general solution because it subsumes all other possible solutions. Any flow of information throughout any network of modules can obviously be emulated by a star-shaped network, in which the central hub is added to connect the modules at the points of the star.

We have extracted some basic concepts, and shown how they come back in several places in the above theory. The theory looks complicated, but there seems to be a chance that it can be simplified to only four main processing modules, two of which can be trivial in the computer model. Namely, a Planner and Predictor, with trivialised Perceiver and Executor.

There are other important concepts we need too, like the concerns, and like a memory, and like world knowledge, but these are passive and representational. So far, I have focused on process. The modules I mentioned may be thought of as processors, because they are specified by what they do, not when they do it. Since the cognitive processors occur in several stages of the core emotion process, they can no longer be ordered linearly in a time-line. Since the theory was presented as a sequential emotion process, design decisions therefore have to be made as to the order of processing in the architecture.

Universal Control.

Parallelism. The architecture has several modules which process information in the central memory, and return new information to it. That is the meaning of having a single central interface. A design decision now has to be made to determine in what order the information is processed.

Which modules must operate first? In a procedural programming language there would be a top-level procedure that would call the various modules in some particular order sequence, but to favour one sequence over all others at this stage would be an ad hoc decision. The most general, least presumptive, decision here is to make the architecture parallel by design. Thus, the question of the time-course of processes is to let all the processors run in parallel. Not to specify any particular temporal order, but to let each module take information as it needs it, and make its outputs available as they are produced.

Just as the choice of a single central interface was most general because it allows all other potential choices to be emulated, so the choice to make the modules parallel is most general, because it allows all other potential sequencing strategies to be emulated. Whether any particular flow of information through all the modules is actually emulated by this architecture is now a matter for the information itself to determine – it is not prejudged by the system designer.

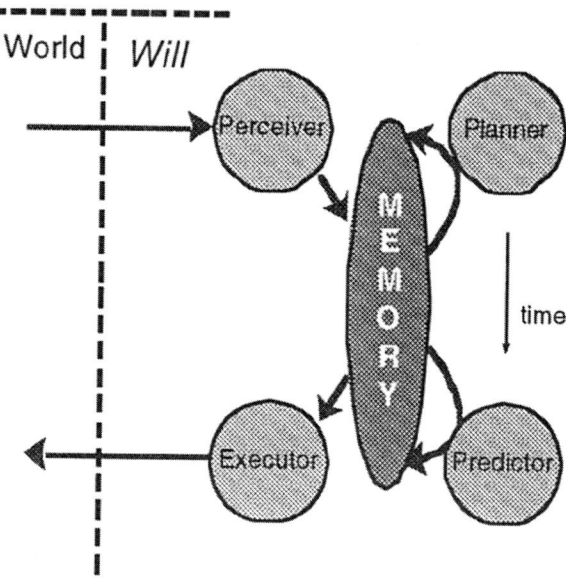

Fig. 2. Module integration

Attention. The final major design decision is to choose a control principle. The modules operate in parallel, and communicate globally, but what do they operate *on*? They are all service functions in that they each have their own task to do repeatedly, as if they run in little cycles, but we have to say which particular task they must do next. The Planner, for example, makes plans from goals and beliefs; but *which* goals and data does it choose to work on at any particular time?

The initial functional answer to this question is that the Planner, or any other module, ideally chooses to work on the most *important* data at all times. The question therefore reduces to one of the determination of importance. This is where Frijda's theory of emotion provides a valuable insight. We can use the *concerns* to determine importance by checking all data for concern-relevance (by matching) and then pick the most relevant data item.

An obvious optimisation would be to check all the items in Memory only once, and thereafter store the result with the item so that it does not have to be recalculated unnecessarily. Most contents in Memory will in most cases remain constant for most of the time, after all. When an item in memory is first created (such as a belief that Viennese people probably eat müsli for breakfast like everyone else, say) is changed, then it needs to be evaluated for concern relevance. When an item is updated (such as when the Viennese are observed breakfasting on chocolate cake), then it likewise has to be *re*-evaluated for relevance. In short, any item that is written into Memory, whether it be a new item, or a change to an existing item, *when* it is written, must be checked for concern relevance. To show this architectural role of the concerns, they are drawn as a shell around the Memory in Fig.3. All information going into Memory, no matter where it comes from, must pass through the concerns layer in order to get evaluated for concern relevance.

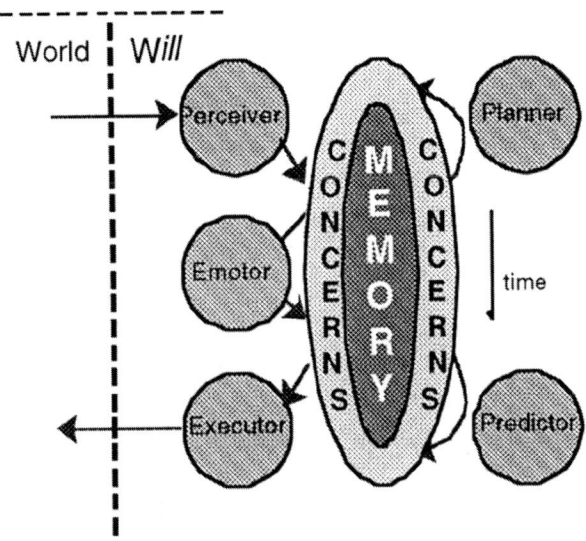

Fig. 3. Full architecture

The final module to be added to the architecture in Fig.3 is the Emotor, which models the remaining, specifically emotional processes required by the theory. These are the secondary appraisal, and action tendencies. Discussion of the Emotor will be left until we get to the working implemented model, below.

4.2 Model Architecture

The architecture arrived at in Fig.3 is not just an emotion model. It is a basic autonomous agent built on AI technology. As I have argued elsewhere, it offers solutions to long-standing but neglected problems in AI: namely, the problems of integration [16] and motivation [3]. The fact that the architecture was intended as a model of emotion does not mean that it is no more than that. On the contrary, since the only theoretical novelty introduced was the *concern*, and since the design process was deliberately minimalist, the architecture is in a sense the most general one possible, within certain limits imposed by the reasonable assumptions made.

Optimisations Possible. From the basic architecture modifications and extensions can be made in order to optimise its functioning, and in this way more specific architectures can be derived that may turn out to correspond more accurately to psychological reality. In other words, the structure of the mind may be like the *Will* architecture only at the most abstract level. In practice, there may be certain extra interfaces between modules, and there should certainly be extra functions, with learning being an obvious one that does not occur in the architecture so far.

As an example of how one might wish to change the architecture in order to optimise it, consider how the Emotor is connected up. In Fig.3 it reads from Memory, and writes its results back to Memory, but there is another natural choice. Since emotional reactions are a type of reaction, one might prefer to do as many researchers in A-Life (and others) do with the concept of *reactivity*. Since reactions may need to be fast, those researchers often [10, 2, 12] connect them, in terms of *Will*'s architecture, directly from the Perceiver to the Executor. Such direct mappings from system input to output are usually called *behaviours*. The idea is that response is more tightly coupled to the environment, and "hardwired" without using the higher level, more intelligent cognition available (the Planner and Predictor). Some researchers take the view that planning as such is not necessary at all, since it can be bypassed in this way and one can still have a viable creature [2, 19].

Emote-Memory Route. While that alternative is certainly feasible and interesting, I have chosen the information route via Memory as shown in Fig.3 for these reasons: (i) it is motivated by the Occamy principle of design, (ii) it means that the whole architecture can still be founded on a single coherent organisation, in which all the modules are managed in the same way, (iii) the architecture is therefore more plausible from a biological and an implementational point of view, (iv) there are already many researchers experimenting with the direct information route from Perceiver to Executor, but as yet almost nobody has considered the route via Memory (but [4] has a similar notion in his "cognitive reactivity"), and (v) the direct route can easily be seen as just an optimisation of the Memory route.

In addition to these reasons, there are functional reasons to prefer the Memory route, like the advantage gained from ensuring that the Emotor only reacts to the most significant information, and the possibility for other modules to sanction reactions proposed by the Emotor. Sometimes reaction tendencies are inappropriate, but a direct Emotor-to-Executor mapping would not allow sanity checking.

Summary of Architecture. The foregoing discussion to motivate the design of the architecture was rather involved, but the resulting architecture itself is simple.

There are several active modules, all running in parallel, and all connected to the central workspace called Memory. Modules can only communicate via the Memory. Input and output modules are of course connected to the outside world as well as the Memory. This is a kind of blackboard architecture.

Each cognitive module operates in short cycles. In a cycle it first gets a problem (called the *focus* item) from the Memory, solves the problem in some way, reading any other information that it may need from the Memory, and then writes back a solution if it finds one. A problem is an item from Memory that needs to be processed. How it should be processed depends on the module.

The control principle is *attention*, based on concern-relevance. Concerns guard the Memory, attaching a *charge* value to every item that is written into it. Items that are more concern-relevant get a higher charge. It is the item with the highest charge that is given to a cognitive module as the new focus item at the start of a cycle. In this way, the items in Memory compete for attention from modules in order to be processed.

The major modules in Will as implemented are the Planner, Predictor and Emotor. Along with the general attentional processing based on emotional significance, which is primary appraisal, the Emotor implements secondary appraisal. From all the appraisals on the focus item, the Emotor produces action tendencies appropriate to the emotion, and installs these into the Memory as intentions to act. Unless it is changed in the meantime by other modules, the Executor module will later begin a new cycle with the emotionally produced intention (it will "notice" it), if it has enough charge to become the focus, and it will execute the action.

Charge Principles. The charge on a Memory item is based on concern-relevance, which is how much intrinsic emotional charge it has. But it is also modified by various other factors in Will, including surprise and uncertainty. Events are unexpected if they were not already written in Memory, or if they were expected to be different. In the context of the Will model, clear reasons can be given for why it is functional to attend more to unexpected events.

If an item is uncertain, then charge has to be calculated from it appropriately. In the current Will model, an average is taken of the charges that would come from each of the possibilities permitted by the uncertainty. But other schemes could easily be imagined.

Autoboredom. Charge has to go down sometimes, as well as up, otherwise attention would soon become fixated on a single focus item. Various schemes are possible to reduce charge, but so far I have only implemented one in Will. Some people find it a most natural principle, the notion that charge should decay with time. To support it, they point to indications that neural synaptic connections lose their strength with time. But I have not implemented this principle. It has several problems: (i) it confuses biology with psychology, (ii) it is ad hoc, assuming more than is strictly necessary to solve the problem – namely the involvement of time as an independent cognitive variable, and (iii) it doesn't solve the problem anyway. If item charges decay with time, then they *all* decay, so that the top item is bound to stay at the top even if its absolute charge falls. It does not matter how fast charge falls, or whether it falls linearly with time, or exponentially – if the same decay applies to all items, then they all maintain their rank ordering.

The method I implemented in W*ill* is to cut charge from the top event only. Even then the charge does not decay with time, because that would be ad hoc again. Instead, the top item (the *focus*) loses charge every time a cognitive module *fails* to process it; such as when the Planner fails to find a new plan for the focus goal. It could be that the Planner has already found a plan for it in a previous cycle, and it only fails now because it succeeded before. In that case, the focus event loses a proportion of its charge and is less likely to command attention because there is nothing more that can be done with it by one or more modules. Since there is no more profit to be had by "thinking" about the focus event, W*ill* in effect gets "bored" by it, and goes onto something else. If the event was very highly charged, it should take longer to lose the focus, but eventually even the most significant events automatically become boring in this way – hence the name *autoboredom* for this *discharge* principle.

The principle is crude, certainly, even though it's far better than the idea that charge should just decay with time. There are many promising ways to experiment with all the control principles mentioned. But they will have to wait for further research.

4.3   Model Example

The architecture is still abstract, so it has been instantiated to a working model, which inhabits a real domain. It plays the Prisoner's Dilemma with the user, interacting through a terminal keyboard and screen.

The Prisoner's Dilemma. The Prisoner's Dilemma is a mathematical game intended to model social dilemmas. Both players simultaneously make a move, which is either to cooperate (c), or to defect (d). They are then rewarded accordingly. If one player defects and the other cooperates, then they get $5 and $0 respectively, as shown in Tab.2.

Table 2. Payoffs for the Prisoner's Dilemma

		User	
		c	d
Will	c	3 / 3	5 / 0
	d	0 / 5	1 / 1

That is just one round. The game becomes interesting when several rounds are played, allowing players to take "revenge" on each other for defecting in earlier rounds. The game can be made to model the natural evolution of cooperation between players, which has all sorts of very interesting and important consequences [1]. However, for the purposes of this paper it is just a game which allows some form of interaction between players (the emotion model is one, the User is the other), and presents opportunities for several different emotional reactions.

Event Types and Relations. There are move events, and there are payoff events. There are two players of the game (*will* and *user*). The possible moves are c and d (cooperate and defect). The possible payoffs are \$0, \$1, \$3, and \$5. When the user plays c, the event is represented as $move(user, c)$.

It is not necessarily known what move the user shall play next, although it is known that he shall play either c or d. In such cases, the partial representation $move(user, \{c, d\})$ serves.

Events are ordered in time. In general the ordering is partial, but in the Prisoner's Dilemma the only temporal relations between events that we need are immediate temporal precedence ($\rightarrow$), and simultaneity ($\&$). Thus, the players always move simultaneously (so that neither is aware of what the opponent plays until both play their moves at once). Players are paid simultaneously also, and immediately after they move.

Using this grammar, the beliefs about the world can be represented in structured expressions. For example, the beliefs that Will defects, while the User plays his own move; and that then both players get the appropriate payoffs, as far as they can be deduced on that information, is represented like this:

$$move(will,\ d)\ \&\ move(user,\ \{c,\ d\}) \rightarrow$$
$$payoff(will,\ \{1,\ 5\})\ \&\ payoff(user,\ \{0,\ 1\}).$$

One virtue of this scheme is that it allows the representation of uncertainty, because arguments can be constrained to small sets, but without requiring the complexities of probabilistic algebras.

Causal Rules. In order to be able to deduce that certain payoff-events must follow a pair of move-events in a round of the Prisoner's Dilemma, and to be able to perform more general causal reasoning, the domain knowledge includes a set of causal rules. The rule that produces inferences that rounds of the Prisoner's Dilemma repeat forever is:

$$payoff(will,\ WP)\ \&\ payoff(user,\ UP) \rightarrow$$
$$move(will,\ \{c,\ d\})\ \&\ move(user,\ \{c,\ d\})$$

which says that every pair of payoffs is followed by a following round's pair of moves. Names in large letters are variables, like Will's and the User's payoffs (WP and UP) above. The rule also introduces the move arguments at their least constrained values, because in general other knowledge will be required in order to infer what the User is likely to play in the new round.

The rule which specifies the way payoffs relate to moves played is:

$move(will, WM)$ & $move(user, UM) \rightarrow$
$$payoff(will, WP) \text{ \& } payoff(user, UP),$$
where $payoff\ matrix(WM, UM, WP, UP)$

The variables for the players' moves and payoffs are related in this causal rule by an auxiliary condition expressed in the *matrix* predicate. It is the logical representation of the matrix shown in Tab.2.

In order to start the game it is only necessary to define the initial moves of both players, without saying what those moves are:

$$move(will, WM) \text{ \& } move(user, UM)$$

Once the Memory is initialised with this belief, further beliefs can be generated by means of the other causal rules. This initial belief will itself be modified as the system comes to believe that one player or the other will play some particular move.

The knowledge representation scheme is a variant of the predicate calculus, of the sort familiar from much of AI work. It can be given a formal semantics and so on, but for present purposes it is enough to understand it intuitively.

Concerns. The aim of the game is to win money, so W*ill* has a concern to maximise \$'s from every opportunity. The opportunities are the "payoff" events, because they have a "get money" feature. The features of an event are matched against the concern, which is represented as a simple scale:

$$\$ \text{ concern} = [0 \rightarrow 2 \rightarrow 5]$$

This means that the least preferred amount of money to win is \$0, the best outcome is \$5, and the *set-point* is \$2. The purpose of the set-point is to show where the average or expected outcome is. A win of \$2 will result in a valence of 0, meaning the event is not felt as relevant by that concern. Other wins are positive or negative:

$$\text{win } \$0 \text{ valence} = -2 \times \text{IMP}$$

$$\text{win } \$3 \text{ valence} = +1 \times \text{IMP}$$

$$\text{win } \$5 \text{ valence} = +3 \times \text{IMP}$$

Where "IMP" is a factor for the *importance* of the concern.

There is also a concern for *moral behaviour*.

$$\text{morality concern} = [0 \to 0.8 \to 1]$$

This means that the worst outcome for an event with a morality feature is a morality value of 0, maximum morality is 1, and the set-point or null-point (the satisfaction level) is 0.8 units. The general knowledge in *Will* records that "move" events have moral value, and that to move c has moral value 1, while the move d has 0 moral units. The representation means that c moves are *felt* as slightly (0.2) positive (because one expects that most people are usually moral); but d moves are appraised with more negative valence (-0.8).

The move by the User is as relevant to *Will* as is *Will*'s own move: the User is also moral or immoral. But the User's payoff is not relevant to *Will*, because the $ concern only matches *Will*'s own wins.

The concern to win money is set to be more important than the concern for moral behaviour.

Cognitive Modules. The input and output modules are not interesting. They only act as buffers between the external events (perceptions and actions), and internal representations of them. The important modules are the more cognitive ones: the Predictor and the Planner.

The Predictor reasons forward in time, as might be expected, predicting consequences from existing beliefs about causal events. The Planner reasons backward, in order to make decisions about causal events that would bring about the desired consequences. Not just any decision can be made, however: the domain representation defines which types of event are *Will*'s own actions, and thus possible subjects for decision. In the Prisoner's Dilemma, the only type of event that *Will* has direct control over is one that matches *move(will, WM)*, where the variable *WM* here represents any possible moves.

World Model. Like any agent, *Will* must have some kind of world model in order to be able to interact intelligently with its environment. Since it is a symbolic architecture, its world model is symbolic too. What is normally called a world model in AI takes the form in *Will* of both types of memory: the episodic Memory blackboard proper, holding factual beliefs, and the semantic causal rules. The most important part of *Will*'s environment is the User, and he can be modelled as a causal rule or two. For example, the belief that the User always defects would be represented as:

$$move(user, UM) \to move(user, d)$$

which says that given any belief that the User plays a move, then the move that the user plays is d.

Note: there are subtleties involved to ensure that the conclusion is drawn concerning the same event in both sides of the causal rule, but they are skipped over in this paper.

The Emotor Module. An important part of emotion is already modelled by the system as described up to now: roughly speaking, the part up to and including *affect*, *primary appraisal* and *control precedence* [8]. The other parts of emotion are modelled by the separate Emotor module. These parts are *secondary appraisal* and *action tendency*.

The emotion of anger can be characterised approximately as the intention or tendency to harm someone because of an immoral (unjustified), harmful action of his, such as an insult. On the other hand, one feels pride when one has performed some good or difficult act, and one then tends to jump about and laugh for joy, like a soccer player who's just scored a goal.

These simple examples show that emotion is arbitrary, in a sense. They are designed into us: they didn't have to be that way. It might have been that one would feel angry at oneself after scoring a goal, or feel proud when insulted. Such emotional reactions would be bizarre indeed, but not logically impossible. Emotional variation like this may just "emerge" from deeper mechanisms, but for theoretical perspicuity they are literally programmable in W*ill*.

The parts of the Emotor module that can be programmed are its appraisals and its action tendencies. The example emotions of anger and pride are used to illustrate this.

Some Appraisals. Different emotion theorists suggest that there are different sets of appraisal categories that cause emotions. Here are some common and important ones. In terms of Frijda's terminology, they are primary and secondary appraisal categories. In order to allow appraisals (and later action tendencies) to bear upon a focus, the representation is again in a predicate/argument form. Say that O is some other agent (not the Self), and G is a goal.

- *Valence* : Can be ±. This says how un-/pleasant the emotion is.
- *Un-/Expectedness* : Was the (perceived) event expected?
- *Control* : Does the Self have control over this situation?
- *Agency* : Who is responsible for this event? Also called "causal attribution". Difficult!
- *Morality* : Was the event (action) moral?
- *Probability* : How probable is it that the event will actually happen?
- *Urgency* : How urgent is the situation?

Some Action Tendencies. Unlike appraisal, the concept of action tendency is almost unique to Frijda's theory, because most emotion theories satisfy themselves with trying to explain what emotions are caused by; not with what they cause in their turn.

Here are some examples:

- *hurt(O)/help(O)*: Want to hurt or help O.
- *try_harder(G)/give_up(G)*: Try harder or give up the goal G.
- *approach(O)/avoid(O)*: Want to approach or stay away from other agent O.
- *fight(O)/flee(O)*: Want to fight or run away from O. Here O can also be a situation.

– *exuberance/apathy* & *inhibition*: general level of activation and mood is high/low.

Some "true" Emotions in Will. Here are some examples of emotions in *Will* as it plays the Prisoner's Dilemma. They are "true" examples in that they use action tendencies and appraisals: they come from the Emotor.

Happiness

Appraisals:	valence = positive
	agency = world
Action tendency:	happy_exuberance

Anger

Appraisals:	valence = negative
	morality = negative
	agency = User
Action tendency:	hurt(User) → play D,
	attend(User)

Pride

Appraisals:	valence = positive
	morality = positive
	agency = Self
Action tendency:	exuberance → verbal,
	attend(Self)

4.4 Model Performance

Table 3 shows an edited printout of a session with *Will*. The genuine output of the program is a lot like this, but I have changed it in small ways to make it easier to follow.

Each paragraph of output is labelled with a unique number, and the name of the cognitive module that produces it. All output is only for logging purposes, except for emotional expressions (in quotation marks, like "I'll get you back for that!"), and except for the outputs from the special module called the Umpire. That is not a part of *Will* at all, but a separate program that sits between *Will* and the world outside (that is, the User). The Umpire holds the moves of both players so that neither player can know what the opponent is going to play before he has played his own move as well. The Umpire then gives out the winnings to both players.

Messages from the cognitive modules show what *Will* is "thinking". Line 1 shows that *Will* has noticed that (is attending to, is aware of the fact that) he is going to play a move in round 1 of the game, and that the move he shall play is either c or d. At this point, the focus of attention is evidently that event, because it has the highest charge. Charges of events are not shown because they would complicate the table too much, but it is clear that the charge of the $move(will, \{c, d\})$ event referred to in line 1 is high because of the concern for moral behaviour. Since there is a possibility that *Will* may play c, which

Table 3. Example session with *Will*

1. Planner: Notice that I play **c** or **d** in round 1.
   a   Decide that I play **c** in round 1.

2. Predictor: Notice that I play **c** in round 1.
   a   Predict that I win $ **0** or $ **3** and User wins $ **3** or $ **5** in round 1.

3. Predictor: Notice that I win $ **0** or $ **3** in round 1.
   a   Predict that I play **c** or **d** and User plays **c** or **d** in round 2.

4. Predictor: Notice that I play **c** or **d** in round 2.
   a   Predict that I and User win $ **0** or $ **1** or $ **3** or $ **5** in round 1.

5. Planner: Notice that I play **c** or **d** in round 2.
   a   Decide that I play **c** in round 2.

6. Executor: Tell the Umpire that I play **c** in round 1.

7. UMPIRE: Round 1. What do you play? ...**c**.

8. UMPIRE: Round 1. You play **c** and *Will* plays **c**.

9. Perceiver: Hear from Umpire that User just played **c** and I just played **c**.

10. Emotor: Notice that I just played **c** in round 1.
    a   *Appraisals*   *Action tendencies*
    b   intensity = 0.4   exuberance = 0.4
    c   valence = +0.4
    d   agency = myself   *emotion* is pride
    e   morality = 0.4
    f   [0.4] express pride

11. UMPIRE: Round 1. You win $ **3** and *Will* wins $ **3**.

12. Perceiver: Hear from Umpire that User just won $ **3** and I just won $ **3**.

13. Emotor: Notice that I did win $ **3** in round 1.
    a   *Appraisals*   *Action tendencies*
    b   intensity = 4.0   jump_for_joy = 4.0
    c   valence = +4.0
    d   agency = world   *emotion* is joy
    e   morality = 0.0
    f   [4.0] express joy
    say: *"La la la!"*

14. Emotor: Notice that I did win $ **3** in round 1.
    a   *Appraisals*   *Action tendencies*
    b   intensity = 2.7   jump_for_joy = 2.7
    c   valence = +4.0
    d   agency = world   *emotion* is joy
    e   morality = 0.0
    f   [2.7] express joy

Table 3. Example session with *Will* (continued)

15. Emotor: Notice that I shall win $ **0** or $ **1** or $ **3** or $ **5** in round 2.

a	*Appraisals*	*Action tendencies*
b	intensity = 3.0	jump_for_joy = 6.0
c	valence = +3.0	
d	agency = world	*emotion* is joy
e	morality = 0.0	
f	[6.0] express joy	
say:	*"Yabba-dabba-doo!!"*	

. . .

16. UMPIRE: Round 2. You play d and *Will* plays c.

. . .

17. Emotor: Notice that I shall win $ **0** in round 2.

a	*Appraisals*	*Action tendencies*
b	intensity = 3.6sentiment = −0.21	
c	valence = −3.6	∴ urge = 8.2 (= |int − sent|)
d	agency = user	hurt(user) = 6.2
e	morality= −1.6	*emotion* is angry revenge
f	React soon (round 3) to hurt(user): decide that I play d.	
g	[8.2] express anger	
say:	*"Hey! I'll get you for that!"*	

. . .

18. UMPIRE: Round 3. You play c and *Will* plays d.

would be good according to that concern, or *d*, which would be bad, then the net charge over both alternatives is calculated from a formula that takes into account the uncertainty between them. Exactly what this formula is does not matter so much, especially since it is easy to change, and is in any case dependent on the chosen representation for uncertainty. The important point is that there is a way to calculate the overall charge of a partially known event, from the charges of each of its possibilities.

Cognitive Processing. The Planner decides in line 1a to play the move *c* in that event. It has decided to do this because according to the concern for morality the move is preferable, and because it knows that *Will*'s own moves are under its own control, so that the decision is one that *Will* can make. The decision is made by the Planner simply changing the representation of the focus event in Memory to *move(user, c)*.

The next module cycle is one by the Predictor, in lines 2 and 2a. The Predictor notices the newly changed event, again because it evidently has the highest charge in Memory. Using a causal rule, the prediction is then made that the following event is to be one in which the User wins either $3 or $5, simultaneously with Will's winning either $0 or $3. The prediction is written into Memory, and the Predictor cycle ends.

Cycles in which modules fail to make any changes to Memory contents (such as new decisions, inferences, or predictions) are not shown in Tab.3. Their effect is only to lower the charge on the focus event.

The next module that does change something in Memory is the Predictor, which processes the round 1 payoffs event, in order to predict the start of round 2. Although the User's and Will's payoff events were inferred together, on line 2a, only one half of that prediction is used on line 3 to drive the next cycle of the Predictor. This is because it is only Will's own payoff that is concern-relevant. Any other event representations in Memory may be used by the Predictor, along with the focus one, in order to make new predictions, but it is only the focus event that actually starts the module off on a new cycle.

By line 5, the round 1 action move(user, c) has become the focus event. It was not highly charged when first created by the Planner on line 1a, because otherwise it would have been executed immediately. Lines 2–4 intervened because their focus events were then more highly charged, but by line 5 they are not any longer. This is because those event representations have lost charge each time a module has tried and failed to process them further. Once the Planner had successfully made a plan to play the move c on line 1a, for example, there was nothing more for it to do with the round 1 move event, and so in later cycles the Planner failed to make any new decisions to improve that event. By the control principle called autoboredom earlier (Sect.4.2), the charge on the representation of Will's round 1 move dropped automatically by a certain proportion every time the Planner, or in fact any module, failed to process it. No such failures are shown in Tab.3, but there must clearly have been some because otherwise Will's attention would not have moved onto other events. By line 5, the focus of lines 2–4 have also dropped, so that now the round 1 move is the focus again, which means the Executor in its cycle notices it, and executes it.

In all this attentional processing, causing the charges on event representations to rise and fall, precisely how fast or by how much is not very important. The essential point is that the parameters can be changed by the programmer in order to experiment with different values. As long as autoboredom decreases charge by some factor, it does not matter so much what the factor is.

The Umpire has got Will's move for round 1, and in line 6 asks the User for his. In line 8 the Umpire reports to both players what the moves were, and in line 10 tells them about their payoffs. Between those lines, other module outputs can be seen, showing that after Will has made a move he doesn't just stop and wait for the world to do something; he continues to show cognitive activity in the normal parallel fashion.

Affective Processing. One thing that happens, while the User and Umpire are responding, is that Will has a first weak emotion. The emotion is one of pride, caused by Will's move in round 1, when he played c, which is a moral move. The appraisals in paragraph 10 also show that there is a small positive valence resulting from the concern relevance of the event, and that the agent (animate cause) of the event is Will himself. The intensity of the emotion is given by the charge on the representation of the focus event (another simplifying design decision). According to the emotion rules given earlier, these appraisals result in the action tendency to be exuberant with general positive activation. There is no action in the Prisoner's Dilemma that could intuitively express pride or joy, but verbal expressions can be printed on the screen as direct messages from Will to the User. The value of the emotion is only 0.4, which is below the threshold for verbal expression (arbitrarily set at 3), so Will says nothing.

Later emotions that Will has are in paragraphs 13–15. First there's joy about winning $3 in round 1. The Emotor cycle in paragraph 13 expresses this joy in song, on line 13say. The next cycle of the Emotor is focused on the same event, so it is a continuation of the same emotion episode but now the intensity (identified with *charge*) has fallen because other cognitive modules have failed to process the focus event further (the principle of autoboredom again). The strength of the action tendency has fallen from 4.0 in line 13f to 2.7 in line 14f, which is below the threshold of 3.0, so that the joy is not expressed. In this way, the emotion has weakened through time, but not because of any neural mechanisms or other low-level issues; it is pure, functional cognition that has done it.

The next cycle (line 15) of the Emotor concerns the round 2 payoffs. Because of the round 2 move that has already been played, the only payoffs that Will can get in round 2 are in fact $0 or $3, depending on what the User plays. But Will has not yet realised that, and still thinks that $5 is a possibility (which came from the inference in line 4a). A possibility of a high payoff is relevant to the concern for winning money, so the charge on the event is high enough to cause, through the rules for generation of action tendency, a joyous urge strong enough to express itself in line 15say.

Some lines of output are then missed out in Tab.3, until line 16, which shows that the User has played *d*. Since that has the consequence that Will only wins $0 in round 2, Will naturally gets emotional about that. In paragraph 17, the focus event is winning only $0, for which the User is blamed (the appraisal for agency is "user"). Since the User played *d*, which is in any case seen as immoral, the emotion rules mobilise anger, creating the action tendency to hurt the User. Note that this action tendency has an object, and the object is the perceived cause of the sorry event; namely, the User.

The strength of the urge to *hurt(user)* is modified by the current emotional attitude or *sentiment* towards the User. The sentiment is calculated (using programmable rules not shown) from previous interactions with the present User character, as well as a baseline set by "personality". The sign of the sentiment is at present negative (-0.21) so that, when added to the valence of the emotion, it tends to strengthen negative action tendencies and weaken positive ones. Whether this model of sentiment is consistent with all types of emotional reaction is not obvious, but at least in cases such as the anger shown in Tab.3 it seems reasonable, and it has the additional virtue of simplicity. The effect in paragraph 17 is to strengthen the angry reaction, so that Will reacts more angrily to the User because of not liking him.

The action tendency is expressed in action, as well as the less interesting verbal output in lines 17g and 17say. The action arises from line 17f, which maps the action tendency into an appropriate action. To *hurt* an opponent in the Prisoner's Dilemma is effectively defined as defection; playing the *d* move. The angry reaction can be seen in line 18, which shows that W*ill* has indeed carried out his threat to "get the User back."

Tensed Thought and Emotion. An interesting theoretical question arises regarding the timing of emotional reactions. Since the focus of an emotion can have any *tense* —can be any time in the past, present or future —the question is when the reaction should take place. W*ill* could be angry about something the User did long ago, for example, or has only threatened to do in the future; but should the angry reaction take place now, or only immediately after the stimulus event? The implementation of the reaction mechanism in the prototype of W*ill* actually reacts "now".

The fact that W*ill* effectively can react angrily *in advance of* what he imagines (for whatever reason) the User shall do in the future may seem strange to some readers. But there are many examples that make it seem more reasonable, such as when you know that the government wants to pass a new law that you despise, but has not passed it yet.

In cases of personal relationships, anticipatory anger like this can even have a preventive or controlling effect, preventing the other person from doing what he planned originally. When anger is purely reactive, it appears irrational, but in cases of anticipatory anger it can be seen to have a direct purpose after all.

In addition, some other emotions, like jealousy and fear, are (almost) always future-directed. It is clear in those cases that the "reaction" must precede the stimulus event if it is to be of any use. The point is to run away *before* the tiger gets you.

4.5   Model Evaluation

The emotion model presented may or may not serve as a model of personality, as hypothesised earlier in Sect.2.8. I have conducted no experiments to determine whether it does, but we can compare the model's performance with the theories of personality overviewed in Sect.2.

W*ill*'s Personality Parameters. According to the definition of personality proposed in Sect.2.6, personality is individual variability in reactive bias, "within the fringe of functionality." The personality parameters in W*ill* are therefore those internal variables that can be varied without making the agent dysfunctional. There are several programmable parameters like that. These include:

-- CHARGE. how many concerns there are, and what they are; relative importance of the concerns;

- the factor of surprise in charging event representations;
- the factor of uncertainty in same;
- the proportion of charge lost when a cognitive module fails on the focus event;
- EMOTOR. The appraisal categories available;
- how the appraisal values are calculated;
- the action tendencies available, and how they correspond to appraisals;
- the relative strengths (availabilities and predispositions) of the action tendencies;
- the inbuilt sentiments for particular objects.

Changing or re-programming any of these would change the reactive style of the model, without making it dysfunctional. Making these parameters extreme, such as making the surprise factor in charge calculation very large and *negative*, so that surprising events actually get very *little* attention, could make the model dysfunctional; but there is a lot of play in these parameters, so varying them amounts to changing Will's personality.

Does Will Have Big Traits? According to the Big Five theory, Will should display certain traits in order to have a personality. It does quite poorly in this comparison. This is how Will matches up on each trait:

⇓ Openness – No, not really modelled. Will does not appear to have broad interests, to be creative or untraditional.

⇑ Conscientious – Yes, about half of the meaning of conscientiousness is possible. There is a concern for honesty and fairness, which is domain dependent. Concerns for being organised, self-disciplined, hard-working and clean could no doubt be programmed in the same manner. The architecture would then fully display this personality trait; the difficulty is in formalising what these terms mean.

⇕ Extrovert – Somewhat. This could correspond to Will's general readiness to express its emotions through verbal statements, and other action tendencies, modelled by baseline level of activation of action tendencies (potentiation).

⇓ Agreeable – No, there is almost no social awareness in Will, so this is out.

⇑ Neurotic – Yes, Will *is* a worrier, worrying about the past and what he could have done differently, and worrying about what might happen in the future, even if there is no profit in worrying about it more. The degree of worry about such things can be controlled by the *autoboredom* principle, and how fast it operates. If it is weak, then emotionally significant situations should tend to occupy attention for longer even if they are actually insoluble.

On average, about half of the Big Five (and thus Eysenck's Big Two or Three) traits are modelled at least partially by Will. It is noticeable that the ones which present difficulties are the more social traits. This is because Will's awareness of other agents as social beings is non-existent.

One insight can be gained from Will regarding *worry*. As pointed out above, Will always worries naturally; it is just a question of how much. Since personality was defined as variation *within* the "fringe of functionality," one might wonder if Will (or indeed anybody) should worry at all. After all, worriers are often told they should not worry about what cannot be helped, because it is irrational – dysfunctional, that is.

What the will architecture makes plain, though, is that a certain tendency to worry *is* functional. If Will focused entirely on the present, it would not be able to learn from the past (Will does not learn, but a Learner module could be added to the architecture as trivially as any other module); and it would be less able to avoid unpleasant futures, even anticipated ones. Once that insight is gained from considering how not worrying at all could actually be harmful for Will, the same can easily be seen to apply to people also.

A further point in the same vein is that worrying is only dysfunctional in cases where it concerns a problem that really cannot be solved (or learned from). Such cases may occur in artificial toy-worlds, but they never do in real life. You can never be absolutely sure that there is no way to avoid some problem; you can only lose interest in it (it loses charge) when the chance of that being so drops below some threshold.

Eysenck's proposal (see [1990] for an excellent review) about the biological basis for the trait of extroversion may be modelled with a small extension to Will. He said that we all desire an optimal level of arousal, and that extroverts have a CNS (central nervous system) with a lower arousal base-level. Hence the extrovert's toleration of and desire for stimulation, which is why extroversion is associated with sensation-seeking behaviour.

The change needed in Will to model this would be to define a parallel for CNS arousal (a good attempt might be the highest charge in Memory) to specify what would be an optimal level for it, and then to add a new concern to keep the two as close as possible. I have not done this in Will, because it would be ad hoc to complicate the model with such extra features, unless one has a good idea about what adaptive value they have. Nevertheless, it could probably be done.

Apart from the Big Five, other traits may be modelled in the architecture, such as the following.

As Gray [9] has suggested, Eysenck's Big Two personality traits may be rotated to get two alternative traits. One is for *anxiety* (neurotic introversion), which is unusually high sensitivity to punishment or non-reward, and the other is *impulsivity* (neurotic extroversion), which is sensitivity to non-punishment or reward. These traits could be modelled in Will simply by changing the formula for calculation of charge, so that it is higher for negative or for positive concern-relevance.

But there is another kind of impulsivity that is variable in the model. The Executor only executes an action when it is the intention with the greatest charge; and the charge has to be greater by a certain threshold. If there are two intentions that are equally charged, then it is as if Will is not certain what to do next, and so does nothing. After a short time, the two intentions should settle to different charges, at which point they hopefully differ by more than the threshold, and the higher of the two can be executed. The threshold parameter would appear to correspond to caution, so that making it smaller would make *Will* more impulsive, tending to perform intentions the moment they "enter the head."

Does *Will* Have a Rotter Personality? Comparison with Rotter's theory of personality is more favourable to *Will*. Much of it is all there, without having to add anything extra to the architecture. In addition, where Rotter focuses more on behaviour, *Will* explicitly models thought reactions, and of course affective reactions, and does so in great detail.

Rotter has expectancies and reinforcement values (Es and RVs), which have direct parallels in *Will* (namely, predictions, made with causal rules, and concern relevance giving rise to positive and negative affect, or feeling). They can also depend on the situation as Rotter requires: fully, in the case of prediction; less so in the case of affect. Concerns are represented in terms of a set-point, deviation from which causes affect. Since the set-point is supposed to model a kind of global, background expectancy, that is something which can change in time and context. However the present implementation does not explore this issue. Relative importance of concerns could also be made context-dependent, but this is not implemented either.

Rotter's notion of need potential (NP in equation 3 of Sect.2.3) emphasises that people only tend to do things that they think will achieve the goal, no matter how much they may desire the goal. Obviously, *Will* is the same, because if a goal is unachievable the Planner cannot even find a plan for it, so no intentions are generated. But it goes a little further, in that the model also predicts that people should stop worrying about unachievable goals after many failed attempts to plan for them. This is a consequence of the autoboredom principle.

The question of acquired RV's would correspond in *Will* to new concerns acquired by association, or derived from primary concerns. There isn't a learning capacity in the model at present, but I imagine that a standard learning algorithm could be incorporated into the architecture, almost as easily as the Emotor was added to it.

The I–E dimension for a person's perceived "locus of control" has no direct parallel, but the related concept of "attributional style" finds a parallel in *Will*'s appraisal for *agency*. People vary in how much they tend to attribute the cause of some event to themselves. Even a single person can vary this attributional style from time to time. For example, there is the "self-serving bias," in which people attribute the cause of good events to themselves. Sporting encounters are good examples.

When Brazil beat Holland in the recent football World Cup in Italy, the match itself was a draw, and had to be decided on a penalty shoot-out. In a Brazilian bar in Amsterdam, where the match was being avidly followed by Dutch and Brazilian supporters together, the interviewed Dutch football fans thought it was a poor way to settle a match in which their side had been the equal of Brazil, because a penalty shoot-out is "little better than a lottery;" but the Brazilian fans thought it was fair because their side deserved to win, "having played better." Some months later, the situation was reversed when the Amsterdam team (AJAX *!*) won the championship for the best club team in the world by beating a Brazilian team. This time the penalty shoot-outs were in favour of the Dutch. The match was an almost perfect mirror image of the previous one, and so were the opinions. This time the Brazilian fans expressed the opinion that they lost "because a penalty shoot-out is no better than a lottery." Strangely, they still thought their team had played better in the match, even though they lost. As well as losing the match, the Brazilian fans were clearly suffering from a severe case of self-serving bias. But it's not just Brazilian psychology. The self-serving bias is universal: we all do it.

There are other biases of causal attribution, but there is no consensus as to why they happen. What is clear is that the process of causal attribution is very difficult. There are no best answers, so there is latitude for individual variation, and the "fringe of functionality" is quite broad. Therefore, one could predict from the cognitive difficulty of the problem alone, that causal attributional style would be a personality variable according to the definition in Sects.2.5 and 2.6. There are no ideal solutions to the problem of who caused what, only heuristic ones, all of them reasonable at least some of the time, and so an agent is relatively free to choose any one of them. A habitual style will form, or be inborn, and then a be part of the personality.

An example of causal attribution at work in W*ill* is shown in Tab.3, on line 17d. The User has played d, and this has caused W*ill* to get a \$0 payoff in that round. The Emotor evaluates the cause of an event by applying the causal rules in reverse, possibly chained onto other causal rules. When an agent is found that performed a causing event, that agent is considered to be causally responsible for the caused event. If the event in question is itself an action, then it is trivially caused by the agent who performed it. But in the case of line 17d, the causal rules of the domain state that there are two joint causes of the unpleasant payoff event: namely, W*ill* only got \$0 partly because he himself played c. So in a way W*ill* could blame himself for his own misfortune. As shown in Tab.3, however, W*ill* considered that the User was wholly to blame for the incident. This is because I have implemented a crude self-serving bias such that, in cases of divided attribution, the burden must fall on the User.

It would be more satisfying to be able to show how the self-serving bias could emerge naturally from cognitive processing, without being literally programmed in. But at least this shows that even some quite involved personality aspects can be set into the model.

One aspect of Rotter's personality parameters that he emphasised is their dynamic nature. Since the RV's and E's that determine action are estimates, they may "change with thought." While that is an aspect that makes experimental measurement of those variables difficult, since it is hard to control how much a person thinks, it is an aspect that is utterly natural to model computationally. In the example session with W*ill* in Tab.3, many "thoughts" were shown, including emotions in successive stages of development. Of course it is still a problem to find a way to experimentally verify that the dynamism is correct, but to model it is at least a necessary step.

Does W*ill* Have a Bandura/Mischel Personality? The main personality variables put forward by Mischel have equivalents in W*ill*. The competencies and expectancies are obviously equivalents to W*ill*'s cognitive modules and domain knowledge. The only exception is the expectation of *self-efficacy*, which, like the similar I-E dimension in Rotter's theory, has but a limited match in the architecture.

The encoding strategies determine how a person selects and elaborates sensory information. The approximate correspondents in W*ill* would be the attentional mechanism, which selects information and causes it to be elaborated; and the emotional appraisal categories, which are programmable set ways of seeing and categorising situations.

Where Mischel has subjective values, for individual evaluations of events, Rotter has *RV*, and W*ill* has his concerns with importance ranking. The correspondence is exact.

Self-regulation is a sophisticated concept in Mischel's theory, because it involves a self-concept. There is no self-concept in W*ill*, and nor will there be, because I have no idea what a self-concept is. However, W*ill* does represent standards of behaviour, and does use those to regulate its behaviour. For example, without the concern for fair play, W*ill* would defect more often. So there is some regulation in W*ill*, but it is not done with self-concepts. It just arises from the way the concerns are integrated into the whole architecture.

5 Conclusion

Several issues have been touched on in this paper. Personality theories have been summarised, and a species-unspecific definition of personality has been proposed that applies to artificial Cognitive Science/AI models as well. The relation of personality to emotion was considered, that led to the hypothesis that the two are members of a single family of phenomena that also include mood and sentiment (affectively loaded attitude). I suggested that the same underlying mechanisms may be made to explain all these phenomena, and illustrated the ideas with a prototype emotion model. The model was then compared with the major theories of personality to evaluate it as if it were originally intended to be a personality model.

The Big Five trait theory of personality is the one that W*ill* compares least favourably against, with about 50% of the theory that can claim to be implemented in the model. Against Rotter's and Mischel's cognitive-behavioural (social learning) theories it does much better, implementing and accounting for the greater part of them. The most obvious weakness in the model is its lack of social awareness, making those aspects of personality that are to do with how people relate to each other impossible to model. Other weaknesses, such as the lack of a learning capacity, are easier to fix.

Before coming to write this paper, it had not occurred to me that an emotion model such as the *Will* model might also serve as a model of personality. It seemed to me, as far as I thought about it at all, that "personality" is a specifically human quality, inapplicable to artificial systems like robots. For some reason, I uncritically believed all those science-fiction notions that robots could be intelligent like us, but could never have what *we* would call "personality." But now, having compared the structure and performance of *Will* with some of the major theories of personality, it suddenly seems more plausible. More than that, it seems feasible. And more than that; according to the definition of personality proposed in this paper, it is almost inevitable.

The new definition of personality in this paper was deliberately chosen in order not to be species-specific. That being so, it is perhaps less surprising that it applies to some artificial agents. One may wonder whether the appellation "personality" is not by this means too easily given away to them. Would a car have personality by this definition; or a cappuccino machine? Yes, if they act in accordance with their function, or within the fringe of functionality, and if they display choice in their reactions (which could just be designer choice). Indeed, people do refer to their cars as if they had personality sometimes, and this is why.

The next question is whether machines can have human-like personalities. In this case, the answer is a much more qualified "yes." Just as there is an arbitrariness about emotion, so there is about having a *human* personality. Our personalities are as individual as our emotions, and that is where a model like *Will* can be said to have more personality than a car can.

The programmable personality parameters in *Will* include the charge manipulation parameters in the attentional mechanism, the appraisal categories, action tendencies, and concerns, all of which can be set at different relative strengths. In this programmability, human-specificity can be built in as required, but with different settings other personalities would also be possible, the like of which have never yet existed. What they may be is beyond science-fiction to imagine, but it is unlikely that they will all be dull, unemotional computers like HAL in *2001*.

There are some potentially valuable applications to the computational modelling of personality. Some researchers [18] have already begun to look at how such work can contribute to out understanding of personality disorders. The idea that machines might have personality may chill some people, so the potential turn back to applications in psychotherapy may ironically be the twist that finally humanises AI, an otherwise cold science.

References

1. Axelrod R. (1984) *The Evolution of Co-operation*. New York: Basic Books
2. Brooks R.A. (1991) Intelligence without representation. *Artificial Intelligence*, **47** pp.139-159

3. Carbonell J.G. (1982) Where do goals come from? In: *4th Annual Conference of the Cognitive Science Society.* Ann Arbor, Michigan.pp.191–194

4. Castelfranchi C. (1995) Guarantees for Autonomy in cognitive agent architecture. In: Wooldridge M., Jennings N.; pp.56–70

5. Engler B. (1993) *Personality Theories (4th edition).* Boston: Houghton Mifflin

6. Eysenck H.J. (1990) Biological Dimensions of Personality. In: Pervin L.A. (ed.) *Handbook of Personality: Theory and Research,* Guilford Press, New York, pp.244–276

7. Frijda N.H. and Swagerman J. (1987) Can computers feel? Theory and design of an emotional system. *Cognition and Emotion* **I(3)** pp.235-257

8. Frijda N. (1987a) *Emotions.* Cambridge University Press, Cambridge, UK, 1987

9. Gray J.A. (1994) Personality dimensions and emotion systems. In: Ekman P., Davidson R.J. (eds.) *The Nature of Emotion (Fundamental Questions).* Oxford University Press; pp.329–331

10. Kaelbling L.P. (1987) An architecture for intelligent reactive systems. In: Georgeff M.P., Lansky, A.L. (eds.). *Reasoning about Actions and Plans: Proceedings of the 1986 Workshop.* Los Altos, California. Morgan Kaufmann; pp.395–410

11. Maslow A.H. (1970) *Motivation and Personality.* (Revised by R. Frager J. Fadiman, C. McReynolds, R. Cox.) New York: Harper & Row

12. Meyer J.-A., Wilson S.W. (eds.)(1991) *From animals to animats: Proceedings of the first international conference on the simulation of adaptive behaviour.* Cambridge, MA: MIT Press

13. Mischel W. (1968) *Personality and assessment.* New York: Wiley

14. Mischel W. (1979) On the interface of cognition and personality: beyond the person-situation debate. *American Psychologist* **34** pp.740-754

15. Moffat D., Frijda N.H., Phaf R.H. (1993) Analysis of a model of emotions. In: Sloman A. et al. (eds.) *Prospects for Artificial Intelligence.* IOS Press, Amsterdam; pp.219–228

16. Moffat D., Frijda N.H. (1995) Where there's a *Will* there's an Agent. In: Wooldridge M., Jennings N.; pp.245–260

17. Pervin L.A. (1993) *Personality: Theory and Research (6th edition).* New York: Wiley & Sons

18. Pfeifer R., Leuzinger-Bohleber M. (1986) Applications of cognitive science methods to Psychoanalysis: A case study and some theory. *International Review of Psycho-Analysis* **13** pp.221–240

19. Pfeifer R., Verschure P.F.M.J. (1991) Distributed adaptive control: a paradigm for designing autonomous agents. In Meyer, J.-A. & Wilson S.W. (eds.); pp.21–30

20. Phares E.J. (1991) *Introduction to Personality (3rd edition).* New York: Harper Collins

21. Rotter J.B., Chance J.E., Phares E.J. (1972) *(Applications of a) Social Learning Theory of Personality.* New York: Holt Rinehart Winston

22. Rotter J.B., Hochreich D.J. (1975) *Personality.* Glenview, Illinois: Scott, Foresman

23. Sloman A. (1995) Exploring design space and niche space. In: *Proceedings of the 5th Scandinavian Conference on AI,* Trondheim, May, IOS Press, Amsterdam

24. Swagerman J. (1987) *The ARtificial Concern Realization System ACRES: A Computer Model of Emotion.* Doctoral dissertation, University of Amsterdam

25. Tate A. (1977) Generating project networks. In *Proceedings of the 5th International Joint Conference on Artificial Intelligence (IJCAI'77),* Massachusetts Institute of Technology, Cambridge, MA, pp.888–893

26. Watson J.B. (1919) *Psychology from the standpoint of a behaviorist.* Philadelphia: J.B.Lippincott

27. Wooldridge M. and Jennings N. (eds.) (1995) *Intelligent Agents - Theories, Architectures and Languages.* Springer Verlag, LNAI 890

What Sort of Control System Is Able to Have a Personality?

Aaron Sloman

School of Computer Science
The University of Birmingham
Birmingham, B15 2TT, England
A.Sloman@cs.bham.uk.ac
Phone: +44-121-414-4775

Abstract. This paper outlines a design-based methodology for the study of mind as a part of the broad discipline of Artificial Intelligence. Within that framework some architectural requirements for human-like minds are discussed, and some preliminary suggestions made regarding mechanisms underlying motivation, emotions, and personality. A brief description is given of the 'Nursemaid' or 'Minder' scenario being used at the University of Birmingham as a framework for research on these problems. It may be possible later to combine some of these ideas with work on synthetic agents inhabiting virtual reality environments.

1 Introduction: Personality Belongs to a Whole Agent

Most work in AI addresses only cognitive aspects of the design of intelligent agents, e.g. vision and other forms of perception, planning, problem solving, the learning of concepts and generalisations, natural language processing, motor control etc. Only a tiny subset of AI research has been concerned with motivation and emotions, or other things that one might regard as relevant to personality.

Partly inspired by Simon's seminal 1967 paper [8], I have been trying since the late 70s, in collaboration with various colleagues and students, to address these issues. They are intimately bound up with deep and difficult problems about how human minds work, and I don't expect answers to be found in my lifetime, though that's no reason for not trying to make a beginning. Doing this requires thinking about the design of 'complete' agents (whether human-like or not), not just specific cognitive mechanisms. That's a very difficult task, since we know so little about so many of the components and underlying implementation mechanisms. Nevertheless, by combining design of 'broad' but temporarily 'shallow' architectures with various other kinds of research on more detailed mechanisms we can hope gradually to make progress towards complete and realistic designs and theories.

In order to make clear the framework within which I am working, I'll start by making some general comments on the scope and methodology of AI. I'll then describe a scenario within which some of us are exploring possible architectures to account for aspects of motivation, emotion and personality. And I'll then sketch some preliminary ideas about an explanatory architecture, which is not offered as a complete specification, but a partial, high level overview of a family of possible architectures. At the end I have included an edited transcript of some tape recordings following the discussion after my presentation at the workshop in Vienna in June 1995, as this may help to remove some common misunderstandings.

Why include a section on the goals of AI? Part of the reason for this is that most people think of AI in terms that are too narrow. I shall try to offer an alternative vision of AI that is broad and deep, within which a study of personality can be accommodated. It also helps to identify many unsolved problems and weaknesses in current research.

2 How Should We Identify Aims of AI?

There are various approaches to defining the aims of AI, including the following:

1. Try to articulate what you yourself think you are doing and what larger set of goals it fits into. This is what many AI practitioners do. Some are unaware of what lots of others do.

2. Repeat some definition of AI that you have read, especially if originally produced by one of the founders or 'gurus' of AI. This is what many undergraduates, recent graduates, recent recruits, journalists, and outsiders do.

3. Look at what actually goes on in AI conferences, AI journals, books that claim to be on AI, AI research labs: Then try to characterise the superset. This could be what a sociologist or historian of science might do. Many AI people now tend to go only to their specialist conferences and read only their specialist journals, so they lose the general vision. So also do many external commentators on AI.

4. Like (3) but instead of simply characterising the superset, try to find some underlying theme or collection of ideas which could generate that superset.

The last is what I have tried to do. This is what I have learnt:

2.1 What Are the Aims of AI?

AI is (as I have claimed in various previous publications):

The general study of self modifying information-driven control systems,
− both *natural* (biological) and *artificial*,
− both *actual* (evolved or manufactured) and *possible*[1].

I include the study not only of individual agents, but also societies and the like: social systems add new constraints and new design possibilities, relating

---

[1] Including what might have evolved but did not, or might be made, even if it never is.

to communication, cooperation and conflict. By the 'general study', I mean to include: not just the creation of any particular such system, but an understanding of what the options are, and how they differ and why, including what the trade-offs are.

From this standpoint, Cognitive Science is the subset of AI that studies human and other animal systems. AI thus defined has a number of sub-activities, not often thought about, which I'll now summarise.

3 Sub-tasks for AI

This general study of behaving systems is *not* a search for a particular algorithm or design. Even if we had a truly marvellous AI system equalling or surpassing humans in many respects, that would not be enough. For we'd need to be able to *understand* what we had done, and why certain aspects of the design were good and why alternatives would not be as good. Such understanding involves knowing not only what a particular design is and what it can do, but also how it relates to other possible designs. It also involves knowing which aspects of the implementation are essential and which are not.

In short we need to understand the space of different possible architectures, i.e. the different regions of design space and their properties. In particular, for different classes of designs and mechanisms we need to understand what are they good for or not so good for. Namely, which collections of requirements do different designs fit into? These questions can arise at many different design levels[2].

3.1 What Is a Niche?

Using terminology from biology, and slightly generalizing it, I use the word 'niche' to refer to a collection of requirements for a working system, such as an engineering requirements specification. Any particular design may fit a niche more or less well.

A niche is not just a physical thing nor a geographical region. A chimpanzee, a squirrel, a parrot, or a flea might each be placed on the same branch of the same tree in the same forest, yet each would be in a different niche from the others. E.g. they need to perceive different things in the environment, and when they perceive the same thing they may use the information for different purposes. Similarly, different software packages, such as a compiler, an editor, a database, a spreadsheet, an internet browser, will all occupy different niches, within the same computer.

A niche is an abstraction, not a portion of the world. A particular physical location may instantiate several different niches at the same time. The bee and the flower which it pollinates, are located in different niches, though their niches

---

[2] Some of the issues are discussed, though in the more general context of understanding complexity and simplicity, by Cohen & Stewart [4]

are related: anything meeting the functional requirements of each of them will help to define part of the niche for the other.

The specification of the niche for a particular type of agent could include: (a) the ontology of the environment, as sensed and acted on by the agent, (b) the dynamics possible within that ontology (which events and processes can occur), (c) the means of sensing the environment available to the agent, (d) the types of actions required of the agent, and (e) a collection of possible tasks and constraints, where the set of actual tasks may be dynamically changing. Exactly what is included will depend on how precisely the niche is specified.

For example the tasks might include finding and consuming enough food to keep alive, finding a mate, reproducing, looking after young, learning about a social system, fitting into the social system, etc. Some constraints are imposed by laws of nature, e.g. physical constraints, and others by a legal system ruling out certain means of achieving goals, or a set of conventions for communication. A niche may be made more constraining by adding additional requirements, e.g. specifying what sort of food is to be used, or which other sorts of agents are to be aided in some way. Because any particular portion of the world can instantiate several different sets of descriptions simultaneously, it can instantiate several niches simultaneously.

Some niches are determined more or less explicitly in advance by human engineers (or their customers) and guide their design work. Other niches are implicit in a collection of evolutionary pressures that operate on a class of organisms. Just as humans can design things with complementary roles (e.g. plugs and sockets, compilers and machines) so naturally occurring implicit niches may complement one another. One way of looking at an ecology is as a collection of interacting niches, which may be changing dynamically. Different aspects can change independently, e.g. changing climate alters the requirements regarding discovery or creation of suitable nests or shelters, whereas a changing culture, or changing amounts and kinds of knowledge alter the requirements for individual learning, and collaboration or competition with others in the society. In a complex society with systematic division of labour, different social roles will require different individual types of motivation, preferences, ambitions, likes, dislikes, etc. I.e. different personalities will be required. An extreme example is the difference in reproductive roles.

3.2 What Is a Design?

A design, like a niche, is not something concrete or physical, though it may have physical instances. A design is an abstraction which determines a class of possible instances, and where a design is capable of being instantiated in different ways, there will be more specific designs corresponding to narrower sub-classes of possible instances.

Talk about 'designs' does not imply anything about the *process* of discovery or creation of designs[3]. Design production does not have to be top-down: it can

---

[3] 'Design' can be a noun as well as a verb.

be bottom-up, middle-out, or multi-directional. Arguing that only one approach will work, as some defenders of genetic algorithms or neural nets do, is silly: all approaches are liable to 'get lost' searching in design space.

There is no one true road to understanding: we have to follow several in parallel and share what we learn. The approach can be empirical or theoretical. When it is theoretical it may be either intuitive and vague or formal and precise, making use of logic and mathematics. It may but need not include the creation and study of instances of the design. When instances are created (i.e. a design is implemented in a working system), this is often part of the process by which we understand the problem, rather than our top level goal. Investigation by implementation is very common in AI, and is partly analogous to the role of thought experiments in physics.

Designs include specifications of architectures, mechanisms, formalisms, algorithms, virtual machines etc. Where a design specifies a complex structure with interacting components, it will need to include not only structural features but also the behavioural capabilities of the components and their possible forms of interaction, i.e. their causal powers or functional roles within the whole system.

Differences between designs include both (a) different ways of refining a common more general design, e.g. starting with a general parsing mechanism and then applying it to two specific grammars, to produce parsers for those grammars, and also (b) differences that are due to different implementations in lower level mechanisms, such as using different programming languages, or different compilers for the same program, or compiling to different machine architectures, or implementing the same machine architecture using different physical technologies.

In many cases a particular design D can be implemented in different lower level mechanisms. In that case we say D is a design for a *virtual* machine, and different instances of that virtual machine may occur in quite different physical systems, for instance when different physical technologies are used to implement the same computer architecture, e.g. a VAX or a SPARC architecture. Insofar as the process of biological evolution can be seen as a mechanism that explores design space it seems to make use of very different levels of implementation, most of them being the result of previous designs, whether of reproductive mechanisms, chemical structures and processes, neural mechanisms, or mechanical structures.

Often it is impossible or difficult to create instances of a new design directly, so part of what has to be designed includes new production processes. This point is often stressed (e.g. by [4]) in criticising the notion that DNA fully determines the development of an embryo, for that ignores the role played by the mechanisms that 'interpret' the DNA.

Human design capabilities are enhanced by development of new design and manufacturing tools. Thus closely associated with any particular design may be a set of more generic 'meta-designs' for design and production mechanisms. The latter have a niche that is determined by the kinds of designs they are required to enable or facilitate.

The less specific a design the more scope there is for varying the implementation details. One of the things we don't yet understand well is which classes of designs are neutral between very different kinds of implementations, e.g. which high level designs for intelligent human-like agents are neutral as to whether the components are implemented in a collection of neural networks and chemical soups or in a collection of symbol manipulating systems, or some mixture of mechanisms.

So, we don't yet know which high level aspects of the design of a human mind are neutral between implementation on human brains and computer-based implementation, though much prejudice one way or the other abounds. Answering that question is among the long term objectives of AI as defined above.

A related question is the extent to which complex behavioural capabilities can be explicitly built in in advance, or whether mechanisms capable of implementing such capabilities cannot be directly programmed, but must 'program' themselves through processes of development, learning and adaptation. E.g. it may be physically impossible, in any kind of factory, directly to assemble a fully formed adult human brain with all the information needed for normal adult functioning already in it.

In that case any system containing such a brain will have to have learnt a great deal for itself. Thus part of a requirement for its early personality will be a set of motivations and capabilities capable of driving such a learning process.

If we wish to understand how to give a synthetic agent a personality we need to understand what sort of niche makes having a personality relevant to the requirements the agent has to fit into, and what sorts of designs are capable of meeting such requirements. I've tried to show that that is a far more complex question than it might at first appear.

3.3 Studying 'Niche-Space' and 'Design-Space'

The general study, which I have claimed constitutes the scope of AI as it is actually practised in all its forms, involves at least the following aspects, though not all are found often in AI work.

1. **The study of 'niche-space'**
   This is the study of collections of requirements and constraints for agent designs, each collection being a 'niche'. Besides particular niches we need to understand dimensions in which niches can vary, and also the dynamics of changes in interacting niche systems. Although this is not very often made explicit, there are examples in AI research, including the study of different requirements for learning systems, and the analysis of different sorts of perceptual tasks (e.g. [6, 12]). Marr misleadingly described this as the computational level of analysis. Many of the papers by myself and my colleagues are concerned with requirements for motivational mechanisms in human like systems (e.g. [9] (chapter 6), [10, 11, 13, 14, 3]).

2. **The study of 'design-space'**
   This includes analysis and comparison of design possibilities at different levels of abstraction, including high level architectures, low level mechanisms,

forms of representation and reasoning, types of long term and short term memory, types of perceptual mechanisms, types of learning mechanisms, and so on. This is found in much of the discussion in research papers comparing work by different authors. Unsurprisingly, it is rare to find discussions of designs or requirements for complete agents.

3. **The study of mappings between design-space and niche-space**
   These mappings are correspondences between designs (or classes of designs) and sets of requirements. For any given region of niche-space there are usually alternative designs, none fitting the niche perfectly. The different styles and widths of arrows in Fig. 1 are meant to indicate different kinds and degrees of match.

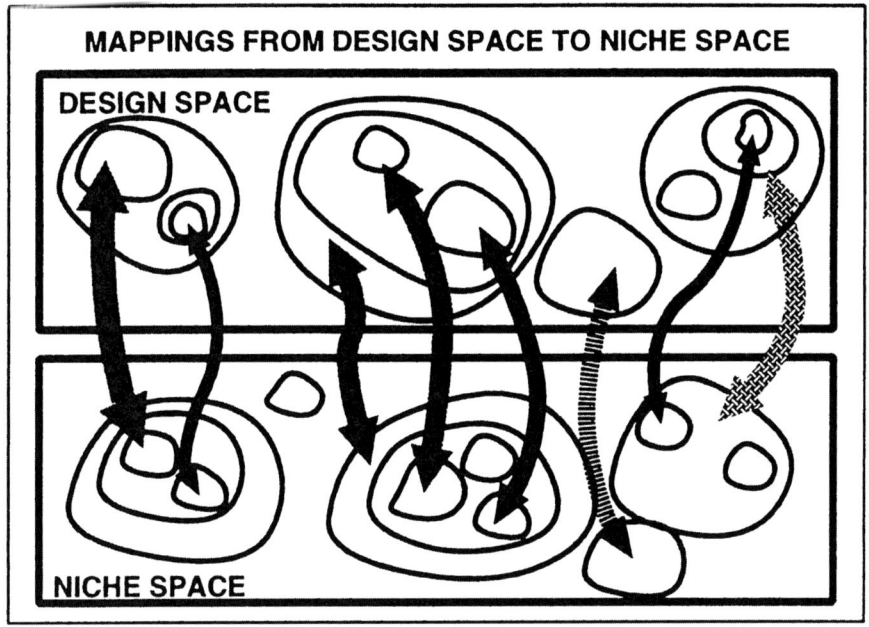

Fig. 1. Mappings between design space and niche space

A niche is a set of requirements. Mappings can vary in degree and kind of goodness. Various kinds of trajectories in design space and niche space are possible.

In particular, there is no 1 to 1 mapping. There are many trade-offs and compromises, and no unique criterion of optimality for satisfying a niche. Neither is there a simple numerical measure of goodness of fit between a design and a niche. Design D1 may be better for niche N than design D2 in some ways, and worse in others. E.g. it may be able to catch a wider range of edible prey because it can run faster, but not be so good at distinguishing edible from inedible items, because of its perceptual limitations. A full analysis of the variety of mappings requires an analysis of the logic of 'better', which is a far more complex concept than most people realise. E.g. we need to understand how to handle multiple partial orderings concerned with different types of comparison.

4. **Analysis of different dimensions and levels of abstraction**
   This involves looking at niches and designs from the standpoint of several different disciplines (e.g. neural, psychological, social, philosophical, linguistic, computational, etc.)

5. **The study of possible trajectories in niche-space and design-space**
   AI, like many other sciences, is concerned with processes that are extended in time. When a complex system interacts with its environment that is external behaviour. In many cases this will involve internal behaviour (e.g. compression and changing stresses within a bouncing ball). Some internal behaviour is information processing, including processes of development or learning, such as happens in a foetus as it develops to a normal infant, or happens in an infant after birth. Many of these changes produce changes in the capabilities of the system. These are changes in design, even though no external agent has redesigned anything.
   In other words, something that develops, or learns, follows a trajectory in design space. And because it can meet different sets of requirements and satisfy different constraints as a result of the changes, there are corresponding trajectories in niche space[4].
   Explorations of learning systems then, are concerned with the study of mechanisms that can move themselves around design space (and niche space) partly as a result of interacting with an environment. The trajectories that are possible may depend on the particular environment - so from that point of view a niche may be part of the 'design' of a larger system.
   One of the interesting questions to be investigated is which sorts of trajectories are possible and which are not. Just as some designs may have features that make direct implementation impossible, so that self-adaptation and learning during development are required, it could also turn out that there are some trajectories in design space that are simply impossible for any individual, though they can be achieved by evolutionary processes operating on a gene pool distributed in a collection of individuals.
   For example, given the physics and chemistry of our universe, it seems to be impossible for any individual to transform itself from an elephant into an ape, or from a flea into a human being, although such transformations might be logically possible. It's likely that neither organism includes the potential for such drastic changes, even if they are produced by gene pools which do. There may also be types of transformations of information processing capabilities that are not possible for an individual. For example it may be impossible for a new born mouse to learn to understand any human language, even though a new born human can, and a mouse and a human share an enormous biological heritage.

---

[4] Though remember we are not talking about movement of a point in either space, but movement of some sort of region, which may have fuzzy boundaries.

Thus some trajectories within design space and niche space may be possible for a gene pool but not for any individual agent.

It might also turn out to be impossible for some of the forms of conceptual development exhibited in the history of human science and culture to occur within any one individual, no matter how long that individual lives. Perhaps a mixture of interleaved individual development and social learning is required to produce transitions such as those leading from ancient Greek science to quantum physics. For example this might be the case if the process necessarily involves 'bootstrapping' through mistaken or confused cognitive states which, once they have been entered cannot be left, even though they may be part of the environment in which a new generation learns while avoiding those states.

The same may turn out to be true for evolution of tastes, aesthetic preferences, art forms, moral values, and types of personalities. These are all topics for further study under the general heading of exploration and analysis of possible trajectories in design space and niche space.

Figure 1 gives a very rough indication of the sort of thing I have been discussing, though the use of a 2-D surface oversimplifies by suggesting that there is a unique level of analysis for designs and niches. This is not the case.

3.4 Discontinuities in Design Space and Niche Space

A point that is often not noticed, and which is important both for AI and for the theory of evolution is that the spaces are discontinuous.

Changes in designs can include either continuous variation or discontinuities. Some regions of design space have smoothly varying properties, e.g. changing speed, electrical resistance, or fuel consumption, or size. Others involve small or large discontinuities, like the change from having one wheel to having two, or three or four. In information processing systems, there are a lot of discontinuities in design. If you remove a conditional branch from a program, that's a discontinuity. You can't put back a half of it or a quarter, or an arbitrary fraction.

On the other hand, some discontinuous spaces may be capable of being embedded in continuous spaces, as the integers are embedded in the reals. Thus (as pointed out in [16] a feed-forward neural net can be thought of as a large collection of condition action rules, all activated in parallel, with many conditions sharing certain actions, and many actions sharing certain conditions, where the weights determine a degree of influence of a particular rule. So in this case the degree of influence between a 'condition' and an 'action' can vary continuously between 0 and some significant value, even though such variation is not possible for conditional branches in ordinary software.

In conventional software, it may be possible to get something approximating such continuous variation by adding a randomiser to each condition, and gradually changing the probability with which the condition will be triggered. Nevertheless the difference between the design that allows a certain condition to play a role, however small, and the design that has no such condition at all, is a discontinuity. A structural change is needed to get from one to the other.

This is one example of a research topic regarding the structure of design space. We need to find out how many kinds of discontinuities there are, and which, if any, of them can be embedded in more complex designs that smooth out the discontinuities[5]. Where there are irreducable discontinuities we need to understand how they relate to possible trajectories in niche space and to developmental or evolutionary mechanisms that are capable of producing such discontinuities[6].

3.5 AI and Philosophy

I hope the discussion of design and niche spaces and possible trajectories makes it clear why it is too limiting to conceive of AI as the search for any particular design, or a class of designs meeting any particular set of requirements. That may be a useful practical goal, but it is not enough for a deep study of mind.

In particular, the design of any particular architecture is but a part of a broader study, which is to try to find out what sorts of architectures are possible, and how they meet different sets of requirements, i.e. how different areas of design space correspond to different areas of niche space.

This enables us to generalise the old philosophical question 'What is a mind?' and replace it with: 'What sorts of minds are possible, and how are they different and what sorts of mechanisms and evolutionary or developmental or learning processes can bring them about?'

Whereas older philosophers tried to say 'A mind has to be this, that or the other', I suggest the answer has to be of the form 'Well, if you design the thing this way, you have one kind of mind, if you design it that way, you have another kind of mind' and so on.

It's the differences and similarities between the different designs and how they relate to different niches that are important, not necessary or sufficient conditions.

In order to pursue this study we need a set of techniques and conceptual tools. I'll now describe some of them.

4 Requirements for a Study of Design Space and Niche Space

At the very least we need the following.

---

[5] One reason for doing the latter is that it may allow 'hill climbing' in the search for good designs, e.g. using evolutionary algorithms, something I've learnt from my colleague Riccardo Poli.

[6] It is not always acknowledged that Darwinian evolution *requires* discontinuous change between generations, even though the discontinuities may be small.

4.1 A Language for Describing Niches (Sets of Requirements)

Some of the work by engineers in developing formalisms for expressing requirements may be helpful. Similarly some of the work done by biologists in comparing the niches of different but related organisms may be helpful. I suspect both have barely scratched the surface of what is required. Any satisfactory language will have to take account of the fact that a niche is an abstraction, not a physical environment.

Moreover, a niche has to be described from the 'viewpoint' of a type of agent.

A part of a design may correspond to part of a niche (as lighting system, fuel delivery system and steering mechanism in a car each comprises a part of the total design meeting different sub-requirements). Within each sub-niche and sub-design further decomposition is possible, e.g. the lighting system includes control switches, wiring, lamps, reflectors, power source, etc. Some sub-systems may share components with others, e.g. the battery is a part of several different sub-systems, and therefore occupies several niches simultaneously.

Some aspects of a sub-niche may be defined by 'other' features of an agent – the same agent or other agents. For example, an individual that cannot think very quickly but lives in an environment in which things change rapidly may need the ability to solve some problems very rapidly without deep thinking[7].

The language for niches will have to evolve as our theories of possible designs evolve.

4.2 A Language for Formulating Designs

Much of the important specification of designs for behaving systems is concerned with what I have called [16] the 'information level'. This is

1. Below Newell's 'knowledge level' and Dennett's 'intentional stance' level of description
2. A level concerned with designs (i.e. part of Dennett's 'design stance') but also involving semantic content of information that is acquired, created, manipulated, stored, or used.
3. A level at which information can be processed without presupposing rationality (as Newell's 'knowledge level' and Dennett's 'intentional stance' both do. In particular, evolution or other designers can produce systems that work in given situations even though they are not rational, e.g. because they blindly follow rules. In particular, where an agent is part of a larger system, e.g. a society or a species, what is rational from the viewpoint of the larger system need not be rational from the viewpoint of the agent. This may be important in trying to understand features of motivation and personality in human-like agents. For example a concern with reproduction and care about one's offspring pervades human personality (well most human personalities, if not all), and yet from the point of view of an individual the cost of reproduction and caring for the young is so high that it is highly irrational, especially for women.

---

[7] A standard answer is pattern recognition capabilities.

4.3 A Language for Describing Mappings

We need to describe mappings between regions of design space and regions of niche space. For example, designs need to be evaluated relative to niches, but, as already indicated:

1. This will in general not be a simple numerical evaluation.
2. It will have to include descriptions of trade-offs, and possibly multiple coexisting partial orderings.
3. It may in some cases be related to evolutionary 'fitness' criteria, e.g. effectiveness in promoting survival and reproduction of a collection of genes, though other kinds of fitness will often be relevant.
4. It will not in general determine unique design solutions for particular niches (as shown by biological diversity).
5. It may have to include potential for future trajectories leading to a better fit between niche and design, either by individual development or learning, or by a succession of evolutionary stages.

All this may be a far cry from the current contents of AI books and journals. However, I expect it to be increasingly important over the next few decades, as more people come to understand the issues and grasp the shallowness and narrowness of much of current AI with its swings of fashion regarding particular mechanisms and architectures.

4.4 Resources and Methods for Exploring Agent Designs

It is commonplace for people in AI, and some of their critics, to make unnecessarily limiting assumptions about the methods, mechanisms or methodologies that can be used in AI.

1. AI can use whatever mechanisms will do the job: connectionist or neural mechanisms, chemical soups, or anything else. Restricting AI to use only a certain class of mechanisms would be like restricting physics to the experiments and mathematics available to Newton.
2. AI is not committed to the use of any particular class of representations. It is not committed to the use of logic, or Lisp-like languages. It is part of the aim of AI to find out which formalisms are well suited to which purposes.
3. It has been fashionable in recent years to criticize 'toy' problems (e.g. simulated worlds). However, working on carefully chosen toy problems is part of a 'divide and conquer' research strategy, required for science. Controlled simplification helps in hard science. Using complicated robot eyes and arms does not necessarily cause one to tackle deep problems, as many frustrated students have found.

One important sort of simplification is to study what Bates et al. [1] call 'broad and shallow' architectures, containing many functionally distinct components, each simplified. This may be one way of finding things out about some of the high level features both of design space and niche space (e.g. building systems and then discovering that they lack certain qualities that one had not previously realised were important). Even when we learn that certain architectures don't work, the study of why they don't work can be an important contribution to knowledge, and help us to a fuller appreciation of alternative designs.

Moreover, for us the broad and shallow approach is not a *permanent* commitment. It may help to clarify requirements for progressive deepening of the design. In some cases this can be done by incorporating what has been learnt via a narrow and deep approach. In other cases it may draw attention to what is missing from such an approach, e.g. a study of visual perception that assumes the sole function of vision is to produce information about the structure and motion of objects (criticised in [12]).

5   Expanded Objectives

Our explorations are both scientific and concerned with practical engineering applications.

5.1   Scientific Objectives Include

1. Trying to understand human capabilities
2. Trying to understand other animals
3. Trying to understand the space of possible designs and how they relate to different niches (capabilities, etc.)
4. Trying to understand which sorts of trajectories in design space and niche space are possible and under what conditions.

Too much AI work merely produces one implementation, without any analysis of the design, the region of niche space or alternative designs. However, this may suffice for certain engineering objectives.

5.2   Engineering Objectives Include

1. Trying to design useful machines that can do ever increasing subsets of what can currently be done only by humans and other animals.
2. Trying to design machines that (for certain jobs) are better than humans or other animals. Often these are not 'stand-alone' machines but components of other machines.
3. Trying to make machines better suited to interact with humans (this depends on learning more about humans).

Other, less obvious, practical objectives include:

4. Developing new educational strategies and technologies: you can't improve human learning without knowing how it works normally.

5. Understanding ways in which the human mind or brain can 'go wrong' may help us design better therapies. You can't easily fix something if you don't know how it works normally!

6. Designing new forms of recreation, new toys[8].

A requirement for progress in all of this is the production of better tools, and that has been a constant feature of AI research. So we can add:

7. Meta-design: Designing new tools and techniques, including programming languages and forms of representation, to help with the process of exploring and implementing designs.

6   The Cognition and Affect Project

The Cognition and Affect project at the University of Birmingham has been concerned with all the above issues for several years, although severely limited resources have forced us to concentrate our main efforts on tiny subsets of the task. The project has come up with some partial requirements for human-like designs, a preliminary partial specification of a type of architecture that might explain human like capabilities, and some preliminary attempts to map that architecture onto the phenomenology of common human emotional states, especially grief [19].

Our work has included the following:

• Collecting 'requirements' for human-like intelligence, such as:

1. The ability to handle multiple independent sources of motivation, some to do with physiological needs, some to do with the individual's preferences, tastes and ambitions, and some to do with the needs of the culture,

2. The ability to cope with many concurrent processes (perception, plan execution, planning, thinking, etc.)

3. The ability to cope despite limited multi-processing capabilities for 'high level' processes.

• Exploring a variety of designs and design fragments, including:

1. Attention-filtering mechanisms to 'protect' resource-limited management processes.

2. Motive generation and reactivation mechanisms.

3. 'Mood' changing mechanisms.

4. Meta-management mechanisms that help to control the resource-limited management processes.

5. Aspects of a control hierarchy that accommodates both long term and short term change.

---

[8] This depends on the scientific and engineering advances.

- Producing ideas that can influence therapies, e.g. for problems involving control of attention.

- Producing interactive demonstrations that might be used for teaching psychologists, therapists or counsellors[9].

Notes:

1. We are particularly interested in 'broad' architectures, so initially they are very 'shallow'. Deepening can come later.
2. Often the process of working out an implementation reveals inadequacies in theories, long before there's a running program to test! At present that's the most important role of implementation.
3. It's inevitably a multi-disciplinary exercise requiring contributions from philosophy, psychology, psychiatry, neuroscience, biology, etc.
4. It's very difficult!

More information is available from our ftp site:
    <URL:ftp://ftp.cs.bham.ac.uk/pub/groups/cog_affect>

6.1 The Minder Scenario

In order to focus our investigations and provide possibilities for useful implementation with restricted resources, we developed a specification for an extendable scenario in which to study some of the processes that interested us [2, 3].

The scenario involves a simple 2-D nursery (or creche) which has a collection of robot 'babies' (minibots) that roam around in various interconnected rooms, and a *minder*[10] with a mobile camera and a mobile hand or 'claw'. The minder has to look after the babies, keeping them out of various kinds of trouble and rescuing them when they get into trouble, until they develop to the point where they can leave the nursery.

Types of problems the babies can encounter include the following:

1. They can fall into ditches and die.
2. Their batteries may run down, so that they need recharging, at a recharge point.
3. If the charge gets too low, they die.
4. Overcrowding can cause some babies to turn into 'thugs', which then have a tendency to damage other babies.
5. Damaged babies need to be taken to the medical centre for repair.
6. If the damage is too great the babies die.

The scenario can later be modified in many ways. The babies can either move around at random or act on goals with some degree of intelligence, exactly what

---

[9] So far only very primitive implementations exist.

[10] In previous papers, we referred to the minder as a 'nursemaid'.

sort of intelligence determines the niche for the minder. The scenario can either have a fixed set of babies, all to be kept alive till they are ready to be discharged, or a steady stream of incoming babies, so that the minder's task is to maximise the rate at which mature surviving babies can be discharged. The minder might be given an auditory sense as well as the camera, e.g. so that sounds of trouble can trigger visual investigation. Predators could make the task harder, and so on.

Initially there was only one minder with a movable claw and a movable camera with a restricted view (e.g. limited to one room at a time). The minder had no other embodiment, since our main task was to design its mind, and that was a big enough task. The camera could look at one room at a time and be moved around, either at random, or by cycling around systematically, or under the control of an attentive process driven by current goals. Alternative more complex scenarios are being investigated. We are also looking at even simpler agents in the context of evolutionary experiments, led by Riccardo Poli.

We chose a simple world, with as little complication in physics, perception, motor control, as possible, because that's not what we are interested in. We are interested in the mind, and the control of the mind, and this environment was designed to give the mind some hard control problems.

Later work could add a more complex body e.g. with auditory sensors, a more complex shape, more parts for manipulating things, richer visual processing, and so on. Similarly the 2-D domain could be expanded to a 3-D domain, but that would enormously complicate problems that at present are not our main focus of interest. When the time comes we would expect to have to collaborate with a research group that has implemented a much richer 3-D world.

Another development is to have more than one minder, to introduce problems of communication and cooperation, both in planning and in acting. The babies could be given more intelligence and a wider range of personalities, perhaps even allowing some of them to learn to help with the minding (a possibility being investigated by my colleague Darryl Davis, who calls them 'minibots').

Even within a very simple 2-D world, the minding task can be made more or less difficult in various ways, e.g.

- changing the numbers of babies to be looked after,
- altering the relative speeds with which the babies can move and the minder's bodily parts can move,
- more interestingly, altering the relative speeds with which processes occur in the environment and 'mental' processes of various kinds occur in the minder, e.g. analysing perceptual input, generating new goals, evaluating the relative importance and urgency of goals, planning, etc.

The last is particularly important as one of our concerns is to see how requirements related to limited processing speeds for high level 'management processes' constrain the design of an architecture able to cope with asynchronous internal and external events[11].

---

[11] See, for example, [8, 10, 11, 3, 19].

The minder has a collection of different sorts of internal processes, all going on in parallel. Our specifications partly overlap the sorts of things described at the workshop by David Moffat and Bryan Loyall. The internal processes include things like:

- realizing that there is a need to consider some new goal
- deciding whether to consider a particular goal
- evaluating a goal in various ways, e.g. importance, urgency, cost, likelihood of success
- deciding whether to adopt or to reject a goal
- deciding when to act on a goal: meta-planning
- deciding *how* to achieve a goal: e.g. by planning, or selection of an existing plan
- detecting and resolving conflicts between goals and plans
- carrying out a plan and monitoring progress

Some of these tasks turned out to have unexpected complexities. Urgency, for example, turned out to include both 'terminal urgency' of a goal which is a measure of how much time is left before it is too late, and generalised urgency which is a function from length of delay to costs and benefits. E.g. generalised urgency may be cyclic: the benefits may go down then up according to time of day, or the season (e.g. planting grain) [3].

It also turned out that there was no fixed sequence in which management tasks needed to be performed, so that a simple flow chart was not adequate. E.g. sometimes a goal can be evaluated and a decision made whether to adopt it prior to any planning, whereas in other cases at least partial planning may be required to evaluate costs and benefits and potential side-effects[12].

These 'management' processes take time, and some of them take unpredictable amounts of time. Many of the problems would be simplified if the minder (or a person) could think with infinite speed. But our assumption is that in human-like agents there are reasons why processing resources, at least for a subset of the cognitive tasks, will be limited, and the amount of parallelism will be limited.

The limits to parallelism were first observed empirically and informally. Later we found a number of *design* factors explaining why it is to be expected that the amount of concurrency in management processes should be limited. The reasons are summarised in the appendix.

Our SIM_AGENT toolkit [18] was designed to support exploration of interacting agents with rich internal architectures in which we could vary relative processing speeds between objects and agents and between components within an agent. The toolkit makes it easy to change the speeds of sub-mechanisms within a simulation, both inside the mind and in the simulated environment.

One of our conjectures is that where some of the high level 'management' processes (such as occur in humans, though not necessarily in microbes or ants or rats) are limited in both speed and amount of parallelism, an extra level is

---

[12] [3] gives more details.

required in the architecture, which provides what we call 'meta-management' processes, recursively defined as processes whose goals involve management or meta-management tasks. Because the definition is recursive we don't need meta-meta-management mechanisms etc.

For example, a meta-management process might detect that a planning process is taking so long that an urgent goal will not be achieved, and decide to switch the management process to carrying out a partial plan in the hope that the plan can be completed later. Another might detect that the rate of occurrence of new problems is so high that switching between management tasks is preventing any significant progress. This could lead to raising of an 'interrupt' threshold for new goals or other information. Hence the dynamic attention filter in the architecture sketched below.

7 Towards a Broad Architecture for Human-like Agents

AI researchers cannot work on everything at once. Many rightly choose to work on narrow and deep mechanisms, e.g. concerned with vision, or planning, or learning, or language understanding. My main concern is how to put all those mechanisms together. So, like the OZ group at Carnegie Mellon University, I have chosen to concentrate on architectures that are initially shallow but broad, combining many sorts of functionality. Later research can gradually increase the depth, which would simultaneously involve increasing the complexity of the environment making the added depth necessary. We can also later increase the breadth, e.g. adding components to the architecture corresponding to evolutionarily older parts of the human brain that we share with many other animals, but which for now we are ignoring (e.g. the limbic system).

In any case, whether an architecture is a close model of any living organism or not, its study can contribute to the general exploration of niche space, design space and their relationships.

It is not possible here to give a full account of our work. So I'll summarise some of the main assumptions regarding the sort of architecture we have been studying (though alternatives are also under consideration).

7.1 Automatic Processes and Management Processes

It seems clear that there are different routes through human brains from sensors to effectors, from perception to action. Some of these routes seem to be shared with other animals, whereas others involve forms of cognition that may well be unique to humans, or at least restricted to a small subset of animals. The latter probably evolved much later.

Automatic, pre-attentive, processes. In particular, the older routes involve many automatic processes. These can be thought of as essentially being a large collection of condition-action systems which are probably implemented in neural nets, permitting a lot of parallel propagation of activation through the networks. The processes are 'automatic' in the sense that as soon as the conditions for some action occur the action (whether internal or external) is triggered.

Examples include low-level perceptual processing, posture control and many other processes triggered by perception, including internal perception of things like temperature changes, damage to tissues, the need for food or liquid, and other body states. These pre-attentive processes can trigger other pre-attentive processes.

Some of them can generate output, both in the environment (e.g. reflex actions, trained responses) and also internally, e.g. controlling internal states, such as generating new desires and driving learning mechanisms.

Attentive management processes. Other routes from perception to action, at least in humans, include processes that are not automatic in the following sense. When triggering conditions for an internal or external action occur the action does not automatically happen. Instead alternative possibilities are considered explicitly (e.g. doing A or not doing A, using this plan or using that plan) and then a choice made between them. Sometimes very elaborate temporary structures (e.g. new possible plans) have to be created and evaluated as part of this process. In addition arbitrarily complex sets of previously stored information may need to be accessed and derivations made, combining old and new information. In general these processes involve combinatorial search: attempts to find combinations of ideas, or actions that will enable some problem to be solved or task to be achieved. Thus, there is not only selection between complete alternatives: many fragments of a solution may require choices to be explicitly constructed and selections made.

The mechanisms forming the implementation for the attentive management processes may themselves be automatic pre-attentive mechanisms. Something has to work automatically or nothing could ever get started.

Besides the functional differences just described it is possible that management processes and automatic processes use different kinds of representations and different sorts of control mechanisms. For example some neural nets provide mechanisms for mapping inputs in one space to outputs in another space, where both spaces have fixed dimensionality and well defined metrics. This could be very useful in automatic processing, though not so useful in problems requiring creation of novel structures of varying complexity.

The distinction between management processes and automatic processes is indicated crudely in Fig. 2 (due partly to Luc Beaudoin and Ian Wright). The distinction is neither sharp nor very well defined yet. We cannot have good concepts and distinctions until we have a really good theory. In deep science, concepts and definitions come after theory. In shallow science, we often start with operational definitions so that we can get on and measure things, instead of thinking, which is much harder. So in what follows I am using provisional terminology that is part of a boot-strapping process of theory building and concept formation.

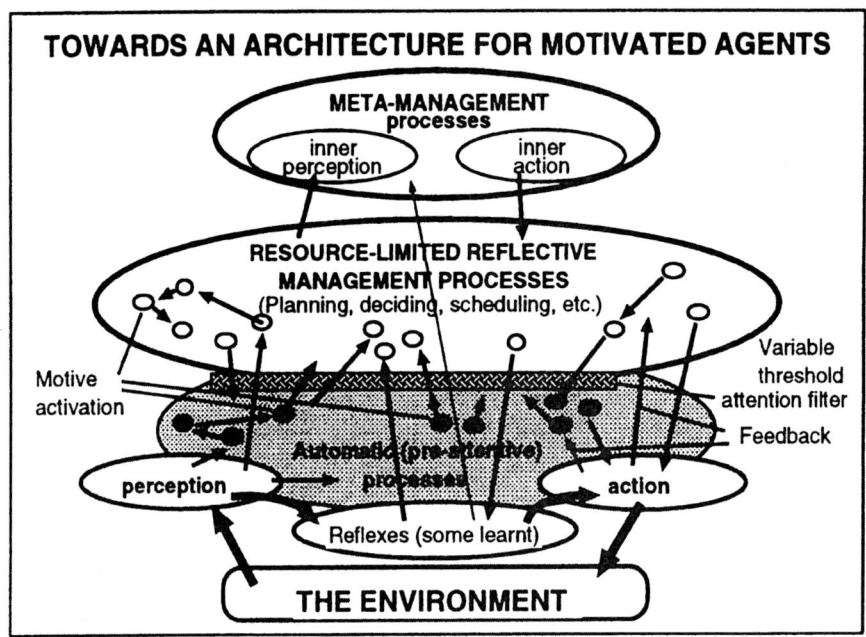

Fig. 2. Towards an Intelligent Agent Architecture

There are several layers of control, involving different routes through the system, from perception to action. Some evolved very early and are shared with many other organisms. Some are newer, and less common.

It seems to be a feature of management processes in humans that they are resource limited, unlike the automatic processes. It is as if the automatic processes have pre-allocated, dedicated, portions of the brain and they can operate whenever they need to, whereas different management processes have to share and re-use relatively slow mechanisms, so that parallelism is restricted, as explained in the appendix.

For example there are different kinds of mental tasks we can perform e.g. counting to oneself, reciting a poem to oneself, counting backwards from 10,000, singing a song silently to oneself, and so on. But we are not able to do several of them fluently in parallel, even though we can alternate between them, and even though there are some things we can do in parallel, e.g. hopping, clapping our hands and talking.

Because both the amount of parallelism and speed of management processes are limited, an interrupt filtering mechanism may be required, to prevent disturbance when the management current task is both very important and very urgent, or likely to fail if temporarily disrupted.

Although some new goals are automatically generated and automatically acted on in the 'older' part of the brain, concurrently with management processes, some tasks (e.g. those requiring planning or investigation) need to be handled by the management system. If they are both urgent or important, this may require interrupting and suspending or aborting some other activity.

Since such interrupts are not always desirable, one way of limiting their potential damage is to have an interrupt filtering mechanism with a dynamically varying threshold. This requires the automatic mechanisms to assign some measure to new goals which will determine their ability to get through the filter. I have called this the *insistence* of a goal. Insistence is one among many features of goals and other information structures controlling processing.

7.2 Processes Involving Motivators

There are many different sorts of processes involving motivators. Motivators are information structures with the potential to initiate or modify internal or external actions, either directly (in the case of innate or learnt cognitive reflexes) or as a result of processes of explicit evaluation of the motivator, acceptance of it, formation of a plan, and plan execution. The following seem to be among the internal behaviours concerned with motivators, which synthetic human-like agents with personalities will require.

- Motivator generation and (re-)activation and setting 'insistence' (interrupt capability).
- Mechanisms to suppress or 'filter' motivators, to protect resource-limited management processes.
- Management of motivators can include the following.
  - Assessing motivators. E.g. importance, likelihood of satisfaction, cost of satisfaction, urgency.
  - Deciding: whether to adopt the motivator, i.e. form an intention.
  - Scheduling: when or under which conditions to execute a motivator.
  - Expansion: deciding how to execute a motivator (planning).
  - Predicting effects. This can occur as part of evaluation or planning or other processes.
  - Assigning an 'intensity' measure. This is not the same as insistence: it influences the ability of the motivator to maintain control once it has gained control.
  - Detecting conflicts between motivators.
  - Detecting mutual support between motivators.
  - Setting thresholds for the management interrupt filter.
  - Termination of motivators. E.g explicit termination on satisfaction, or decay.
  - Detecting the relevance of new events to existing motivators.
- Meta-management: I.e. processes that (recursively) control management or meta-management processes (e.g. deciding which to do when).
- Execution of plans, with or without high level management.

- Learning: improving or extending performance, improving methods for assigning insistence, for assessing urgency or importance, for choosing in cases of conflict, etc.
- Extending the architecture: developing new abilities, or new 'cognitive reflexes'.
- Global switches or modulators: e.g. mood changes, arousal changes, e.g. becoming optimistic and bold, or turning pessimistic and cautious.

7.3   Representing Motivator Structure

In order to be able to engage with all these different kinds of processes, motivators need a rich structure. They often include the following components, though they may have other specific features also. Some of these will vary over time, whereas others define the motivator and are fixed.

1. Semantic content: for example a proposition, P, denoting a possible state of affairs, which may be true or false.
2. A motivational attitude to P, e.g. 'make true', 'keep true', 'make false', etc.
3. A rationale, if the motivator arose from explicit reasoning.
4. An indication of the current belief about P's status, e.g. true, false, nearly true, probable, unlikely etc.
5. An 'importance value' (e.g. 'neutral', 'low', 'medium', 'high', 'unknown'), importance may be intrinsic, or based on assessment of consequences of (doing and not doing).
6. An 'urgency descriptor' (possibly a time/cost function).
7. A heuristically computed 'insistence value', determining interrupt capabilities. Should correspond loosely to estimated importance and urgency. This is used only for attracting attention.
8. Intensity – determines whether a motivator that has already been attended to (thought about, acted on) will continue to be favoured over others that may be considered. This gives motivators a kind of momentum.
9. Possibly a plan or set of plans for achieving the motivator.
10. Commitment status (e.g. 'adopted', 'rejected', 'undecided').
11. Dynamic state (e.g. 'being considered', 'consideration deferred till...', 'nearing completion', etc.).
12. Management information, e.g. the state of current relevant management and meta-management processes.

In most animals, as in current robots and software agents, motivators probably have a much simpler structure. We need to explore the possibilities for a variety of different types of motivator structure. These will require differences in motive generation, in management processes, in meta-management processes and in execution processes.

There may be individual differences among humans too.

Exploring 'design space' will help to show what is possible.

8   Deepening the Design: Visual Perception

Figure 2 is in some ways misleading as it suggests that components of the architecture have a simple structure. In particular, boxes concerned with perception
need to be far more complex than the figure indicates. Attempts over many
years to model visual perception have suggested that at least for a human-like
visual system something with the sort of complexity indicated in Fig. 3 may be
required.

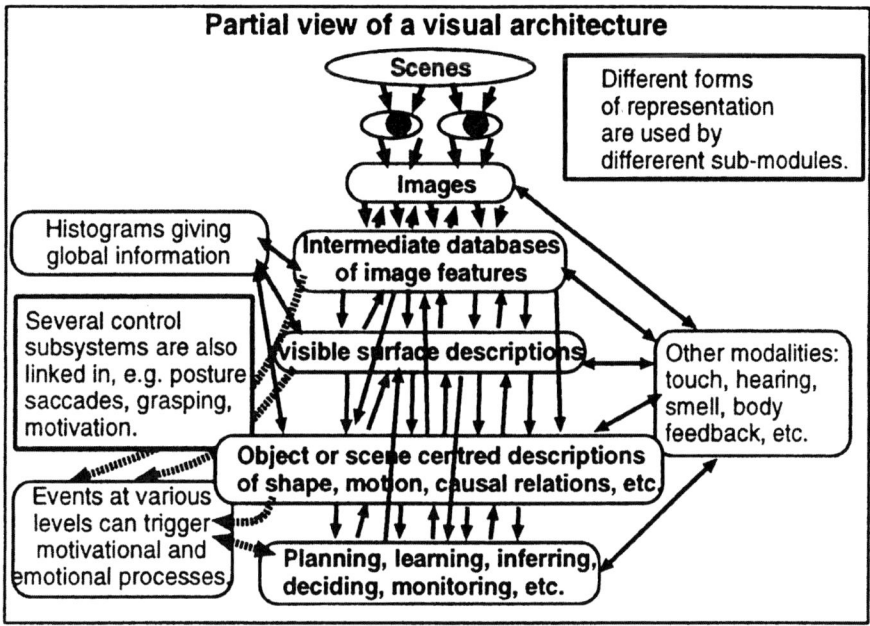

Fig. 3. Sketch of a visual sub-architecture

For example, perception is not just a matter of recognizing patterns in the
sensory input. Different levels of analysis are required. In the case of speech
this is very obvious: besides the acoustic signal there are levels of interpretation
concerned with phonetics, word recognition, syntax, semantics and what the
speaker intends to achieve (sometimes called 'pragmatics').

In the case of vision there is often, though not always, a requirement to go far
beyond the 2-D structure of the retinal image or the optic array and find the 3-D
structure of the environment [6] and many non-spatial properties and relations
of objects including their causal relations and potential for change, what J J
Gibson referred to as 'affordances' [12]. For example, I need to be able to see
not only that a surface is flat and horizontal, but also that I can sit on it and it
will support me and I need to see a cliff as potentially dangerous.

Besides the internal complexity and variety of tasks in visual processing mechanisms, they also have many links to other sources of information besides the visual images. For instance visual processing can be influenced both by input via other current sensors (what is heard or touched) and also by general knowledge about the type of thing being seen. Moreover, instead of having only one form of output, descriptions of spatial structure and motion, as Marr suggests, visual mechanisms may also have many outputs of different sorts to other submechanisms, including posture control and some motive generators. Some of the cross links merely transmit control signals, whereas others transmit information about contents of intermediate databases, or about the environment.

Vision is a primary example of the claim that there are myriad routes through the system, including many routes through the automatic processing mechanisms serving many different purposes, including controlling breathing, heart rate, posture, sexual arousal, various sorts of attraction or disgust, and no doubt many things we don't yet know about.

Visual input is only one modulator of posture. Some aspects will be partly a result of physical structure, e.g. congenital deformities, or a person's height relative to most doorways or other individuals. Other aspects could be due to early childhood experiences, e.g. having a brutal, easily provoked, parent might lead to the development of a very retiring and diffident posture. Visual processing that triggered reminders of unpleasant interactions could influence posture, e.g. producing a tendency to cower, in parallel with more common posture control signals.

Much of the detail concerning what sort of processing occurs and which cross links occur will be very dependent on individual experience, and will form part of a unique personality. An architect will see a building differently from its occupants. Perception of spiders affects different personalities in different ways.

So personality is not just a feature of some high level control mechanism, but is distributed throughout the whole system. Moreover, there isn't *one* thing that is distributed - personality is multi-faceted as well as distributed. That is one of the reasons why it is so hard to change: there is so much to change.

9   Control States in an Intelligent Agent

I have tried to indicate this in Fig. 4, which is an impressionistic diagram intended to suggest dynamic aspects of the human-like architecture, namely existence of different levels of control, with varying types of influence, different life-spans and different degrees of ease of change.

The dark circles represent an event stream, whereas the unfilled circles represent control states, some long term, some short term, some specific and goal-directed (such as desires), some more global (such as moods). Some of the events are physical, e.g. being struck by a falling apple, others mental, e.g. being struck by a thought. Control states are subject to some influences that are bottom-up (event driven) and others that are more top down, e.g. the influence of a longer lasting or more general control state, including aspects of personality.

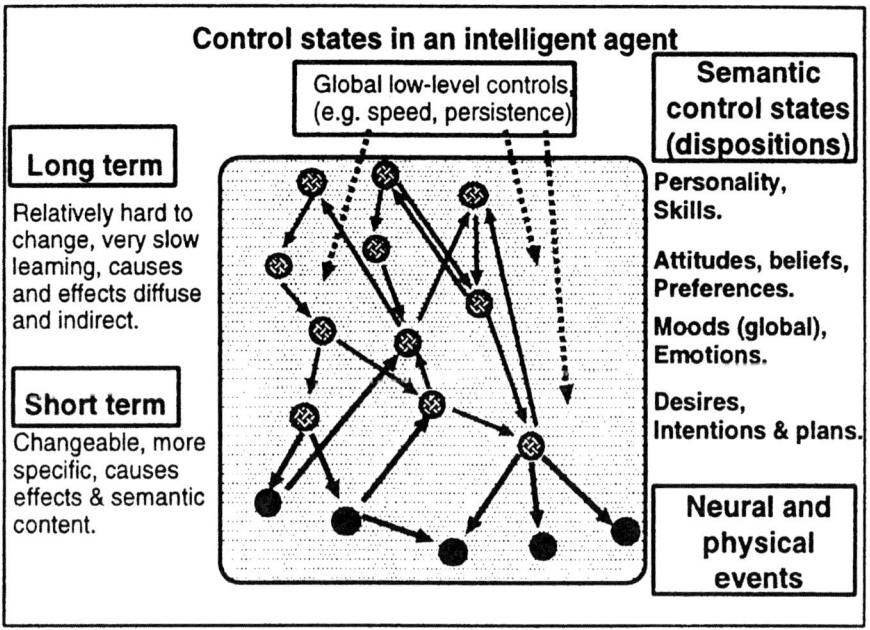

Fig. 4. Control states of various kinds: see text.

A very sudden and intense pain in the hand may produce very specific and short term manifestations, e.g. movement away from the source of the pain. However, a very long lasting intense pain might cause all sorts of complex processes, including going to a surgical specialist, taking drugs, reading about neuroses, etc. (Are such differences in effects produced by similar mental states also found in other animals?)

Some of the mental events and enduring states have semantic content (e.g. attitudes, desires) while some (e.g. moods, states of arousal) merely modulate processing locally or globally, e.g. speed, risk-taking, alertness, amount of deliberation prior to action. The modulation may be quantitative (e.g. speeding up, slowing down) or structural (e.g. switching from one strategy or language to another).

Arrows represent causes of differing strengths and differing time-scales, some deterministic, some probabilistic. Various routes through the system are causal influences linking events and enduring but modifiable states.

The distinction between automatic and attentive processes can be made at all levels in this diagram.

Unfilled circles at lower levels in the diagram are supposed to represent control states that influence events fairly directly, and which are typically also readily changeable from one moment to another, e.g. how thirsty one is, or whether somebody has annoyed one so much that one just wants to walk away.

Higher up the system are things which are more indirect in their influences and also capable of having a broader range of influences, for instance tastes in food or music, or political attitudes. These can influence events only indirectly, via changes to dispositions lower down the system - e.g. creation of new motivators.

A control state is *dispositional* insofar as it can exist without producing any actual change in the event stream, until the conditions are right for it to do so[13]. For example, the brittleness of glass is capable of determining how it breaks, but can persist for a long time without producing any particular manifestation, until the glass is struck hard. Similarly many dormant mental states produce no effects until the conditions are right.

Some of the 'higher level' states also have a very general range of potential influences, whereas others are more specific. For example, a state of nervousness that controls my current posture is very specific. By contrast, my preference for old-fashioned movies as opposed to new ones will not directly influence specific items of behaviour. It might sometimes get me to board a train to go and see some movie I have heard about. At other times, it might make me look closely at something, e.g. a poster advertising a film show. At some other time, it may make me go to a library to read a book.

High level control states can evolve. For instance tastes in films may develop over time. These changes need not be manifest. A high level dispositional mental state S may be changed in such a way that if some new information comes up later S will produce behaviour different from what it would have produced if it hadn't been influenced earlier. Yet the change need not actually be manifested for a long time, if ever.

The fact that some dispositions are never manifested, because their activating conditions do not occur, or because other things suppress their influences does not mean that they do not exist. They are merely dormant.

Moreover, internal influences, when they do occur, need not lead to external signs. People with a lot of self-control often have states that do not manifest themselves externally, whereas others reveal nearly everything. This is another aspect of personality: how much and what sort of control exists over expression of current thoughts, desires, feelings, etc. This can have an important effect on social relations, via complex social feedback loops.

These differences between different levels in the control hierarchy do not correspond in any direct way to the difference between management processes and automatic processes depicted in Fig. 2. Differences in level of the sort discussed in this section can occur in both the management processes and the automatic processes. Understanding these issues requires far more exploration of design space and types of control architectures.

10 Problems in Defining 'Emotion'

One manifestation of personality is the variety of emotional states an individual is capable of. However, discussion of that is bedevilled by the fact that the word

---

[13] This was one of the main themes of Ryle ([7]).

'emotion' has such a wide variety of uses. There seem to be as many different definitions of 'emotion' as there are people claiming to be studying emotions.

At one extreme are people who write as if every motive is an emotion, if it's a strong motive. For instance, for such a person a strong desire for promotion would be an emotion. I'd call it a motive.

Another kind of extreme view defines 'emotion' in terms of particular mechanisms of the brain, e.g. the limbic system. This focuses attention on a concept of emotion that can apply both to humans and many other animals with whom we share an ancient evolutionary history.

Others define 'emotion' in terms of external behavioural manifestations, e.g. whether the corners of the mouth go up or down, whether tears come out of the eyes, whether an aggressive or cowering posture is produced, and so on.

Some define it in terms of the things which are at the boundary between internal and external processes, e.g. muscular tension, proprioceptive sensory information, galvanic skin response, and so on.

In my own work, I have concentrated mainly on a subclass of emotional states that seem to be common in humans but may not occur in all other animals. These are states that deeply involve high level cognitive processes and which are often socially important, for example grief, anger, excited anticipation, dismay, pride in achievement: the kinds of emotions that poets and novelists write about.

These are all states in which there is a partial loss of control of high level cognitive processes. These are clearly included in common non-technical uses of the word 'emotion', but to avoid confusion with other technical definitions our project often uses the word 'perturbance' to label such phenomena. The word is intended to resonate with the concepts of 'perturbation' and 'disturbance'.

10.1   An Example of Perturbant Emotional States

I once heard a woman interviewed on the radio who was talking about her grief. Her teen-age son had been killed in a road accident a year before.

She did not talk about the state of her limbic system, nor about whether her muscles were tense or not, nor her facial expressions, or her posture, nor whether she was sweating or not. What she talked about was her state of mind.

One of the themes that kept coming up was the extent to which she was unable to control her own mental processes. She was constantly drawn back to thinking about this child, about what he would have been doing now, about whether she could have prevented the accident, about whether to keep his room as it was when he died, as opposed to letting one of the other children move in and use it. Her inability to control what she was thinking about meant that she could not pay attention to normal tasks and carry them out properly.

She found this inability to get on with her life very debilitating. It made her miserable, and it affected other people also. She could not do most of the other things she was supposed to do, including looking after her children. And that made her very depressed.

She was grieving, and she was depressed, and she felt guilty about her inability to cope and she desperately wished her own life could end somehow, though she did not wish to take it herself. So she had several emotions piling up on top of one another.

The possibility of several different sorts of mental states occurring simultaneously, is one of the kinds of consequences of the type of architecture I have been talking about, whereas some theories of emotions claim that only one can occur at a time. The links between the architecture and states like grieving is discussed more fully in [19].

Grieving is not the only case. I suspect most people have experienced such states. For instance, a person who has been humiliated by someone else, or who made a fool of himself in public may remain concerned about it for some time after, not in the sense that they simply wish it had not happened (which seems to be Frijda's sense of 'concern' in [5]), but in a stronger sense: it holds their attention. They can't put it out of their mind. They are drawn back to it, even when they don't wish to be.

Anger is another common example. Consider someone who has done something that you did not like. It stopped you in achieving your goal. You may wish he hadn't done it. You may wish to do something in return to stop him doing it to you again. However, merely desiring revenge is not yet the sort of perturbant state I am talking about, though it is an aspect of anger. In addition you may find that you are partly out of control. The desire to get your own back is something you can't put out of your mind. It continually tends to draw your attention away from other things. However that is a dispositional state, and like other dispositions it may temporarily be swamped by more powerful influences, e.g. seeing a child in sudden danger.

I suspect that such states cannot occur in most other animals. Although they may share the states and processes that occur within what I have called the 'automatic' part of the architecture, they do not have the sort of architecture that makes it possible for them sometimes to be in control of their thought processes and sometimes not. A rat may sometimes be terrified, but can it lose control of thought processes if it never has control?

10.2 Why do Perturbant States Occur?

The possibility of perturbant states is inherent in the sort of architecture I have been discussing, though not because the architecture evolved in order to produce perturbant states. Similarly the possibility of thrashing is inherent in many multi-processing computer operating systems, but not because that is something intended by the designers. The possibility *emerges* from other functional aspects of the design.

In this case we have management mechanisms whose parallelism is limited, and consequently they need to be protected by some kind of filtering mechanism. I've suggested that new motivators (and other information items) may be assigned a level of insistence which determines their ability to get through the filter and interrupt management processes. Because the insistence level is assigned by *automatic* processes it may not be possible to prevent a high level of insistence being assigned to goals that have already been rejected, or which conflict with some high level objectives.

When attention is frequently interrupted and held by items that have been assigned a high insistence level which is *inconsistent* with goals or strategies selected by the meta-management processes, then the agent has partly *lost control* of his or her thought processes.

A full account of such perturbant states would show how they are dispositional states that can persist even though temporarily dormant because other more insistent and more acceptable thoughts and goals grab and hold attention [11, 19].

11 Conclusion

This exploration of niche space and design space and their relationships is a multi-disciplinary affair, and includes not only: exploration of various architectures, mechanisms, formalisms, inference systems, and the like (aspects of natural and artificial designs), but also the attempt to characterize various kinds of behavioural capabilities and the environments in which they are required, or possible.

I do not believe we can understand human personality except in the context of a study of possible designs for human-like agents in human-like niches. This study is also a prerequisite for constructing synthetic agents with aspects of human personality, attitudes, emotions and motivation in synthetic agents. In this and other papers I have tried to show how such features may be explained on the basis of an underlying information processing architecture and its design requirements.

The implications of such a study are profound: e.g.

- for engineering,
- for biology,
- for psychology,
- for philosophy,
  and
- for our view of how we fit into the scheme of things.

12 Acknowledgements

This work was supported by the UK Joint Council Initiative, the Renaissance Trust, and a grant from the University of Birmingham.

I am grateful to Robert Trappl and colleagues at the Austrian Research Institute for Artificial Intelligence. In particular Gerda Helscher prepared the transcript of my talk and the discussion from the audiotapes.

Thanks to Luc Beaudoin, Ian Wright, Tim Read, Christian Paterson, Chris Complin, Riccardo Poli, Darryl Davis, all past or present members of the Cognition and Affect project at Birmingham. Additional papers by the group can be found at the ftp site:

<URL:ftp://ftp.cs.bham.ac.uk/pub/groups/cog_affect/0-INDEX.html>
or via this Web page:
<URL:http://www.cs.bham.ac.uk/%7Eaxs/cogaff.html>

A   Discussion

What follows is an edited transcript of the discussion leading on from the talk. Some parts of the tape were very unclear and some of my editing may be wishful thinking. The transcript has not been checked with other participants, and as I do not have access to the original audio tapes I may have taken some wrong decisions regarding ambiguous or incomplete portions of the transcript. I have moved some portions of the discussion back into the main paper, where they seemed most relevant.

Editor's note: for reasons already phrased by the author, the discussants have been anonymized (D:).

A.1   Metric for Success of the Design

D: What's the metric of success for the design of the minder?
Sloman: At the moment, we don't have any well-defined notion of success for our experiments, but you could easily use a measure of how many babies the minder manages to keep alive over a period of time.

For the existing simple implementation, we can vary the relative speeds of (a) movements of the babies (b) movement of the minder's hand, and (c) internal processing in the minder. We then find that, for instance, for some settings, it's impossible to keep even more than two babies alive, and for other settings more babies can be kept out of trouble, though that depends on the initial geographical distribution of the babies and their behaviour, which has random elements.

Another sort of evaluation, which would be appropriate when we have a full implementation including the meta-management processes, would be to see what happens when we make external events generate new goals faster than they can be handled by the management processes, and then see whether introduction of meta-management processes improves success at keeping the babies alive.

A.2   Physical and other Resource Limits

Several points of clarification emerged regarding the claim that management processes were resource limited.
D: ...contrast with automatic processes that you could do, many of them at one time?
Sloman: That's the point. There's, as far as I know, no particular reason why parallelism should be limited in the pre-attentive parts of the architecture. Whereas physical limits, such as having only two hands ...

D: That's right. That's right. That's all I was getting at. There are physical resource limitations.

Sloman: Yes. On the other hand, for a distributed robot, even that might not be the case. You might have a robot with many hands, like an octopus, doing many things at once, which would have fewer physical limits to parallelism than we have.

But I am not talking only about physical resource limits. I am talking about limitations of information processing resources.

An interesting question is whether it is just a fact of how we evolved that we have these resource limits, or whether there are good design reasons for this[14].

In this case, I think there are good design reasons for limits to parallelism.

One of them has to do with the fact that if you want to learn from what you do, you had better not do too many things at once, or you will have to solve a complex credit assignment problem, i.e. deciding which combination of what you did was responsible for the good or bad things that happened unexpectedly. The number of possible combinations is an exponential function of the number actions, and can therefore rapidly become intractable, especially where effects can be delayed.

Another type of limit may arise from the need for a long-term memory store, which is content-addressable and makes use of a highly parallel associative engine, but can only be given *one* question at a time to answer.

Another type of limit may be concerned with the requirements for building temporary structures of unbounded complexity, during planning and problem solving.

Another may be due to the need to have a single coordinated process at the 'top level' to reduce the risk of independent sub-processes taking mutually inconsistent decisions ([9], chapters 6 and 10).

There may be other reasons, design reasons not accidents of history, why sophisticated agents are limited in the number of 'management' tasks that they can do simultaneously.

The more automatic processes are not limited in their parallelism because they don't access common information stores, and they don't do sophisticated learning, and they don't have to build temporary structures of unknown complexity in re-usable workspaces. Notice that I am not saying that automatic processes never build complex structures: visual and language understanding processes almost certainly do. It may be that one effect of certain forms of training is the allocation of dedicated portions of the automatic mechanisms to tasks which thereafter can run in parallel with higher level processes. Learning to sight-read music is a spectacular example.

When the circumstances are appropriate, the automatic, mechanisms just get on with their tasks, with minimal mutual interference.

The meta-management processes, that I mentioned earlier, have to do with working out what to do next within this resource limited system. And one dif-

---

[14] That's always a good question to ask whenever you discover a fact about human psychology.

ference between different architectures might be whether meta-management is present or not.

If we had good ways to study mental architectures, we might find out which organisms do and which do not have architectures of the types discussed here. I suspect we will find many organisms that share with us only what I have called the automatic processes. But my impression is that very few species also include the attentive management processes and the meta-management processes for controlling them.

Perhaps even birds that perform complex nest-building tasks have only automatic mechanisms that respond to triggers and produce stereotyped responses, unlike a human house builder who sometimes explicitly considers alternative structures, alternative materials, and alternative construction sequences before acting.

Perhaps only a few other species, e.g. bonobos, chimps and nothing else, have such meta management processes. Perhaps only humans have them.

So, this whole approach defines a research programme for biologists.

A.3   How is Filtering Implemented

D: Can you say a little bit more about internal perception and internal action, or —

Sloman: Preferably not right now. Ok? Because there is just too much.

By the way, David Moffat mentioned the filtering mechanism, which his system doesn't need, though I have claimed it is needed because some new goals need to be able to interrupt management processing whereas others should not.

Now, I have a totally open mind as to how that's implemented. It might be implemented by neural nets, which don't have an explicit filter, but just allow certain subnodes to become active under some conditions and not under others, because of the operation of excitative and inhibitory links.

Alternatively there might be a separate mechanism with an explicit threshold set by higher level processes.

The important point is not how it's implemented, but the sort of function that is needed within the total architecture.

D: Can you try ... to explain the requirements for the nursemaid project, characterizing that as some kind niche that will then require certain kinds of design to give us a sense of what you are doing.

Sloman: At the moment, the niche for the minder is rather simple. But it has a number of features which were chosen to drive the research.

One is that the world has a number of different things happening independently, which are capable at any time of generating new goals. So it's not like a system where you have a 'user' giving a command, and the system makes or selects a plan and after completing it comes back for the next command, like a simple computer interface. The minder, like a typical windowing interface, must have asynchronous perceptual monitoring of the environment, concurrently with everything else that's going on inside it, e.g. planning, problem solving, etc. So, that's an example of a requirement that forms part of the niche.

Another requirement is that the speed at which things happen in the environment should be such as to make these internal resource limits significant, so as to show up the need for an internal architecture that gets round the problem of the resource limits.

What that means is that you can't have a system which deals with each new goal by immediately investigating fully what its potential consequences are and what the costs and benefits of achieving it are, and deciding whether to adopt it, and if so when and how it could be achieved, and so on.

That is not possible because such processes could interfere with other important current planning or deliberation processes. This would not be a problem if management mechanisms supported unlimited parallelism or had no speed limitations, or if things happened so slowly in the environment that all internal processes could run to completion in any order without opportunities being missed.

Another requirement was that the environment should be unpredictable. That means that the system cannot decide in advance when to interrogate the environment and build that into its plans. That is why asynchronous concurrent perceptual processes are needed.

Gap in transcript due to tape change.

In a slightly more sophisticated simulated world, the minder might be aware that something over there is crying for help, but it does not know what or why, or where exactly. So it now has a further task, which is deciding whether to go and find out exactly what the problem is. This contrasts with the simplest version where the minder always knows exactly what the problem is, and its management task is deciding whether to act on this problem or another problem, or how to achieve particular goals, e.g. helping a baby with low charge recover by taking it to the recharge point, or picking up and moving a baby that has got too close to a ditch.

The current domain gives the minder a small collection of requirements to be satisfied, subject to trying to keep as many babies out of trouble as possible. Those requirements already make our design problem non-trivial, but we can go on adding more requirements. For instance we could add the requirement to be able to cooperate with another minder, in order to be able to do things sensibly. For instance, if there are two minders and two babies are in trouble, the minders shouldn't each go to the baby nearest to the other minder.

A.4   Comparison with Real-time Scheduling Systems

D: ...(??)...that's the kind of problem that's solved better by a computer dedicated to doing real-time scheduling, and not by a person.

So, what is it about this problem of trying to schedule these different tasks, that is so particular to humans?

Sloman: If you have a computer of infinite speed, there will be infinitely many different designs that will all be functionally equivalent. Ok?

D: Ok, you have some optimal conditions of performing these various tasks?

Sloman: I am not defining a notion of optimality. I am assuming that there is going to be a certain minimal architectural structure, because I think that's how we (humans) do things. I then try to see how to make that work.

But I am perfectly open to someone else deciding to explore different sorts of assumption from the sort we are talking about, or even running genetic algorithms to see what would evolve naturally in a whole variety of situations. Maybe we will find a collection of different solutions, or solutions which work in different ways.

One of the things about the mapping between niche space and design space, which was on the slide is that there are different styles of arrows, because there isn't a simple notion of a design fitting or not fitting a niche. There may be different ways of fitting and many trade-offs.

You may have something that works very well under normal circumstances, but perhaps a slight change of circumstances makes it go wrong, and other designs which don't work as well in normal conditions, but work better in abnormal conditions. Similarly one design may be better as regards speed or precision, and another may be less costly in fuel, or easier to build.

So, there is a whole variety of different kinds of issues. And I suspect we don't yet understand what all those issues are. So, we have to explore that. That's a partial answer to your question about alternative solutions.

A.5 Predictability and 'Cognitive Friendliness'

D: Did I understand you right that you said the environment should be unpredictable?

Sloman: Not that it *should be*. It *is*. And we want to try to understand what the implications of being able to deal with an unpredictable environment are.

D: Are you saying this environment (i.e. the minder scenario) is unpredictable?

Sloman: Yes. The minder does not know what each baby is going to do.

D: Yes. But you have a lot of these constraints. You know that they won't be in that other room.

Sloman: It's partly predictable. Yes. Every environment is partly predictable. In fact, I believe that is in part a result of co-evolution between us and our environment.

D: I think that this is what makes you able to live at all, these persistent features of the environment.

Sloman: Yes. I have a concept of the cognitive friendliness of the environment. There are different dimensions of cognitive friendliness.

Some of them have to do with the availability of detailed information. So, for example, if we didn't have all this electromagnetic radiation bouncing off the surfaces of things onto detectors in our retinas which are very well tuned to those frequencies, the environment would be cognitively less friendly to us than it is.

Another type of cognitive friendliness concerns the amount of information and the complexity of processing required to discriminate objects, and whether the physical structures of objects that are importantly different in their behaviour are hard to differentiate. For instance, suppose some trees produced edible fruit and others produced poisonous fruit and the only way to tell which was which was to count the leaves on the whole tree to find whether the number was odd or even. That would be cognitively unfriendly.

But by and large, things evolve so that this sort of case does not occur. So, yes, you are right, our environment not totally unpredictable.

A.6   How Many Levels of Management

D: (transcript unclear) raised a question about the meta-management processes being defined recursively, and how many levels of management might be required.
Sloman: In practice, the recursion probably runs out after two or three steps.
D: Yes. So one got this feeling that you have, that that is sufficient independent of the niche characteristics. Is that because you have performed an exploration of a large number of what niche spaces might be? Or just sort of a priori –
Sloman: It seems to me to be an empirical fact that we have something like this meta-management ability. Up to a point it works. However, I would not say it's *sufficient* in any general sense, because it doesn't solve all the problems.
D: So, you think that the niches that people actually encounter seem to motivate these three levels and nothing more. But an exploration of more different niches might lead to additional aspects of architecture.
Sloman: It might. But some of those additional aspects could require more concurrency at management levels, which I have claimed we don't have, for reasons explained previously.

Thus limits to concurrency could rule out coexisting processes involving management, meta-management, meta-meta-management, etc.

But of course, if you build a robot system, you might be free to put together whatever mechanisms you like, and you might find a totally different architecture, which, for instance, was much better than the sort of mechanism I have discussed. The control system required for a complex automated factory might be an example of a different sort of architecture.

So, I regard it as an open question, whether certain niches which are in some ways like ours, but in some ways different, would require very different architectures. And maybe even for niches like ours, there may be different successful solutions – different sorts of mind.

A.7   Why Filtering is Needed

D: So, the meta-management was supposed to identify processes that are identified with control, self-control.
Sloman: Processes that control management or meta-management.
D: So, this is your explanation for human emotion being –
Sloman: Oh, I haven't said anything about how meta-management relates to emotions.

I previously talked about the grieving mother, not being able totally to control her thought processes. And, that's linked to the fact that we need the attention filter, or something equivalent to a filter, which means that not every new *potential* user of high-level resources will automatically get those resources.

We can imagine designs which once they have started to attend to a problem are never diverted from it until that problem has been solved. But such single-mindedness could be disastrous in cases where something more important and more urgent turn up. So new motivators should be able to capture attention and re-direct management processes sometimes.

However, we can't just let every new motive have that effect, because the management processes have limited parallelism and some tasks are urgent and important and intricate, requiring full attention to all details. I don't want the brain surgeon who is operating on my brain to be distracted by every sound or thought about whether to have a holiday in Spain. Similarly if someone is giving you intricate instructions on how to defuse a deadly bomb, you had better listen all the time, because you might miss some crucial information otherwise.

So, we want to allow the possibility of interruption of high-level management processes, but we also sometimes want to prevent that. And that's where this notion of dynamically variable filtering mechanism comes from.

Exactly how it varies is an open question. I originally started with the idea that that a simple one-dimensional threshold might be enough, but Luc Beaudoin, in his PhD thesis suggested that instead of a simple numerical filter something more qualitative would be required, so that, for example, the whimpering of a baby, however quiet, could divert attention even when much louder noises from the kitchen could not. The type and level of threshold would then be determined by meta-management processes that determine whether the current management tasks should be easily interruptable.

A.8 Insistence Levels are Unreliable

The automatic processes that generate new potential distractors and assign insistence values to them cannot themselves be fully intelligent, because they would themselves then need all the resources that the filter mechanism must protect from disruption. So the insistence assignment mechanisms must use 'quick and dirty' heuristics which give an approximate estimate of importance and urgency, perhaps based on previously learnt patterns. So they will sometimes get things wrong, allowing dysfunctional types of interrupts to occur.

How insistence assignments occur and what sorts of filter thresholds are set up in various kinds of circumstances will be yet another way in which personalities can vary.

It seems that many - not all – but many of the things that we call human emotional states are cases where something continues to grab attention, whether you want it to or not. Now, sometimes you don't mind because there is a kind of pleasure in being partly out of control. E.g. sometimes being passionate thought to be a good thing. Or people put themselves on roller-coasters, where they get into a situation where they are partly out of control, and they do it freely. There are all kinds of strange things people like to do to themselves.

So, I am claiming that the aspect of emotional states which I call perturbance, which has to do with management processes being partly out of control, can occur only in the context of an architecture with sufficient richness to support the possibility of management processes being controlled, so that on some occasions that control can be lost. That seems to require meta-management processes that can monitor, and evaluate and control management processes.

And I don't believe our architecture is the only one or the right one, though it does seem to make sense of such processes. There may be other architectures which could do just as good a job, or a better one.

A.9   Could Current Network Server Architectures Suffice?

D: I have a comment, and I think it's worth looking at it just a second:

If you go back to the babies problem, I am pretty convinced after that comment that you could probably formulate that as a network server model for real-time systems. There's nothing in that that's particularly unusual: you have got resource limitations, you have got reconfigurable networks. You might have a very complicated system, but you are basically serving customers.

And if you allow this system to run in an experimental situation for some period of time, you can probably collect enough statistics to define your heuristics or optimizations, or your local optimizations, that will give you a static state behaviour. Well, if you don't have static state behaviours, then you either have a situation where everyone is happy, or where someone is frantic or desperate, if you want an emotional content. But there's not anything in your example which I find to violate the kinds of formal models that people already use for those kinds of situations. In other words, I am not convinced that this has to be approached as an AI problem, first.

Sloman: Well, there are networks where there is a lot of distributed control about routing. We are not talking about that. We are talking about something like, say, a file-server, which is serving lots of different computers.

So, the next question is, how many different sources of motivation does your network server have.

D: Well, all those things that can request output, each of which is like a baby.

Sloman: Right. So, we have a class of requests for some services, which can arrive asynchronously and have varying importance and urgency.

D: Yes, it may have finite buffers, which, if they overflow, it's equivalent to death or injury.

D: I think maybe there is a better problem domain which would express your ideas better, because –

Sloman: There may be millions of analogous problem domains. But the question I was going to ask was, where does the need to plan come into the network server?

D: It depends on whether you believe the problem has a solution, in which case you try to perform an optimization, or whether you simply do the best you can.

It seems to me that there are just numerical algorithms, or statistical algorithms, to maximize the likelihood of successful operation.

Sloman: What I am claiming is that a human being, in this situation, will find things difficult. And that's partly what I want to explain.

I am not trying to find an optimal engineering solution to the problem. If I were I would be looking for a different sort of architecture with different sorts of mechanisms.

D: Right. You wouldn't consider an architecture with a planner, and then a planner and a meta-management.

You would collect statistics, trying out a few ways of doing the plans, figure out the best strategy, on the basis of the distribution of baby arrival times, and distribution of baby death times.

Sloman: Yes, and in fact, a real nursemaid might actually eventually learn some of that, and use that to control fast heuristics for deciding what to do. Learning of that kind is something that we eventually need to build into our system.

Such mechanisms, designed by evolution and tuned by adaptive processes in individuals, could play an important role in the automatic processes that we share with other animals. But they are not flexible enough when you need to deal with circumstances that can change too much for statistical adaptive processes to cope, e.g. because you need to be able to construct new plans, make complex inferences, form complex new systems of concepts.

The niche to which a human architecture is fitted is far more complex than a typical network server's niche, at present anyway.

D: But is it so complicated that you need this kind of system. Or is there a point at which you can just have this kind of scheduling system, which is optimized under these conditions do this.

Sloman: No matter what the external problem is, there will always be an architecture that solves this problem quite differently from the way we do, by having very much faster processing internally, and different kinds of memory, or whatever. So, to that extent, I am not claiming uniqueness.

D: Yes, I meant, the distinction is not to solve the nurse-maid problem, to create the optimal nurse-maid. The goal is not to make that particular nurse-maid work well, but to make the nurse-maid that's ... (tape not clear)

Sloman: And if it turns out to be too easy to do it in the nursery domain, I have indicated that there are lots of ways of making the environment more complicated, and more like real human life.

However, I regard as obviously false the claim, fashionable in some quarters, that human-like intelligent agents never have to do any explicit plan construction and problem solving prior to performing actions. For example before coming to this workshop I had to explore alternative dates and modes of travel and create a plan, including deciding whether to go to the airport by train, coach or car. That took time and interfered with other activities, such as planning lectures, etc.

So the kind of niche that defines our research problem *requires* the minder to be able to perform planning tasks that take time, even if a competent engineer could find a solution for *this* simple domain that made use of pre-stored plans and condition-action rules.

A.10   How Should an Artificial Domain be Evaluated for Realism?

D: Well. You will have to be able to evaluate whether this is or isn't comparable to humans. You need some kind of metric given this artificial world, saying what is or isn't, comparable, and saying what a human would do under these circumstances.

And given it's not an optimization problem, where you can say you have or haven't got an optimal solution, what sort of things are you using to develop intuitions for saying whether the decisions you have made are the ones that a person would make?

Sloman: I don't have any direct answer to that. First of all, there is no such thing as *the* decision a person will make, because people are all different. So, there might be classes of decisions, and we might have to find a framework within which one –

D: But you have to be able to say that this time it didn't make the right decision . . . and say: something is missing from the architecture.

Sloman: Yes, and you might say that the reason it did not make the right decision is the same as the reason why a human being in the same situation might not make the right decision.

So, it made a 'right' decision in terms of the time pressure.

D: Allowing for that, you have to be able to characterize what's happening.

Sloman: Sorry, I started by making the negative point about the difficulty of making the comparison with humans, which I shouldn't have done. It's a distraction. And I'll now try to give the positive answer.

First, at a lower level, we have direct ways of evaluating the system in the way you are asking for e.g. by asking human beings to drive the simulation and comparing their behaviour with that produced by a software system.

We also have indirect ways, which will take a long time.

One of these indirect ways is by looking to see how well this framework generates new explanations for things that psychologists and psychiatrists and social workers and teachers are concerned about.

So, for example, recently, with two of my students, I produced the previously mentioned paper on emotions like grief [19]. What triggered this was my reading an autobiographical report of a particular experience of intense and long lasting grief, written by someone whose much loved friend had died following a long illness.

In our paper we made a first shot at trying to show how the phenomena might come out of something like our architecture. In fact, the process of doing that forced us to pay attention to some things missing from the architecture, including support for experiences of pleasure and pain, and certain kinds of self-consciousness and self-evaluation, to define what it meant to be in control of one's own thought processes.

This led to further developments in the design, though not yet to implementation. Thus comparison of a model with detailed phenomenological reports is one sort of evaluation.

Another is what happens when I show a paper like that to experts from other fields, e.g. clinical psychologists. To my pleasure and surprise, some of them are already saying, that the paper is relevant and helpful to them. In fact, when it was read by the editor of a journal on Philosophy, Psychology and psychiatry, he immediately wanted to publish it. That does not prove that our ideas are correct. It's only a partial initial indication that we may be making progress in a useful direction.

I regard this as a kind of indirect test, which doesn't say our ideas are right. It just says that we seem to have some useful ideas that other people haven't got. But it may turn out that something else is even better. And that's how I think all science goes. You never can prove anything conclusively correct or incorrect: you can only gradually get closer and closer to accurate theories.

A.11 Testing by Running a Simulation

D: So, you point to some event that's happened in a simulation. And you say: why did this happen? You may find as well as getting behaviour that seems to correlate with what people do, you also observe behaviours that don't correlate with what people do. And you may find an explanation in terms of some features of the architecture. Will you then go to a psychiatrist and say, do you ever come up with an example of this?

Sloman: We might. And that would be interesting. However, as I explained previously I think the problems we are addressing are enormously complex and certainly will not be solved in my lifetime. Moreover our current thinking may be limited by our current understanding of architectures mechanisms and formalisms.

So for some time I don't expect that the main form of test will come by studying the actual behaviour of a working implementation of our ideas. Rather, an earlier phase, the mere task of planning the implementation is making us discover gaps in our thinking, making us understand the problem better, sending us back to the drawing board to extend either the requirements specification (the niche description) or some aspect of the design.

For that we don't need implementations yet, though we do need to be trying to produce them.

However, implementations also have a cosmetic value. People will pay more attention to our ideas if we can show them something working. It proves it's not all empty hand-waving if it can drive development of a real implementation, unlike many so-called theories. And we also hope eventually to produce a nice teaching tool for psychology students and others.

D: But don't you get something out of running the implementation?

Sloman: I will get nothing out of running it, I think. That's my guess.

D: ...

Sloman: Well, what I really want to do, is explore and understand design space. When I said I get nothing out of running it, that was a bit extreme – certainly it has some impact on our thinking.

And we may well get surprising behaviour. We may have to say, oops, there is something we haven't thought about, which we have to get back to and try to understand.

But equally, I personally don't want to do a long line of experiments comparing an implementation with human behaviour when I know in advance that there will be large discrepancies because our implementations in the foreseeable future will be very much oversimplified, and also because people are so variable.

I regard it as more important to do a deep analysis of the problem, asking what effects differences in designs will have in different situations. E.g. how will they affect speed or correctness or precision of performance? I always want to move up to a higher level of understanding of what's going on, and then perhaps do some tests to see whether the understanding is right. But mainly that test will consist in seeing whether the ideas are implementable.

But I don't simply want to run a lot of tests to see what the program does if, instead, I can formulate theoretical predictions of what the architecture is and is not capable of. Of course, sometimes we get useful surprises from running the programs. But that in itself will be of no value, unless it can be related to a theoretical explanation of what's going on. When you have understood something general, as a result of that surprise, that will be of value.

A.12 Can the Architecture Model Different Personalities

D: A different question: Given the architecture you propose, how do you start to model different personalities? Will they be just variations of the different components, like the way you said the filter, or the change of management strategy, or would it be something that would be completely different?

Sloman: In a real biological population, which is to have a social structure and a lot of cooperation, the same general system has to generate some differences within individuals to start with, e.g. to support divergence of function in the society.

Some of these differences will then be amplified by differences in individual experiences, e.g. either growing up in Vienna or growing up in an African jungle, or whatever.

Although there may be minor variations within the architecture, I would expect many different kinds of personalities to be accommodated within the same general architecture, e.g. different sorts of motive generators, different strategies for evaluating and comparing motivators, different ways of assigning priorities and thresholds, different meta-management strategies, and also many differences within the pre-attentive automatic part of the architecture, about which I have said very little because that's not the main focus of my research.

In the long run, we need to explore types of genetic differences in human beings and see whether we could find ways of implementing them. That raises many interesting questions: What is it that makes some of us want to be surgeons, and others want to be philosophers, while some people are happy to be airline pilots or bus drivers? There clearly are different kinds of life-styles and life preferences.

I do not claim that this is all genetically determined. It depends also on the extent to which individuals absorb information and strategies from the environment, e.g. how they generate new perceptual categories and new motivators, or motivator-generators, or motivator-comparators through the process of growing up in a particular culture. Some of these may be regarded as a change of architecture, e.g. acquisition of new types of abilities and new links between components. Remember that personality is not one thing but a large collection of information and control structures distributed throughout the system.

That's really long term research.

I suspect we can explain within our general *sort* of architecture some very interesting individual variations in terms of the kinds of ways different things are valued, and how different agents react to the same situation.

There won't be enough variety in our little toy domain to support all of that. We would need a much richer scenario to support individual variations of the sort that humans have, including different environments in which they develop. There may be a large set of detailed problems that each individual has to solve because of the structure of the environment and which produce long term changes affecting future processing and behaviour.

So, a full study of personality would require us to investigate the whole range of different ways in which individuals can vary, both genetically and in their development, despite sharing a common generic architecture, at least at birth.

Whether and how we will ever be able to implement them, I don't know. Only a tiny subset will be done in my life-time, that's for sure.

References

1. Bates J., Loyall A.B., Reilly W.S. (1991) Broad agents. Paper presented at AAAI Spring Symposium on Integrated Intelligent Architectures. (Available in *SIGART BULLETIN* 2(4) Aug. 1991 pp.38–40

2. Beaudoin L.P., Sloman A. (1993) A study of motive processing and attention. In: Sloman, A., Hogg D. Humphreys G. Partridge D., Ramsay A. (eds.) *Prospects for Artificial Intelligence*, IOS Press, Amsterdam, pp.229–238

3. Beaudoin L.P. (1994) *Goal processing in autonomous agents*. PhD thesis, School of Computer Science, The University of Birmingham

4. Cohen J., Stewart I. (1994) *The collapse of chaos*, Penguin Books, New York

5. Frijda N.H. (1986) *The Emotions*, Cambridge University Press

6. Marr D. (1982) *Vision*, Freeman

7. Ryle G. (1949) *The Concept of Mind*, Hutchinson

8. Simon H.A. (1967) Motivational and Emotional Controls of Cognition. Reprinted in: *Models of Thought*, Yale University Press, pp.29–38

9. Sloman A. (1978) *The Computer Revolution in Philosophy: Philosophy, Science and Models of Mind*. Harvester Press (and Humanities Press), Hassocks, Sussex

10. Sloman A., Croucher M. (1981) Why robots will have emotions. In *Proc 7th Int. Joint Conf. on AI*, Vancouver

11. Sloman A. (1987) Motives Mechanisms and Emotions. *Cognition and Emotion* **1** (**3**), pp.217–234,
    Reprinted in Boden M.A. (ed.) *The Philosophy of Artificial Intelligence*, OUP, 1990

12. Sloman A. (1989) On designing a visual system (Towards a Gibsonian computational model of vision). *Journal of Experimental and Theoretical AI,* **1**(**4**), pp.289–337

13. Sloman A. (1992) Prolegomena to a theory of communication and affect. In: Ortony A., Slack J., Stock O. (eds.) *Communication from an Artificial Intelligence Perspective: Theoretical and Applied Issues*, Springer, Heidelberg, Germany, pp.229–260

14. Sloman A. (1993) Prospects for AI as the general science of intelligence. In: Sloman A., Hogg D., Humphreys G., Partridge D., Ramsay A. (eds.) *Prospects for Artificial Intelligence*, IOS Press, Amsterdam, pp.1–10

15. Sloman A. (1993) The mind as a control system. In: Hookway C., Peterson D. (eds.) *Philosophy and the Cognitive Sciences*, Cambridge University Press, pp.69–110

16. Sloman A. (1994) Semantics in an intelligent control system. *Philosophical Transactions of the Royal Society: Physical Sciences and Engineering* **349**, 1689, pp.43–58

17. Sloman A. (1995) Exploring design space and niche space. In: *Proc. 5th Scandinavian Conf. on AI*, Trondheim, IOS Press, Amsterdam

18. Sloman A., Poli R. (1996) SIM_AGENT: A toolkit for exploring agent designs. In: Wooldridge M., Mueller J., Tambe M. (eds.) *Intelligent Agents Vol II (ATAL-95)*, Springer-Verlag, 392–407,
    (Also Cognitive Science technical report: CSRP-95-4)

19. Wright I.P, Sloman A, Beaudoin L.P. (to appear) Towards a Design-Based Analysis of Emotional Episodes. With commentaries. In: *Philosophy Psychiatry and Psychology*

Personalities for Synthetic Actors: Current Issues and Some Perspectives

Paolo Petta, Robert Trappl

Austrian Research Institute for Artificial Intelligence*, Vienna, and
Department of Medical Cybernetics and Artificial Intelligence, University of Vienna
{paolo, robert}@ai.univie.ac.at

1 Introduction

The content of the present volume depicts a lively area of research where a number of impressive results have already been achieved and successfully carried across to commercial applications. As illustrated in the overview given in the introductory chapter, these efforts were originally motivated by a wide variety of different objectives, which in turn fostered the exploration and adoption of a whole spectrum of personality engendering architectures and processes. Resuming and furthering this discussion, we will now proceed to analyse the current limitations and shortcomings of the various approaches and point out possible directions to extend the cover functionalities or amend existing problems. Adding to that, we will give a brief description of some further lines of research which we expect to become of practical relevance in this area, thereby suggesting starting points for future directions of research, in which interdisciplinary efforts will continue to play an essential role.

If we now pick up and continue to follow the thread laid down in the first chapter, we find two dimensions along which to structure our comments. The first one concerns the different kinds of basic approaches to how to create synthetic actors with personalities: here we will contrast lines of research applying detached drama-theoretic techniques "from the outside"—where actors are seen as remotely controlled puppets engaging in fictitious interactions—to such that pursue the modeling of characters endowed with a "self" and which typically draw upon results from physics, biology, and the cognitive sciences. Within this second group, we will then make a further distinction: surface models are aimed at achieving external behaviours and display of traits which convey the impression of believable personalities, thus placing the emphasis on achieving the effect of a believable performance, if possible under preservation of real-time responsiveness and performance. On the other hand we find the deep generative cognitive models, in which issues such as emotions and personality are not considered and covered as ends to themselves, but rather are integrated in the respective architectures as necessary components for the achievement of rationality and social competence.

* The Austrian Research Institute for Artificial Intelligence is supported by the Austrian Federal Ministry of Science, Transport, and the Arts.

2   Issues in Drama Theory Approaches

The applications developed by David Blair [8] and Barbara Hayes-Roth [26] are situated in the domain of virtual drama. In this context, the principal interpretation of cyberspace is as a medium of artistic expression, to be used to convey the conceptions of some author to the recipient spectators or, respectively, the participating, engaged users of the systems. As an important resource to achieve this goal, they tap into the pool of techniques offered by the research area of drama theory. Drama theory is a generalisation of game theory and decision theory, in which the metaphor of drama (explained in the following) is applied to human interaction [5]. The resulting drama theoretic analyses focus on how characters frame, resolve and are transformed by interactions, paying also particular attention to the issues of irrationality and emotions.

One particular aspect we want to briefly go into in this context is the important distinction between the frequently confused concepts of *drama* ("the doing thing"), which designates an activity, and *theatre* ("the seeing place"), which essentially describes a finished performance. The technologically mediated shared experience of a virtual environment is closer to an active play than the passive consumption of a canned presentation. Consequently, a straightforward application of established traditional stage techniques to virtual reality settings is often inappropriate, because the latter are more process-oriented and as such not directly comparable to theatre or film. This is also why *improvisation*—dramatising freed from the strait-jackets of precisely prescribed scripts—has been proposed as the most promising candidate for successful supervised activities in virtual worlds [4, 27].

While David Blair's work anticipates and calls for the development of tools for human users aiding in the development of adequate solutions, the efforts of the group led by Barbara Hayes-Roth challenge quite directly the present limitations of natural language understanding and, in particular, natural language dialogue systems. It will be interesting to see how the safe and narrow boundaries of the scenes inspired by the commedia dell'arte and classical drama that are presently covered in the Virtual Theater project can be expanded in the future. In particular, this will mean tackling the problem of having to integrate deeper or in any case more comprehensive knowledge about the fictitious world the improvising agents "act in" and world knowledge of the human spectators with the current abstract and shallow representation in terms of scripts and traits. At present, the latter solution not only suffices but indeed *succeeds* by virtue of the very detachment of the underlying agents from what (also) to them is but a staging, however, to paraphrase the closing remark of [26]: "Just how far can you get by acting *only*?", i.e. without common sense [13] or world knowledge [24]. It would seem that the integration of at least some of these properties will be inevitable in the (not so) long run.

3   Issues in the Shallow Representation of Emotions

Virtually all of today's implemented performing systems featuring synthetic actors endowed with first person point of view reduce the concept of *personality* to some kind of a "deliberate misinterpretation", namely solely to *behaviour*. Frequently the scope is narrowed even further to cover only individual behaviour, while behaviour of populations (social behaviour, territorial behaviour in animals, etc.) is by comparison all but neglected. The embodied folk psychology stereotypes captured in theories such as the cognitive appraisal theory of emotion described by Ortony, Clore, and Collins [38] and implemented by the research groups at CMU [31] and NYU MRL [23] fall mostly into this category: they achieve efficient surface modeling at the cost of the danger of encountering breakdown situations entailed by the well-known brittleness that comes along with it. On the other hand, a big alleviating factor in this particular kind of applications is given by the circumstance that the coverage obtained by basic attitudes and behaviours can be expected to be broad enough to ensure that such breakdowns will occur only rarely. Furthermore, as illustrated in [20], reducing environmental dependencies to a minimum permits to build up quite large numbers of emotion-induced actions (well over a thousand in the given case) without having to worry about unintended side-effects and interdependencies. In addition to that, advantage can be taken of the user's presupposed goodwill, who in general will not expect "living" entities—and "animals" in particular—to react properly and understand everything all the time (cf. "Why Julia Wins" in [22] for a more detailed discussion of related aspects).

In spite of all these assets, these architectures do remain limited to essentially "canned" performances and competence. In this regard, an often voiced criticism referring to the Tok architecture used to animate the Woggles in the Edge of Intention scenario [42] concerns its lack of dynamic and autonomous extension of the available collection of explicitly modeled behaviours. This limitation comes from the difficulty of arranging for "interesting" situations that can be recognized by the virtual actors and which lead to the acquisition of behaviours which are also understandable and "interesting" for the human user. First solution proposals to this big obstacle have now been appearing especially in the research area of embodied systems, discussed below.

The specific problems encountered in the distributed deployment of object oriented approaches, as is the case for the inverse causality technique used in [23], have also been extensively discussed. The recent advent of more adequate support for the development and maintenance of ontologies and efforts towards the realization of interlinguas and facilitator/mediator services will contribute to the amelioration of this situation.

4   Issues in Generative Architectures for Emotions

4.1   Virtual Embodiments

Work on deep or generative models of personalities is being carried out following both bottom-up and top-down approaches (or even combinations of the two). Either one can exploit today's achievements in "virtual biomechanical engineering" which, as illustrated in the pertinent chapters [2, 47, 35], has reached a very high level of fidelity that is increasingly being matched by other system components based on mathematics and natural laws, such as the modeling of elements of the environment and synthetic sensing. It has become increasingly evident that these sophisticated models provide essential contributions for the progress of research in the area, as the virtual embodiment of synthetic characters provides an (and, given the current state of the art in the natural language processing area, we may well even dare say: *the*) important means of conveying information about their internal state (but see also e.g. [31] for effective circumvention of the current impasse). As such, the (geometric) rendering of the synthetic actors forms one of the main means for evaluating the performance of an application. Conversely, the availability of virtual sensors complements the crucial role of the embodiment of an architecture according to the ever more widely accepted paradigm [45, 12, 17] (the related additional insight that emotions are an integral necessary part of rationality is discussed below).

Successful re-use of components (e.g., the Edge of Intention user interface developed in the Oz project and Ken Perlin's procedurally animated actors, both of which have been used in the context of the Barbara Hayes-Roth's Virtual Theater Project [26]; or the motor system of the Hamsterdam architecture [10] used in PHISH [43]) not only allows single research groups to concentrate their research on focussed topics, it also ensures that the results are tied into a generic shared framework and thereby goes some way towards preventing overspecialization (and possibly even effective decoupling) of architectural elements. Yet another benefit results from the existence of interface specifications to functionalities provided by "lower" subsystems, as they entail constraints on design choices for the implementation of higher level cognitive modules. The resulting close integration of all parts of an architecture also addresses the issue of avoiding arbitrariness in design decisions, and thereby does away with one of the two major causes of the often-criticised "boxology" design approaches (see also below). Finally, the openness of the resulting systems, namely their compatibility stemming from the use of shared or similar interfaces to the simulated environment, is indeed nothing less than a necessary precondition for any research in the field of social phenomena, which governs the area of personality theory.

For all these opportunities and help provided by the available physical models, the real difficulties and challenges now lie in the explicit modeling of those parts of the individual systems which are to supply the actual "personalities". We hasten to stress that this separate discussion of this particular topic is not intended to run counter to our position exposed above, in which we advocate the importance of a unified treatment of physical and cognitive aspects (where the latter includes emotion as part of rationality)—the different personality engendering machineries may be integrated with (or even include) the bodily subsystems to any degree, and actually will have to be, as perhaps already well illustrated by the documented effects of different parametrizations of the Sense-Control-Act loops on the "personality" expressed in Jack's walking gaits alone [2] and exacted by e.g. de Sousa's and Damasio's theories discussed below.

4.2 Generative Architectures

The paradigm shift advertised by the introduction of artificial life as new research area has also brought about fundamental contributions to our subject domain, raising the attention to issues of relevance for the modeling of whole populations and, consequently, of social behaviours. The coverage and performance achieved by bottom-up approaches has been continuously expanded, as for instance exemplified by the line of research being pursued at different laboratories at MIT. The development of action selection algorithms [32, 33] which was related to work on behaviour-based systems [12] with additional important inspirations from [36] was followed by a computational framework and its instantiations [9, 10] which also integrates important findings from the area of ethology [48, 29, 30, 3]. Recent efforts now start to make first breaches into the barrier of solely animalistic behaviour, e.g. endowing synthetic characters with more sophisticated ways of acting in order to achieve their goals [43].

On the opposite front, the difficulties encountered with the top-down design of formal models of generative personality processes have been widely acknowledged, e.g. as in the following quote from [21]:

> ... We are dealing with a *weak* theory, as opposed to the *strong* theories often found in physics and other hard sciences. As Cohen and Nagel pointed out, in order to deduce the proposition P from our hypothesis H, and in order to be able to test P experimentally, many *other* assumptions, K, must be made (about surrounding circumstances, instruments used, mediating concepts, etc.). Consequently it is never H alone that is being put to the test by the experiment—it is H and K together. In a weak theory, we cannot make the assumption that K is true, and consequently failure of the experiment may be due to wrong assumptions concerning K, rather than to H's being false. ... In other words, failure does not lead to any certain conclusion. ... Psychology also needs a similar concentrated effort involving what Kuhn calls "the ordinary business of science," in order to resolve the many anomalies still remaining. [p.250]

We already pointed out in the opening chapter of this volume how similar critical attitudes played an essential role as motivation for the research carried out by Aaron Sloman [44] and Dave Moffat [37]. As discussed in detail in their respective papers, an important problem in devising comprehensive cognitive architectures lies in the danger of unwarranted overspecialization: this state of affairs may already come about just as a consequence of the holistic approach which opens up a plethora of opportunities for arbitrary design decisions. However, there already do exist some attempts to alleviate the present lack of methodologies and associated tools[2], providing support for principled designs [1]. Recent results from neurophysiology contribute with additional design constraints as the hypothesis of the existence of numerous emotion systems is corroborated. These systems are being mapped to structures of emotionally relevant brain pathways, e.g. the fear system of the human brain detailed in [19].

5 Outlook

In this concluding section we touch upon some other recent results which we see as holding great promise to provide valuable contributions to our area of research. This will also allow us to point out interesting directions for future investigations. Perhaps the single most important development in recent years is the increased awareness of the relevance of a different kind of "holism" than the one mentioned previously, namely of the tight interrelationships between the environment, the "body" and the "mind" of a cognitive entity [45, 12, 17] (following the earlier works including [49, 34]). In particular, the *design stance* [18]—i.e. viewing rationality as the solution to certain design problems—has proven a fruitful source of guidance and inspiration for a multitude of lines of research. Theoretical analyses such as [45] and [17] provide a valuable and continuously growing "checklist" of relevant phenomena to be covered as well as characterizations of the performance of the human system in coping with these problems. For instance, Damasio's "somatic markers" point to one approach to attack the issue of how to characterize *states*, a necessary precondition for learning (see e.g. [11]).

In the same context, the understanding gained from rigorous investigations into indexical "first person point-of-view" [28] is of obvious relevance. With the availability of applicable formalisms these results will readily be taken into account in the design of future architectures. As another example taken from the area of learning, the results concerning situated cognition obtained from experiments with physically realized three-level-architectures (e.g. [46]) should also be find consideration in the virtual domain.

Concurrently, fundamental critiques to established approaches and techniques along with proposals of alternatives e.g. [7] replenish the pool of resources to tackle current impasses with—take as an example the issue of what Mark H. Bickhard terms *system detectable error*, "representation must be capable of being in error in such a way that that condition of being in error is detectable by the agent or system that is doing the representing" [6]) and which John L. Pollock [39, 40] approaches as *defeasible epistemic reasoning*, "reasoning can lead not only to the adoption of new beliefs but also to the retraction of previously held beliefs" [40].

---

[2] E.g. in the form of executable specification languages [14, 16] which have already been successfully applied in some investigations (e.g. [15]).

The family of belief-desire-intention architectures has been the focus of intensive research over the past years [41, 50, 51, 25]. We expect that implemented frameworks such as the OSCAR architecture [40] interfacing "epistemic" and "practical" reasoning while also providing support for the inclusion of so-called "quick and inflexible" black-box modules implementing heuristics and skills should quickly attract the interest of members of our research community. To appropriately cover all aspects of personality as a social phenomenon it will furthermore be inevitable to broaden the view from the current focus on how "everyone is different" to also cover how some individuals out of a larger group are the "same" and what basic commonalities are shared by all individuals. This in turn entails a number of additional requirements to be added to the research agenda, including the provision of virtual environments that are complex and persistent and the implementation of synthetic characters which can "interface" to these worlds and which exist over extended periods of time.

The issue of communication—especially in terms of natural language dialogue—presently is the area that is arguably in the most dire need of substantial progress. At the same time, the increased availability of high-quality testbeds might prove a decisive contribution towards the solution of present difficulties.

6 Concluding Remarks

We would like to conclude our observations with a call to stay on the lookout for yet other fields and disciplines which have not been considered in the given context up to the present time; the examples contained in this volume showing how results from diverse areas— including e.g. ethology and drama theory—can be successfully exploited document the high returns that can result from such interdisciplinary efforts. At this connection we would like to also extend a special invitation to readers from such other areas who have come to flip through these pages asking them to bring in their knowledge and expertise into what we think today can be rightfully considered as one of the most exciting scientific meeting grounds.

Acknowledgements

The authors gratefully acknowledge the support and valuable inputs provided by Erich Prem and Arthur Flexer.

References

1. Agre P.E., Rosenschein S.J. (eds.) (1996) *Computational Theories of Interaction and Agency*, MIT Press, Cambridge, MA
2. Badler N., Reich B.D., Webber B.L. (1997) Towards Personalities for Animated Agents with Reactive and Planning Behaviors. In: Trappl R., Petta P. (eds.) *Creating Personalities for Synthetic Actors* (In this volume)

3. Baerends G.P. (1975) An evaluation of the conflict hypothesis as an explanatory principle for the evolution of displays. In: Baerends G.P., Beer C., Manning A. (eds.) *Function and Evolution in Behaviour*, Clarendon Press, Oxford

4. Benjamin I., Cooper M. (1995) Actors, Performance and Drama in Virtual Worlds. In: *Proceedings of Computer Graphics International '95*, Leeds, UK, June

5. Bennett P., Howard N. (1995) What is Drama Theory?, Management Science Dept., Strathclyde University

6. Bickhard M.H. (1995) Interaction and Representation, Department of Philosophy, Lehigh University, Bethlehem, PA

7. Bickhard M.H., Terveen L. (1995) Foundational Issues in Artificial Intelligence and Cognitive Science, Elsevier Science Publishers

8. Blair D., Meyer T. (1997) Tools for an Interactive Virtual Cinema. In: Trappl R., Petta P. (eds.) *Creating Personalities for Synthetic Actors* (In this volume)

9. Blumberg B. (1994) Action-Selection in Hamsterdam: Lessons from Ethology. In: *Proceedings of the 3rd International Conference on the Simulation of Adaptive Behavior*, Brighton, England, MIT Press, pp.108-117

10. Blumberg B. (1997) Multi-level Control for Animated Autonomous Agents: Do the Right Thing... Oh, Not That... In: Trappl R., Petta P. (eds.) *Creating Personalities for Synthetic Actors* (In this volume)

11. Bozinovski S.: Emotion, Embodiment, and Consequence Driven Systems (1996) In Mataric M. (ed.) *Embodied Cognition and Action*, AAAI Press, Menlo Park, Technical Report FS-96-02, pp.12-17

12. Brooks R.A. (1991) Intelligence without Reason. In: *Proceedings of the 12 International Conference on Artificial Intelligence*, Morgan Kaufmann, San Mateo, CA, pp.569-595

13. Chaignaud N., Levy F. (1996) Common Sense Reasoning: Experiments and Implementation. In: Wahlster W. (ed.) *Proceedings of the 12th European Conference on Artificial Intelligence (ECAI-96)*, Wiley, Chichester, UK, pp.604-608

14. Cooper R., Farringdon J., Fox J., Shallice T. (1992) New Techniques for Computational Modelling, In: *AISB Quarterly* 81, pp.21-25; also: UCL-PSY-ADREM-TR2. Department of Psychology, University College London

15. Cooper R., Shallice T. (1994) Soar and the Case for Unified Theories of Cognition. Department of Psychology, University College London, UCL-PSY-ADREM-TR10

16. Cooper R., Fox J., Farringdon J., Shallice T. (1995) A systematic methodology for cognitive modelling, *Artificial Intelligence*, to appear; also: UCL-PSY-ADREM-TR14, Department of Psychology, University College London

17. Damasio A.R. (1994) Descartes' Error, Grosset/Putnam, New York

18. Dennett D.C. (1987) The Intentional Stance, A Bradford Book, MIT Press, Cambridge, MA

19. Doux J.le: The Emotional Brain, Simon & Schuster, New York, 1996.

20. Elliott C.D. (1992) The Affective Reasoner: A process model of emotions in a multi-agent system. Northwestern University, Illinois. Ph.D. Thesis

21. Eysenck H.J. (1990) Biological Dimensions of Personality. In: Pervin L.A. (ed.) *Handbook of Personality: Theory and Research*, Guilford Press, New York, pp.244-276

22. Foner L.N. (1993) What's An Agent, Anyway? MIT Media Laboratory

23. Goldberg A. (1997) IMPROV: A System for Real-Time Animation of Behavior-based Interactive Synthetic Actors. In: Trappl R., Petta P. (eds.) *Creating Personalities for Synthetic Actors* (In this volume)

24. Guha R.V., Lenat D.B. (1991) Cyc: A Mid-Term Report. In R.Trappl (ed.): Artificial Intelligence: Future, Impacts, Challenges, Special Issue of *Applied Artificial Intelligence* 5(1), pp.45–86

25. Haddadi A. (1996) Communication and Cooperation in Agent Systems. Springer, Berlin

26. Hayes-Roth B., Gent R.van, Huber D. (1997) Acting in Character. In: Trappl R., Petta P. (eds.) *Creating Personalities for Synthetic Actors* (In this volume)

27. Laurel B. (1991) Computer as Theatre, Addison-Wesley, Reading, MA

28. Lesperance Y., Levesque H.J. (1996) Indexical Knowledge and Robot Action—A Logical Account. In Agre P.E., Rosenschein S.J. (eds.) *Computational Theories of Interaction and Agency*. MIT Press, Cambridge, MA, pp.435–482

29. Lorenz K. (1965) *Evolution and Modification of Behavior*. University of Chicago Press, Chicago

30. Lorenz K., Leyhausen P. (1973) Motivation of Human and Animal Behavior: An Ethological View. New York: D. Van Norstrand

31. Loyall B. (1997) Some Requirements and Approaches for Natural Language in a Believable Agent. In: Trappl R., Petta P. (eds.) *Creating Personalities for Synthetic Actors* (In this volume)

32. Maes P. (1989) The Dynamics of Action Selection. In *Proceedings of the Eleventh International Joint Conference on Artificial Intelligence (IJCAI-89)*. Morgan Kaufmann, Los Altos, CA, pp.991–997

33. Maes P. (1991) A Bottom-Up Mechanism for Behavior Selection in an Artificial Creature. In Meyer J.-A., Wilson S.W. (eds.), *From Animals to Animats*. A Bradford Book, MIT Press, Cambridge, MA, pp.238–246

34. Maturana H.R., Varela F.J. (1980) Autopoiesis and Cognition, Reidel, Dordrecht

35. Magnenat-Thalmann N., Volino P. (1997) Dressing Virtual Humans. In: Trappl R., Petta P. (eds.) *Creating Personalities for Synthetic Actors* (In this volume)

36. Minsky M. (1985) The Society of Mind, Simon & Schuster, New York

37. Moffat D. (1997) Personality Parameters and Programs. In: Trappl R., Petta P. (eds.) *Creating Personalities for Synthetic Actors* (In this volume)

38. Ortony A., Clore G.L., Collins A. (1988). The Cognitive Structure of Emotions, Cambridge University Press, Cambridge, UK

39. Pollock J.L. (1992) How to Reason Defeasibly. *Artificial Intelligence* 57(1)

40. Pollock J.L. (1995) Cognitive Carpentry, MIT Press/Bradford Books, Cambridge (MA), London (England)

41. Rao A.S., Georgeff M.P. (1991) Modeling Rational Agents within a BDI-Architecture. In Allen J. et al. (eds.) *Principles of Knowledge Representation and Reasoning*, Morgan Kaufmann, Los Altos, CA, pp.473–484

42. Reilly W.S., Bates J. (1993) Emotion as part of a Broad Agent Architecture. In: *Working Notes of the Workshop on Architectures Underlying Motivation and Emotion*, Birmingham, England, August

43. Rhodes B.J. (1996) PHISH-Nets: Planning Heuristically In Situated Hybrid Networks, Massachusetts Institute of Technology, Cambridge, MA, Master's Thesis

44. Sloman A. (1997) What Sort of Control System is Able to Have a Personality? In: Trappl R., Petta P. (eds.) *Creating Personalities for Synthetic Actors* (In this volume)

45. Sousa R.de (1987) The Rationality of Emotion, MIT Press, Cambridge, MA

46. Stein L.A. (1994) Imagination and Situated Cognition, *JETAI, Journal of Experimental and Theoretical Artificial Intelligence* 6(4)

47. Thalmann D., Noser H., Huang Z. (1997) Autonomous Virtual Actors based on Virtual Sensors. In: Trappl R., Petta P. (eds.) *Creating Personalities for Synthetic Actors* (In this volume)

48. Tinbergen N. (1951) *The Study of Instinct*, Oxford University Press, Oxford

49. Uexkuell J.von (1928) Theoretische Biologie, Julius Springer, Berlin, (Suhrkamp, Frankfurt/Main, 1973)

50. Wooldridge M.J., Jennings N.R. (eds.) (1995) *Intelligent Agents: Proceedings of the ECAI-94 Workshop on Agent Theories, Architectures, and Languages, Amsterdam, The Netherlands, August.* Springer-Verlag, Berlin Heidelberg New York, LNAI 890

51. Wooldridge M., Mueller J.P., Tambe M.(eds.) (1996) *Intelligent Agents II: Agent Theories, Architectures, and Languages.* Springer-Verlag, Berlin Heidelberg New York, LNCS 1037

Personalities for Synthetic Actors:
A Bibliography

Paolo Petta

Austrian Research Institute for Artificial Intelligence*, Vienna,
and
Department of Medical Cybernetics and Artificial Intelligence, University of Vienna
paolo@ai.univie.ac.at

Overviews

1. Agre P.E. (1996) Computational Research on Interaction and Agency. In: Agre P.E., Rosenschein S.J. (eds.) *Computational Theories of Interaction and Agency*. MIT Press, Cambridge, MA. pp.1-52

   This article gives an overview of this special volume on interaction and agency. Agre advocates a "principled approach" to supercede 'formal or logical approaches' in this area of research, and argues in favour of a balance between theoretical and empirical research. Furthermore, the importance of making the transition from today's typical "one agent in a complex environment" setting to "many agents in complex environment" testbeds is emphasized.

2. Badler N.A., Phillips C.B., Webber B.L., Badler N., Steedman M., Webber B.L. (1990) Narrated Animation: A Case for Generation. In: McKeown K.R., Moore J.D., Nirenburg S. (eds.) *Proceedings of the Fifth International Workshop on Natural Language Generation*. Linden Hall Conference Center, Dawson, Pennsylvania

3. Bates J. (1991) Virtual Reality, Art, and Entertainment. In: *Presence: The Journal of Teleoperators and Virtual Environments* **1(1)** 133-138

4. Bates J. (1992) The Nature of Characters in Interactive Worlds and The Oz Project. School of Computer Science, Carnegie Mellon University. Report CMU-CS-92-200

   These two papers provide an introduction to the research on Virtual Drama carried out at CMU under the direction of Joseph Bates. The key concept of virtual drama and approach of deploying broad and believable agents in order to meet the project goals are illustrated. The relevance of an effective simulation of emotional behaviour for the achievement and maintenance of the the suspension of the human participant's disbelief is highlighted.

---

* The Austrian Research Institute for Artificial Intelligence is supported by the Austrian Federal Ministry of Science, Transport, and the Arts.

5. Beaudoin L., Paterson C., Read T., Shing E., Sloman A., Wright I. (1993) A Summary of the Attention and Affect Project. Cognitive Science Research Centre, School of Computer Science, Univ. of Birmingham, Birmingham, UK

6. Bennett P., Howard N. (1995) What is Drama Theory? Management Science Dept., Strathclyde University

   An introduction to the field of drama theory, explaining its rooting in game theory and decision theory as well as its potential for application in diverse scenarios.

7. Elliott C. (1994) Research Problems in the Use of a Shallow Artificial Intelligence Model of Personality and Emotion. In: *Proceedings of the Twelfth National Conference on Artificial Intelligence.* AAAI Press/MIT Press, Cambridge, MA. pp.9-15

8. Foner L.N. (1993) What's An Agent, Anyway? MIT Media Laboratory, E15-401B, 20 Ames St, Cambridge, MA 02139

   An often cited report lucidly characterizing particular properties of shared virtual environments and their impacts on—in particular, the opportunities offered—the design of believable agents populating them

9. Franklin S., Graesser A. (1996) Is it an Agent, or Just a Program?: A Taxonomy for Autonomous Agents. In: Mueller J., Wooldridge M., Jennings N. (eds.) *Working Notes of the Third International Workshop on Agent Theories, Architectures, and Languages.* ECAI'96, August 12-13, Budapest, Hungary. pp.193-206

   One the first attempts to organize the ever-growing research field of autonomous agents with the use of an encompassing taxonomy. This is an ongoing work project, with refinements of the structures introduced in this paper being presented in subsequent and future publications.

10. Maes P. (1995) Artificial Life Meets Entertainment: Lifelike Autonomous Agents. In: New Horizons in Commercial and Industrial AI. *Communications of the ACM* **38(11)**

    A summary of the the MIT Media Lab's ALIVE system along with a review of application areas

11. Strohecker C. (1994) The "Zircus" Concept Sketch for a Learning Environment and Online Community. Mitsubishi Electric Research Laboratories, Cambridge, MA. Report TR-94-22

    An overview of a guiding vision for the virtual environment being developed. Discussed topics include the overall organization, user interface devices, and the kinds of functionalities to be taken over by synthetic actors.

12. Trappl R., Petta P. (1995) What Governs Autonomous Agents? In: Magnenat-Thalmann N.M., Thalmann D. (eds.) *Proceedings Computer Animation '95, April 19-21, Geneva, Switzerland.* IEEE Computer Society, Los Alamitos, CA. pp.1-10

This paper reviews a number of representative examples of current artificial intelligence research efforts aimed at providing computational models of behavioural and cognitive phenomena.

13. Wooldridge M., Jennings N.R. (1995) Agent Theories, Architectures, and Languages: A Survey. In: Wooldridge M.J. and Jennings N.R. (eds.): *Intelligent Agents. Proc. ECAI-94 Workshop on Agent Theories, Architectures, and Languages, Amsterdam.* Springer, Berlin

    A detailled survey of theoretical intelligent agent research, complemented by the sequel published in the subsequent year and the overview published in the *Knowledge Engineering Review* **10(2)**.

14. Wooldridge M., Jennings N.R. (1995) Intelligent Agents: Theory and Practice. *The Knowledge Engineering Review* **10(2)**

    This important overview paper discusses theoretical and practical issues in the design and construction of intelligent agents along with a review of realized and projected applications of agent technology.

15. Wooldridge M., Jennings N.R. (guest eds.) (1995, 1996) Special Issue: Intelligent Agents and Multi-Agent Systems, Parts 1 & 2, of Trappl R. (ed.) *Applied Artificial Intelligence* **9(4)** & **10(1)**.

    The special issue of the AAI Journal rounds off the comprehensive assessment of the state of the art in intelligent agent research: in addition to a broad panorama of existing applications (including health care management, monitoring of environmental data, transportation scheduling, and implementation of computer game characters), the guest editors share their points of view on the promises and problems of the rapid deployment of this novel technology in real-word settings.

222

Selected Publications from the Center for Human Modeling and Simulation

1. Badler N., Webber B., Esakov J., Kalita J. (1991) Animation from instructions. In: Badler N., Barsky B.A., Zeltzer D. (eds.): Making them Move: Mechanics, Control, and Animation of Articulated Figures, Morgan-Kaufmann

2. Badler N.I., O'Rourke J., Platt S., Morris M.A. (1980) Human Movement Understanding: A Variety of Perspectives. In: *Proceedings of the First National Conference on Artificial Intelligence (AAAI-80)*. Morgan Kaufmann, Los Altos, CA

3. Badler N.I. (1982) Design of a Human Movement Representation Incorporating Dynamics and Task Simulation. Dept. of Computer and Information Science, University of Pennsylvania, Philadelphia, PA. Report MS-CIS-82-14

4. Cassell J., Pelachaud C., Badler N., Steedman M., Achorn B., Becket T., Douville B., Prevost S., Stone M. (1994) ANIMATED CONVERSATION: Rule-based Generation of Facial Expression, Gesture & Spoken Intonation for Multiple Conversational Agents. In: *Proceedings of SIGGRAPH 94 (Orlando, FL, July 24-29), Computer Graphics, Annual Conference Series.* ACM SIGGRAPH, New York. 413-420

5. Monheit G., Badler N.I. (1990) A Kinematic Model of the Human Spine and Torso. Dept. of Computer and Information Science, University of Pennsylvania, Philadelphia, PA. Report MS-CIS-90-77, GRAPHICS LAB 35

6. Pelachaud C., Badler N.I., Steedman M. (1990) Issues in Facial Animation. Dept. of Computer and Information Science, University of Pennsylvania, Philadelphia, PA. Report MS-CIS-90-88, GRAPHICS LAB 36

7. Pelachaud C., Badler N.I., Viaud M.-L. (1994) Final Report to NSF of the Standards for Facial Animation Workshop. School of Engineering and Applied Science, Computer and Information Science Department, University of Pennsylvania, Philadelphia, PA

8. Pelachaud C., Badler N.I., Steedman M. (1996) Generating Facial Expressions for Speech. In: *Cognitive Science* **20(1)**

9. Reich B.D., Ko H., Becket W., Badler N.I. (1994) Terrain Reasoning for Human Locomotion. In: Magnenat-Thalmann N.M., Thalmann D. (eds.) *Proceedings Computer Animation '94, May 25-28, 1994, Geneva, Switzerland.* IEEE Computer Society Press, Los Alamitos, CA. 76-82

See also: <URL:http://www.cis.upenn.edu/ hms/publications.html>

Selected Publications from the MIT Media Laboratory

1. Blumberg B. (1994) Action-Selection in Hamsterdam: Lessons from Ethology. In: *Proceedings of the 3rd International Conference on the Simulation of Adaptive Behavior, Brighton, England, MIT Press.* 108–117
   This paper focuses on the ethological foundations of the behaviour-based Hamsterdam architecture used in the ALIVE system at MIT.

2. Blumberg B.M., Galyean T.A. (1995) Multi-Level Direction of Autonomous Creatures for Real-Time Virtual Environments. In: *Proceedings of SIG-GRAPH'95*
   This paper discusses how different levels of directability can be achieved within the Hamsterdam architecture framework.

3. Foner L.N. (1994) Paying Attention to What's Important: Using Focus of Attention to Improve Unsupervised Learning. Dissertation, MIT
   This work illustrates the relevance of mechanisms aiding in singling out single situations as prerequisite for the subsequent deployment of unsupervised learning procedures

4. Johnson M.B. (1995) WAVESworld. Dissertation, MIT
   WAVESworld is another ambitious virtual agent architecture and environment, with an emphasis on geometric rendering and performance aspects.

5. Maes P., Darrell T., Blumberg B., Pentland A. (1995) The ALIVE System: Full-Body Interaction with Autonomous Agents. In: Magnenat-Thalmann N.M., Thalmann D. (eds.) *Proceedings Computer Animation '95, April 19-21, Geneva, Switzerland.* IEEE Computer Society, Los Alamitos, CA. pp.11-18, also MIT Media Laboratory Perceptual Computing Technical Report No.257

6. Rhodes B.J. (1996) PHISH-Nets: Planning Heuristically In Situated Hybrid Networks, Massachusetts Institute of Technology, Cambridge, MA, Master's Thesis
   This thesis addresses the problem of integrating planning capabilities into a situated architecture. Virtual characters are equipped with libraries of behaviour modules encoding the single available actions. Each behaviour module carries the specification of when its action can be carried out, what the expected outcomes are, and to the fulfillment of which high-level goals it can contribute. The modules are interconnected into a network where links represent causal relations between behaviours. Effects of actions are constrained to being context independent, allowing for a wider range of safe combination of single actions.

See also: <URL:http://agents.www.media.mit.edu:80/groups/agents/papers.html>

Selected Publications from the Virtual Theater Project, Stanford Univ. (CA)

1. Hayes-Roth B., Brownston L. (1994) Multi-Agent Collaboration in Directed Improvisation. Stanford University, Knowledge Systems Laboratory. Report KSL-94-69.ps

2. Hayes-Roth B., Feigenbaum E. (1994) Proposal for a Computer-Animated Improvisational Theater Game for Children. CAIT (Computer-Animated Improvisational Theater) Project, AIS (Adaptive Intelligent Systems) Group, Stanford University

3. Hayes-Roth B., Pfleger K., Lalanda P., Morignot P., Balabanovic M. (1994) A domain-specific software architecture for adaptive intelligent systems. In: *IEEE Transactions on Software Engineering*

4. Hayes-Roth B., Sincoff E., Brownston L., Huard R., Lent B. (1994) Directed Improvisation. Stanford University, Knowledge Systems Laboratory. Report KSL-94-61

5. Hayes-Roth B. (1995) Agents on Stage: Advancing the State of the Art of AI. In: Mellish C.S. (ed.) *Proceedings of the 14th International Joint Conference on Artificial Intelligence.* Morgan Kaufmann, San Mateo, CA. pp.967-971

6. Hayes-Roth B., Brownston L., Sincoff E. (1995) Directed Improvisation by Computer Characters. Stanford University, Knowledge Systems Laboratory. Report KSL-95-04

7. Rousseau D., Hayes-Roth B. (1996) Personality in Synthetic Agents. Knowledge Systems Laboratory, Computer Science Dept., Stanford University, Stanford, CA 94305, USA. Report KSL 96-21

See also:
<URL:http://www-ksl.stanford.edu/projects/CAIT/publicity.html>

Selected Publications from MIRALab (Univ. Geneva), and EPFL (Lausanne)

1. Kalra P.K. (1993) An Interactive Multimodal Facial Animation System. Departement d'Informatique, Ecole Polytechnique Federale de Lausanne. MSc. thesis

2. Magnenat-Thalmann N.M., Kalra P. (1992) A Model for Creating and Visualizing Speech and Emotion. In: Dale R., Hovy E.H., Roesner D., Stock O. (eds.) *Aspects of Automated Natural Language Generation*. Springer, Berlin. Lecture Notes in Artificial Intelligence No.587 . pp.1–12

3. Magnenat-Thalmann N.M., Thalmann D. (1993) *Virtual Worlds and Multimedia*. Wiley, Chichester, UK

4. Magnenat-Thalmann N.M., Thalmann D. (1994) *Artificial Life and Virtual Reality*. Wiley, Chichester, UK

5. Noser H., Thalmann D. (1993) Complex Vision-based Behaviors for Virtual Actors. Computer Graphics Lab, Swiss Federal Institute of Technology, Lausanne

6. Pandzic I.S., Kalra P., Magnenat-Thalmann N.M., Thalmann D. (1994) Real Time Facial Interaction. In: *Displays, Butterworth-Heinemann Ltd.* **15(3)**, 157–163

7. Sanso R.M., Thalmann D. (1994) A Hand Control and Automatic Grasping System for Synthetic Actors. In: Daehlen M., Kjelldahl L. (Guest eds.): *Eurographics'94, Blackwell Publishers* **13(3)** C-167–C-177

See also: <URL:http://miralabwww.unige.ch/Publications-TO.html>

Selected Publications from the Oz Group at CMU

1. Bates J. (1992) Virtual Reality, Art, and Entertainment. In: *Presence: The Journal of Teleoperators and Virtual Environments*, MIT Press, Cambridge, MA

   This article describes the goals of the Oz project at CMU: the concept of virtual drama is explained and the special role broad believable agents play in it.

2. Bates J. (1992) The Nature of Characters in Interactive Worlds and The Oz Project. School of Computer Science, Carnegie Mellon University. Report CMU-CS-92-200

3. Bates J. (1994) The Role of Emotion in Believable Agents. In: Special Issue: Intelligent Agents. *Communications of The ACM* **37(7)**

   This article details the relevance of emotions for synthetic actors to meet the criteria of believability and interestingness in virtual drama performances.

4. Bates J., Altucher J., Hauptman A., Kantrowitz M., Loyall A.B., Murakami K., Olbrich P., Popovic Z., Reilly W.S., Sengers P., Welch W., Weyrauch P., Witkin A. (1993) Edge of Intention. In: Linehan T.E. (ed.) *Visual Proceedings, Computer Graphics Annual Conference Series.* ACM, New York. pp.113–114

   A brief description of the Edge of Intention, a scenario demonstrating the Virtual Drama being researched in context of the Oz project at CMU.

5. Bates J., Loyall A., Reilly W. (1992) Integrating Reactivity, Goals, and Emotion in a Broad Agent. In: *Proceedings of the Fourteenth Annual Conference of the Cognitive Science Society.* Lawrence Erlbaum, Hillsdale, NJ. pp.696–701

   This paper gives an overview of the Tok architecture which integrates Em, an extension of the OCC theory of elicitation of emotions, and Hap, the reactive goal-directed component, while maintaining real-time responsiveness.

6. Bates J., Loyall A.B., Reilly W.S. (1992) An Architecture for Action, Emotion, and Social Behaviour. School of Computer Science, Carnegie Mellon University. Report CMU-CS-92-144

   This paper gives a detailed account of the Tok architecture used in the implementation of the Woggle characters populating the Edge of Intention testbed realized within the framework of the Oz project at CMU.

7. Kantrowitz M. (1990) GLINDA: Natural Language Generation in the Oz Interactive Fiction Project. School of Computer Science, Carnegie Mellon University. Report CMU-CS-90-158

8. Kantrowitz M., Bates J. (1992) Integrated Natural Language Generation Systems. School of Computer Science, Carnegie Mellon University. Report CMU-CS-92-107

This reports covers the GLINDA natural language generation system developed in the context of the Oz project at CMU, illustrating the opportunities arising from its specific application in the context of interactive Virtual Drama scenarios.

9. Kelso M.T., Weyhrauch P., Bates J. (1992) Dramatic Presence. School of Computer Science, Carnegie Mellon University. Report CMU-CS-92-195

10. Loyall A.B., Bates J. (1991) Hap: A Reactive, Adaptive Architecture for Agents. School of Computer Science, Carnegie Mellon University. Report CMU-CS-91-147

11. Loyall B.A., Bates J. (1993) Real-time Control of Animated Broad Agents. In: *School of Computer Science, Carnegie Mellon University.* Proceedings of the Fifteenth Annual Conference of the Cognitive Science Society, Boulder, CO, June
This paper updates the description of the broad agent architecture Tok detailing the design decisions and tradeoffs made to meet the realtime performance constraints.

12. Reilly W.S. (1994) Building Emotional Characters for Interactive Drama. In: *Proceedings of the Twelfth National Conference on Artificial Intelligence.* AAAI Press/MIT Press, Cambridge, MA

13. Reilly W.S.N. (1996) Believable Social and Emotional Agents. School of Computer Science, Carnegie Mellon University. Technical Report CMU-CS-96-138
This thesis covers two aspects of the Tok architecture developed to drive the Woggle characters populating the Edge of Intention world implemented in the Oz project: Em, the emotion engine, along with the specification of a methodology on how to design single agent personalities; and the social capabilities of the agents, aimed at achieving robust behaviour by minimizing the required context dependencies.

14. Reilly W.S., Bates J. (1993) Emotion as part of a Broad Agent Architecture. In: *Working Notes of the Workshop on Architectures Underlying Motivation and Emotion.* Birmingham, England, August
This paper gives a more detailed description of Em, the emotional component of the broad agent architecture Tok, and the various ways this module interfaces to the other subsystems.

See also: <URL:http://www-cgi.cs.cmu.edu/afs/cs.cmu.edu/project/oz/web/papers.html>

Selected Publications of the Cognition and Affect Project at the University of Birmingham

1. Paterson C.J. (1995) The Use of Ratings for the Integration of Planning & Learning in a Broad but Shallow Agent Architecture. The Cognition and Affect Group, Cognitive Science Research Centre, School of Computer Science, Univ. of Birmingham, Birmingham, UK

2. Pryor L., Collins G. (1992) Reference features as guides to reasoning about opportunities. In: *Proc. of the Fourteenth Annual Conf. of the Cognitive Science Society, 1992.* 230–235

3. Read T. (1993) Systematic Design: A Methodology For Investigating Emotional Phenomena. Cognitive Science Research Centre, School of Computer Science, Univ. of Birmingham, Birmingham, UK

4. Read T., Sloman A. (1993) The Terminological Pitfalls of Studying Emotion. Cognitive Science Research Centre, School of Computer Science, Univ. of Birmingham, Birmingham, UK

5. Shing E. (1994) Computational constraints on associative learning. Cognitive Science Research Centre, School of Computer Science, Univ. of Birmingham, Birmingham, UK

6. Sloman A. (1985) Why we need many knowledge representation formalisms. In: Bramer M. (ed.) *Research and Development in Expert Systems, Proc. BCS Expert Systems Conference 1984*, Cambridge University Press. 163–183

7. Sloman A. (1990) Motives Mechanisms and Emotions. In: *Cognition and Emotion* **1(3)**, 217–234 1987, reprinted in Boden M.A. (ed.), *The Philosophy of Artificial Intelligence* "Oxford Readings in Philosophy" Series, Oxford University Press, 231–247

8. Sloman A. (1990) Notes on Consciousness. In: *AISB Quarterly*

9. Sloman A. (1992) Silicon souls: how to design a functioning mind. Cognitive Science Research Centre, School of Computer Science, Univ. of Birmingham, Birmingham, UK. Report Professorial Inaugural Lecture, Birmingham, May 1992

10. Sloman A. (1992) Prolegomena to a Theory of Communication and Affect. In: Ortony A., Slack J., Stock O. (eds.) *Communication from an Artificial Intelligence Perspective: Theoretical and Applied Issues*, Springer-Verlag, Heidelberg, 229–260

11. Sloman A. (1993) Varieties of Formalisms for Knowledge Representation. In: *Computational Intelligence, Special issue on Computational Imagery* **9(4)**, November

12. Sloman A. (1993) Prospects for AI as the General Science of Intelligence. In: *Prospects for Artificial Intelligence (Proceedings AISB 93)*, The University of Birmingham, IOS Press.

13. Sloman A. (1993) The Mind as a Control System. In: *Hookway C., Peterson D. (eds.) Proc. 1992 Royal Institute of Philosophy Conf. 'Philosophy and the Cognitive Sciences'*. Cambridge University Press, 69–110

14. Sloman A. (1994) How to dispose of the free will issue. Cognitive Science Research Centre, School of Computer Science, Univ. of Birmingham, Birmingham, UK

15. Sloman A. (1994) Representations as control sub-states. Cognitive Science Research Centre, School of Computer Science, Univ. of Birmingham, Birmingham, UK

16. Sloman A., Beaudoin L., Humphreys G., Paterson C., Shing E., Read T., Wright I. (1994) Explorations in Design Space. In: Cohn A. (ed.) *Proc. 11th European Conf. on Artificial Intelligence (ECAI 94)*, John Wiley & Sons, Ltd. 578–582

17. Sloman A., Beaudoin L., Wright I. (1994) Computational Modelling of Motive-Management Processes. The Cognition and Affect Group, Cognitive Science Research Centre, School of Computer Science, Univ. of Birmingham, Birmingham, UK. Poster at the Conference of the International Society for Research in Emotions (ISRE), Cambridge July

18. Sloman A., Poli R. (1994) Playing God: A toolkit for building agents. School of Computer Science, The University of Birmingham

19. Sloman A. (1995) Musings on the roles of logical and non-logical representations in intelligence. In: Glasgow J., Narayanan H., Chandrasekaran B. (eds.) Diagrammatic Reasoning: Computational and Cognitive Perspectives, AAAI Press

20. Wright I. (1994) An Emotional Agent. The Cognition and Affect Group, Cognitive Science Research Centre, School of Computer Science, Univ. of Birmingham, Birmingham, UK

21. Wright I., Sloman A. (1995) The Architectural Basis for Grief. The Cognition and Affect Group, Cognitive Science Research Centre, School of Computer Science, Univ. of Birmingham, Birmingham, UK

22. Sanders K.E. (1989) A Logic for Emotions: A Basis for Reasoning about Commonsense Psychological Knowledge. In: *Proceedings of the Eleventh Annual Conference of the Cognitive Science Society*. Lawrence Erlbaum, Hillsdale, NJ. pp.357–363

See also: <URL:http://www.cs.bham.ac.uk/%7Eaxs/cogaff.html>

Computer Animation

1. Christianson D.B., Anderson S.E., He L.-W., Salesin D.H., Weld D.S., Cohen M.F. (1996) Declarative Camera Control for Automatic Cinematography. In: *Proceedings of the Thirteenth National Conference on Artificial Intelligence.* AAAI Press/MIT Press, Cambridge, MA. pp.148-155

2. Kurlander D., Skelly T., Salesin D. (1996) Comic Chat. In: *Computer Graphics Proceedings, Annual Conference Series.* pp.225-236

3. Morawetz C.L., Calvert T.W. (1990) Goal-Directed Human Animation of Multiple Movements. In: *Proc. Graphics Interface '90*

   This paper discribes the GESTURE system which provides a movement lanaguage scripting facility allowing the realistic animation of complex movements of articulated bodies.

4. Perlin K. (1995) Real Time Responsive Animation with Personality. In: *IEEE Transactions on Visualization and Computer Graphics* **1(1)** pp.5-15

   The procedural animation technique developed at the New York University's Media Research Lab allows to attach behavioral characteristics to characters and objects, enabling very high level control. A character can be directed to walk or dance simply by issuing the corresponding command. The single actions and transitions are accurately modeled to achieve a convincing natural appearance; parameter randomization techniques are used to avoid a repetitious impression

5. Perlin K., Goldberg A. (1996) Improv: A System for Scripting Interactive Actors in Virtual Worlds. In: *Computer Graphics Proceedings, Annual Conference Series.* pp.205-216

   Procedural animation techniques achieve realistic appearance while obviating for the need to model the underlying physics. The introduction of an additional level of indirection, in contrast to the familiar "First Person Point of View" used e.g. in most adventure video games, allows not only for the natural introduction of a more efficient human-computer dialog at a higher level, it also introduces the option to display scenes from freely chosen camera angles. The synthetic actors are controlled by scripts, communication among actors is realized via a shared blackboard architecture.

6. Tosa N. (1993) Neuro Baby. In: Linehan T.E. (ed.) *Visual Proceedings, Computer Graphics Annual Conference Series.* ACM, New York. 167

   Combination of a artificial neural network architecture, (essentially facial) animation, and (simple) acousting sensing

Behaviour-Based Systems

1. Balkenius C. (1995) Natural Intelligence in Artificial Creatures. Lund University Cognitive Studies. 37

   This thesis is located in the area of behaviour-based systems and neural networks. Combining ideas from robotics, control theory, machine learning, biology and psychology an artificial nervous system for a simulated artificial creature is assembled out of a multitude of functional subsystems. Goal-directed behaviour is categorized into four different groups, providing a more detailed account for reactive behaviour. Various learning algorithms are developed for this architecture and evaluated, with an emphasis on the relevance of the important role assumed by different types of matching between actual and expected sensory states. The essential roles of emotion and motivation are discussed, and their particular contribution to behaviour coordination is illustrated.

2. Booker L.B. (1994) Editorial. In: *Adaptive Behavior* **3(1)** pp.1–3

3. Brooks R.A. (1985) A Robust Layered Control System for a Mobile Robot. AI-Laboratory, Massachusetts Institute of Technology, Cambridge, MA. Report AI-Memo 864

   One of the first descriptions of the subsumption architecture.

4. Brooks R.A. (1986) Achieving Artificial Intelligence Through Building Robots. AI-Laboratory, Massachusetts Institute of Technology, Cambridge, MA. Report A.I. Memo 899

5. Brooks R.A. (1989) A Robot That Walks: Emergent Behaviors from a Carefully Evolved Network. AI-Laboratory, Massachusetts Institute of Technology, Cambridge, MA. Report AI-Memo 1091

6. Brooks R.A. (1990) Elephants Don't Play Chess. In: Maes P. (ed.) *Designing Autonomous Agents*. MIT Press, Cambridge, MA. Bradford Books . pp.3–16

   One of the standard references for the subsumption architecture

7. Brooks R.A. (1991) New Approaches to Robotics. In: *Science* **13** September, Vol.253, pp.1227–1232

8. Brooks R.A., Lynn A. (1994) Building Brains for Bodies. In: *Autonomous Robots* **1**, pp.7–25

9. Hexmoor H.H., Lammens J.M., Caicedo G., Shapiro S.C. (1993) Behavior Based AI, Cognitive Processes, and Emergent Behaviors in Autonomous Agents. In: *Proc. of AI in Engineering, Toulouse, France*

10. Hexmoor H.H., Lammens J.M., Shapiro S.C. (1993) An Autonomous Agent Architecture for Integrating Unconscious and Conscious, Reasoned Behaviors. In: *Proc. Computer Architectures for Machine Perception*

11. Horswill I. (1996) Analysis of Adaptation and Environment. In: Agre P.E., Rosenschein S.J. (eds.) *Computational Theories of Interaction and Agency.* MIT Press, Cambridge, MA. pp.367–396

12. Kelemen J. (1994) On Rationality of Behavior-Based Agents. In: Trappl R. (ed.) *Cybernetics and Systems '94, Volume II.* World Scientific Publishing, Singapore. pp.1411–1418

13. Mataric M.J. (1992) Integration of Representation Into Goal-Driven Behavior-Based Robots. In: *IEEE Transactions on Robotics and Automation* **8(3)**, June

14. Steels L. (1995) The Homo Cyber Sapiens, the Robot Homonidus Intelligens, and the 'artificial life' approach to artificial intelligence. In: *Proceedings of the Burda Symposium on Brain-Computer-Interfaces, Munich, February*

    An introduction to the bottom-up artificial life oriented line of research at the Artificial Intelligence Laboratory of the VUB in Brussels.

15. Tyrrell T. (1993) Computational Mechanisms for Action Selection. University of Edinburgh. Ph.D. thesis

    This thesis includes a comparative review of various proposed action selection mechanisms: the drive model, Tinbergen's hierarchical mechanism, Lorenz' hydraulic model, Baerends' functional explanations of behaviour, Maes' distributed non-recurrent non-hierarchical spreading activation networks, and Rosenblatt & Payton's and Halperin's connectionist hierarchical feed-forward networks. An extension to Rosenblatt & Payton's mechanism is proposed.

16. Tyrrell T. (1994) An Evaluation of Maes' Bottom-Up Mechanism for Behavior Selection. In: *Adaptive Behavior* **2(4)** pp.307–348

    A critical review of P.Maes' behaviour selection mechanism outlining some deficiencies for which a number of remedies are introduced.

Intelligent Agents

1. Anderson J., Evans M. (1995) A Generic Simulation System for Intelligent Agent Designs. In: *Rosenblit J. (ed.) Applied Artificial Intelligence Special Issue: "Intelligent Control and Planning"*
   This paper includes an extensive review and criticism of prior agent simulation testbeds and introduces the versatile Gensim simulation system which supports the design of complete environments to test intelligent systems.

2. Anderson J.E. (1995) Constraint-Directed Improvisation for Everyday Activities. Dept. of Computer Science, University of Manitoba, Winnipeg, Manitoba, Canada. Thesis
   This thesis presents a formalization of improvisation as a solution to the problem of performing the difficult tasks of everyday activities for which traditional AI planning approaches are not suited. The new approach relies heavily on background knowledge and a comprehensive library of activities. A sample implementation of the proposed approach based on constraint-directed reasoning is described.

3. Bonarini A. (1994) Some Methodological Issues about Designing Autonomous Agents which Learn their Behaviors: the ELF Experience. In: Trappl R. (ed.) *Cybernetics and Systems '94, Volume II.* World Scientific Publishing, Singapore. pp.1435–1442

4. Botelho L., Coelho H. (1996) Emotion-Based Attention Shift in Autonomous Agents. In: Mueller J., Wooldridge M., Jennings N. (eds.) *Working Notes of the Third International Workshop on Agent Theories, Architectures, and Languages.* ECAI'96, August 12-13, Budapest, Hungary. pp.221–232

5. Briggs W., Cook D. (1995) Flexible Social Laws. In: Mellish C.S. (ed.) *Proceedings of the 14th International Joint Conference on Artificial Intelligence.* Morgan Kaufmann, San Mateo, CA. pp.688–693

6. Buerckert H.-J., Mueller J., Schupeta A. (1991) RATMAN and its Relation to Other Multi-Agent Testbeds. DFKI, Saarbruecken, FRG. Report RR-91-09

7. Carmel D., Markovitch S. (1996) Learning Models of Intelligent Agents. In: *Proceedings of the Thirteenth National Conference on Artificial Intelligence.* AAAI Press/MIT Press, Cambridge, MA. pp.62–67

8. Connah D., Shiels M., Wavish P. (1988) A Testbed for Research on Cooperating Agents. In: Kodratoff Y. (ed.) *Proceedings of the 8th European Conference on Artificial Intelligence (ECAI-88).* Pitman, London. pp.445–448

9. D'Inverno M., Luck M. (1996) Understanding Autonomous Interaction. In: Wahlster W. (ed.) *Proceedings of the 12th European Conference on Artificial Intelligence (ECAI-96).* Wiley, Chichester, UK. pp.529–533

10. Davidsson P., Astor E., Ekdahl B. (1994) A Framework for Autonomous Agents Based on the Concept of Anticipatory Systems. In: Trappl R. (ed.) *Cybernetics and Systems '94, Volume II*. World Scientific Publishing, Singapore. pp.1427–1434

11. Decker K., Lesser V. (1993) An Approach to Analyzing the Need for Meta-Level Communication. In: Bajcsy R. (ed.) *Proceedings of the Thirteenth International Joint Conference on Artificial Intelligence*. Morgan Kaufmann, San Mateo, CA. pp.360–366

12. Dignum F., Linder B.van (1996) Modelling Social Agents in a Dynamic Environment: Making Agents Talk. In: Mueller J., Wooldridge M., Jennings N. (eds.) *Working Notes of the Third International Workshop on Agent Theories, Architectures, and Languages*. ECAI'96, August 12-13, Budapest, Hungary. pp.83–94

13. Elliott C.D. (1992) The Affective Reasoner: A process model of emotions in a multi-agent system. Northwestern University, Illinois. PhD. thesis

    This thesis presents an implementation of the OCC theory of the elicitation of emotions, covering the 24 emotion types and around 1400 emotion-induced actions. A number of subtle points and details of the theory are fleshed out and refined in the rigorous implementation process. Special emphasis is placed on the issues of representing the concerns of others and construals, interpretation of events with respect to an agent's concerns. The simulation testbed allows for multi-agent interactions with up to a few dozen agent instances.

14. Elliott C. (1994) Research Problems in the Use of a Shallow Artificial Intelligence Model of Personality and Emotion. In: *Proceedings of the Twelfth National Conference on Artificial Intelligence*. AAAI Press/MIT Press, Cambridge, MA. pp.9–15

15. Gray M.A., Studdard D.P. (1996) Incorporating Emotional Agents Into The Cooperation Mechanism Of The Accord System. In: Mayfield J., Nicholas C. (eds.) *Proceedings Workshop on Intelligent Hypertext*. National Institute of Standards, Gaithersburg, MD

16. Hinkelman E.A., Spackman S.P. (1994) Communicating with Multiple Agents. In: *Proceedings of the 15th International Conference on Computational Linguistics*. Kyoto, Japan. pp.1191–1197

17. Konolige K., Pollack M.E. (1993) A Representationalist Theory of Intention. In: Bajcsy R. (ed.) *Proceedings of the Thirteenth International Joint Conference on Artificial Intelligence*. Morgan Kaufmann, San Mateo, CA. pp.390–395

    This paper attacks the use of normal modal logics for formalizations of intentions while conceding their appropriateness for formalization of belief. A simple representation covering static relations between belief and intention is presented. Coverage of dynamical relations is however deferred to future work.

18. Singh M.P. (1991) Social and Psychological Commitments in Multiagent Systems. DFKI. Report TM-91-08

19. Studdard P. (1995) Representing Human Emotions in Intelligent Agents. Department of Computer Science and Information Systems, The American University, Washington, D.C.. Masters Thesis

20. Walker A., Wooldridge M. (1995) Understanding the Emergence of Conventions in Multi-Agent Systems. In: *Proceedings of the First International Conference on Multi-Agent Systems, San Francisco, CA, June*

    This paper investigates the topic of mecanisms of convention evolution. A new formal model defining the problem domain is introduced along with a rigorous formal methodology used to derive sixteen mechanisms that can be used to reach global agreement relying only on locally available information. These mechanisms are evaluated using a set of specified performance measures.

21. Wallace J.G. (1983) Motives and Emotions in a General Learning System. In: *Proceedings of the 8th International Joint Conference on Artificial Intelligence.* Morgan Kaufmann, Los Altos, CA

22. Watson M. (1996) AI Agents in Virtual Reality Worlds. John Wiley & Sons, N.Y.

    This book is an introduction to the implementation of simple software agents for computer games on popular platforms (MS Windows, Apple Macintosh, the X Window System, and OpenGL) using a VR Agent Toolkit implemented as a library of C++ classes.

23. Weiss G. (1992) Action Selection and Learning in Multi-Agent Environments. Institut für Nachrichtentechnik, TU München. Report FKI-170-92

24. Werner E. (1988) Socializing Robots: A Theory of Communication and Social Structure for Distributed Artificial Intelligence. Universität Hamburg, WISBER. Report Bericht Nr.36

25. Werner E. (1990) What Can Agents Do Together? A Semantics for Reasoning about Cooperative Ability. In: Aiello L. (ed.) *Proceedings of the 9th European Conference on Artificial Intelligence (ECAI-90).* Pitman, London. pp.694-702

26. Zeng D., Sycara K. (1996) How Can an Agent Learn to Negotiate? In: Mueller J., Wooldridge M., Jennings N. (eds.) *Working Notes of the Third International Workshop on Agent Theories, Architectures, and Languages.* ECAI'96, August 12-13, Budapest, Hungary. pp.181-192

27. Zeng D., Sycara K.P. (1996) Preliminary Report on GENERIC NEGOTIATOR. In: Mayfield J., Nicholas C. (eds.) *Proceedings Workshop on Intelligent Hypertext.* National Institute of Standards, Gaithersburg, MD

28. Zlotkin G., Rosenschen J.S. (1993) A Domain Theory for Task Oriented Negotiation. In: Bajcsy R. (ed.) *Proceedings of the Thirteenth International Joint Conference on Artificial Intelligence.* Morgan Kaufmann, San Mateo, CA. pp.416–422

29. (1994) Special Issue: Intelligent Agents. *Communications of The ACM* **37(7)**

Cognitive Science

1. Balkenius C. (1995) Natural Intelligence in Artificial Creatures. Lund University Cognitive Studies. 37

2. Bickhard M.H., Terveen L. (1995) Foundational Issues in Artificial Intelligence and Cognitive Science. Elsevier Science Publishers

   An attack on the fallacies of illict applications of "representationalism", the often tacit assumption that representation is a form of encoding. An alternative conception of representation called interactivism is introduced and explored in contexts such as the frame problem and language. Interactivism is proposed to serve as both an "external" point of reference/comparison to standard approaches and as a true alternative for classes of applications. Food for thought and suggested reading, no matter whether you will subscribe to the authors' view in the end or not.

3. Boden M.A. (1994) Agents and Creativity. In: Special Issue: Intelligent Agents. *Communications of The ACM* **37**(7)

4. Damasio A.R., Damasio H. (1992) Brain and Language. Scientific American. September, 63-71

5. Damasio A.R. (1994) Descartes' Error. Grosset/Putnam, New York

   An often cited work, in which the author attacks the exclusion of emotivity from rationality and also points out various examples for the relevance of the "embodiedness" for human cognition.

6. Prem E. (1996) Motivation, Emotion and the Role of Functional Circuits in Autonomous Agent Design Methodology. Oesterreichisches Forschungsinstitut fuer Artificial Intelligence, Wien. Report TR-96-04

7. Pollock J.L. (1995) Cognitive Carpentry. MIT Press/Bradford Books, Cambridge (MA), London (England)

   This monography describes the architecture for an autonomous rational agent, OSCAR. The comprehensive fleshed-out system (made available on the World-Wide Web) includes emotional components, partly realized as dedicated modules. Based on a doxastic-conative loop, this architecture also heeds the issue of situatedness. Another particular characteristic is the capability of defeasible reasoning which can lead to the adoption of new beliefs as well as to the retraction of previously held ones.

8. Wehrle T. (1994) New Fungus Eater Experiments. *in Proc. From Perception to Action (PerAc'94), Lausanne*

Selected Publications from Related Areas of Psychology and Medicine

1. Britton B.C.J. (1990) The Computation of Emotion in Facial Expression Using the Jepson & Richards Perception Theory. In: *The Twelfth Annual Conference of the Cognitive Science Society.* Lawrence Erlbaum, Hillsdale, NJ. pp.637–645

2. Chwelos G., Oatley K. (1994) Appraisal, Computational Models, and Scherer's Expert System. In: *Cognition and Emotion* **8(3)** pp.245–257

3. Clynes M. (1973) Sentography: Dynamic Forms of Communication of Emotion and Qualities. In: *Computers Biol. Med.* **3,** pp.119-130

4. Doux J.le (1996) The Emotional Brain. Simon & Schuster, New York

5. Elliott C., Ortony A. (1992) Point of View: Modeling the Emotions of Others. In: *Proceedings of the Fourteenth Annual Conference of the Cognitive Science Society.* Lawrence Erlbaum, Hillsdale, NJ. pp.809-814

6. Frijda N. (1987) Emotions. Cambridge University Press, Cambridge, UK

   A comprehensive review of motivational and neurophysiological preconditions for emotions leads to the formulation of a theory viewing emotions as the result of an appraisal process in which the environment is interpreted in terms of one's own concerns. The resulting architecture does not provide all the details required for the specification of an implementation. Additional work in this direction has been carried out e.g. by D. Moffat.

7. Goleman D. (1995) Emotional Intelligence. Bantam Books, New York

8. Izard C., Levi L. (1975) *Emotions—Their Parameters and Measurements.* Raven Press, New York

9. MacLean P.D. (1975) Sensory and Perceptive Factors in Emotional Functions of the Triune Brain. In: Levi L. (ed.) *Emotions - Their Parameters and Measurements.* Raven Press, New York

10. Mandler G. (1975) The Search for Emotion. In: Levi L. (ed.) *Emotions - Their Parameters and Measurements.* Raven Press, New York. pp.1-15

11. MacLean P.D. (1975) Sensory and Perceptive Factors in Emotional Functions of the Triune Brain. In: Levi L. (ed.) *Emotions - Their Parameters and Measurements.* Raven Press, New York

12. Moffat D., Frijda N. (1994) Where's a WILL There's an Agent. In: Wooldridge M.J., Jennings N.R. (eds.) *Intelligent Agents.* LNAI 890, Springer-Verlag Berlin Heidelberg NewYork

    Precursory work to the one reported in this volume on realizing an implementation of Nico Frijda's appraisal theory of emotions.

13. O'Rorke P., Ortony A. (1994) Explaining Emotions. In: *Cognitive Science* **18(2)**

14. Ortony A., Clore G.L., Collins A. (1988) The Cognitive Structure of Emotions. Cambridge University Press, Cambridge, UK

    This monography presents a shallow, trait-based psychological theory of the elicitation of emotions that has been used in many, especially (real-time) performance-oriented projects.

15. Pervin L.A. (1990) *Handbook of Personality: Theory and Research.* Guilford Press, New York

    A standard reference collecting comprehensive reviews of the state of the art in various areas of personality research by recognized authorities in the respective areas

16. Scherer K.R. (1993) Studying the Emotion-Antecedent Appraisal Process: An Expert System Approach. In: *Cognition and Emotion* **7(3/4)** pp.325–355

17. Sousa R.de (1987) The Rationality of Emotion. MIT Press, Cambridge, MA

    A "classic" refutation of the characterisation of emotion as irrational behaviour and pointing out how to the contrary emotions are necessary requisites for rationality

See also: <URL:http://pmc.psych.nwu.edu/personality.html>

Drama Theory and Human-Computer Interaction

1. Barclay D. (1994) The Well-Storied Urn: Computer Hypertext as Multi-Plot. In: *Computers and Writing 1994, Forum*

2. Benjamin I., Cooper M. (1995) Actors, Performance and Drama in Virtual Worlds. In: *in: Proceedings of Computer Graphics International '95, Leeds, UK, June*

   A drama theoretic analysis of applications of virtual worlds for entertainment, education, training and artistic purposes is carried out, leading to a framework for the design of such environments. Drama and theatre are confronted as models of interaction. The advantages of using virtual puppeteer avatars over software agents are identified, on which basis an the possibilities offered by a mixed population of live performers and computer-controlled agents in virtual drama are assessed.

3. Kass A., Burke R., Fitzgerald W. (1995) Interfaces for Supporting Learning from Interaction with Simulated Characters. The Institute for the Learning Sciences, Northwestern University, Evanston, IL. Report TR #64

4. Kautz H., Selman B., Milewski A. (1996) Agent Amplified Communication. In: *Proceedings of the Thirteenth National Conference on Artificial Intelligence.* AAAI Press/MIT Press, Cambridge, MA. pp.3–9

5. Laurel B., Laurel B., Strickland R., Tow R. (1994) Placeholder: Landscape and Narrative in Virtual Environments. In: Computer Graphics. *ACM SIG-GRAPH, New York* **28(2)**

6. Macmillan S.A. (1984) User Models to Personalize an Intelligent Agent. School of Education, Stanford University, Stanford, CA. Ph.D. Dissertation

7. Nass C., Steuer J., Tauber E.R. (1994) Computers are Social Actors. In: Adelson B., Dumais S., Olson J. (eds.) *Human Factors in Computing Systems: CHI'94.* ACM Press, New York. 72–77

   An analysis of the antropomorphic aspects of human-computer interaction.

8. Tice S., Laurel B. (1993) The Art of Building Virtual Realities. In: Jacobson L. (ed.) *Cyberarts: Exploring Art & Technology.* Miller Freeman Inc., Gilroy, CA, USA. pp.280-291

9. Toole J. (1992) The Process of Drama. Routledge, London

Proceedings

Selected AAAI Spring & Fall Symposia Proceedings/Working Notes

1. (1994) *Working Notes: AAAI Spring Symposium Series: Believable Agents.* Stanford University, California, USA. March 19&20

2. (1994) *Software Agents.* AAAI Spring Symposium Series, AAAI Press, Menlo Park, CA

3. (1995) *Interactive Story Systems: Plot and Character.* AAAI Symposium Working Notes. 1995 Spring Symposium, March 27-29, Stanford University

4. Cox M.T., Freed M. (1995) *Proceedings of the 1995 AAAI Spring Symposium on Representing Mental States and Mechanisms.* AAAI Press/MIT Press, Menlo Park, CA

   These proceedings include numerous of articles on the topics of folk psychology and related representations of emotional states

Distributed Artificial Intelligence, Intelligent Agents

1. Agre P.E., Rosenschein S.J. (1996) *Computational Theories of Interaction and Agency.* MIT Press, Cambridge, MA

2. Demazeau Y., Mueller J.-P. (1990) *Decentralized A.I.: Proceedings of the First European Workshop on Modelling Autonomous Agents in a Multi-Agent World.* North-Holland, Amsterdam

3. Demazeau Y. (1991) *Decentralized AI 2: Proceedings of the Second European Workshop on Modelling Autonomous Agents in a Multi-Agent World.* North-Holland, Amsterdam

4. Huhns M. (1987) *Distributed Artificial Intelligence.* Morgan Kaufmann, Los Altos, CA

5. Gasser L., Huhns M.N. (1989) *Distributed Artificial Intelligence, Volume II.* Pitman, London

6. Avouris N.M., Gasser L. (1993) *Distributed Artificial Intelligence: Theory and Praxis.* Kluwer, Dordrecht

7. Lesser V. (1995) *Proceedings of the First International Conference on Multi-Agent Systems.* MIT Press, Cambridge, MA

8. Wooldridge M.J., Jennings N.R. (1995) *Intelligent Agents: Proceedings of the ECAI-94 Workshop on Agent Theories, Architectures, and Languages, Amsterdam, The Netherlands, August.* Springer-Verlag, Berlin Heidelberg New York, LNAI 890

9. Wooldridge M., Mueller J.P., Tambe M. (1996) *Intelligent Agents II: Agent Theories, Architectures, and Languages.* Springer-Verlag, Berlin Heidelberg New York

10. Mueller J., Wooldridge M., Jennings N. (1996) *Working Notes of the Third International Workshop on Agent Theories, Architectures, and Languages.* ECAI'96, August 12-13, 1996, Budapest, Hungary

Artificial Life

1. Meyer J.-A., Wilson S.W. (1991) *From Animals to Animats.* A Bradford Book, MIT Press, Cambridge, MA

2. Meyer J.-A., Roitblat H.L., Wilson S.W. (1993) *From Animals to Animats 2.* A Bradford Book, MIT Press, Cambridge, MA

3. Cliff D., Husbands P., Meyer J.-A., Wilson S.W. (1994) *From Animals to Animats 3.* MIT Press, Cambridge, MA

4. Deneubourg J.L., Goss S., Nicolis G., Bersini H., Dagonnier R. (1993) *Proceedings of the Second European Conference on Artificial Life, Vol I.* Universite Libre de Bruxelles, Brussels, Belgium

5. Deneubourg J.L., Goss S., Nicolis G., Bersini H., Dagonnier R. (1993) *Proceedings of the Second European Conference on Artificial Life, Vol II.* Universite Libre de Bruxelles, Brussels, Belgium

6. Moran F., Moreno A., Merelo J.J., Chacon P., Steels L., Brooks R.A. (1993) *The 'Artificial Life' Route to 'Artificial Intelligence'. Building Situated Embodied Agents.* Lawrence Erlbaum Ass., New Haven. LNAI 929

7. Steels L. (1995) *The Biology and Technology of Autonomous Agents.* Springer, Berlin Heidelberg New York. NATO ASI Series F, Vol. 144

8. Langton C.G., Taylor C.E., Doyne-Farmer J., Rasmussen S. (1990) *Artificial Life II: Proceedings of the Second Artificial Life Workshop.* Addison-Wesley, Reading, MA

9. (1992) *Artificial Life III: Proceedings of the Third Artificial Life Workshop.* Addison-Wesley, Redwood City, Calif.

10. Brooks R.A., Maes P. (1994) *Artificial Life IV: Proceedings of the Fourth Artificial Life Workshop, July 6-8, The Massachusetts Institute of Technology.* MIT Press, Cambridge, MA

User Interfaces

1. (1990) *Proceedings of the ACM SIGGRAPH Symposium on User Interface Software and Technology, Snowbird, Utah, October 3-5.* ACM, New York

2. (1991) *Proceedings of the Fourth Annual ACM Symposium on User Interface Software and Technology, Hilton Head, South Carolina, USA, November 11-13.* ACM Press, New York

3. (1992) *Proceedings of the Fifth ACM Annual Symposium on User Interface Software and Technology, Monterey, California, November 15-18.* ACM, New York

4. (1994) *Proceedings of the Seventh Annual ACM Symposium on User Interface Software and Technology, Marina del Rey, California, November 2-4 (UIST '94).* ACM Press, New York

5. (1995) *Proceedings of the ACM Symposium on User Interface Software and Technology, Pittsburgh, Pennsylvania, November 14-17.* ACM Press, New York

6. (1995) *Proceedings of the Symposium on Designing Interactive Systems: Processes, Practices, Methods, & Techniques, Univ. of Michigan, Ann Arbor, Michigan USA, August 23-25.* ACM Press, New York

Computer Graphics

1. Magnenat-Thalmann N.M., Thalmann D. (1993) *Models and Techniques in Computer Animation.* Springer Verlag, Tokyo Berlin Heidelberg

2. Magnenat-Thalmann N.M., Thalmann D. (1994) *Proceedings Computer Animation '94, May 25-28, Geneva, Switzerland.* IEEE Computer Society Press, Los Alamitos, CA

3. Magnenat-Thalmann N.M., Thalmann D. (1995) *Proceedings Computer Animation '95, April 19-21, Geneva, Switzerland.* IEEE Computer Society, Los Alamitos, CA

4. (1992) *SIGGRAPH '91 Panel Proceedings.* Association for Computing Machinery, New York

5. (1993) *Proceedings of SIGGRAPH 93 (Anaheim, CA, August 1-6), Computer Graphics, Annual Conference Series.* ACM SIGGRAPH, New York

6. (1994) *Proceedings of SIGGRAPH 94 (Orlando, FL, July 24-29), Computer Graphics, Annual Conference Series.* ACM SIGGRAPH, New York

7. Cook R. (1995) *SIGGRAPH '95 Conference Proceedings.* ACM, New York

Index

Page numbers in *italics* designate entire chapters or chapter subdivisions.

Springer
and the
environment

At Springer we firmly believe that an international science publisher has a special obligation to the environment, and our corporate policies consistently reflect this conviction.

We also expect our business partners – paper mills, printers, packaging manufacturers, etc. – to commit themselves to using materials and production processes that do not harm the environment. The paper in this book is made from low- or no-chlorine pulp and is acid free, in conformance with international standards for paper permanency.

 Springer

Lecture Notes in Artificial Intelligence (LNAI)

Lecture Notes in Computer Science